GAME TESTING

GAME TESTING

All In One

Second Edition

Charles P. Schultz
Robert D. Bryant

MERCURY LEARNING AND INFORMATION
Dulles, Virginia
Boston, Massachusetts

Publisher: David Pallai

MERCURY LEARNING AND INFORMATION
22841 Quicksilver Drive
Dulles, VA 20166
info@merclearning.com
www.merclearning.com
1-800-758-3756

This book is printed on acid-free paper.

Charles P. Schultz and Robert D. Bryant. *GAME TESTING: All In One, Second Edition.*
ISBN: 978-1-9364201-6-2

Library of Congress Control Number: 2011932024

121332

CONTENTS

FOREWORD

I n the beginning, there was *Pong*. (Not really, but let's start there anyway.)

In those days you did not have to worry about testing against such variables as operating systems, Web browser compatibilities, or countless different video cards. Today, games are multifaceted, with players playing the same game on different platforms, or even playing online.

In my career as multimedia manager for third party testing house, VeriTest, and later as co-owner of 20/20 Labs, I always wanted a "bible" on game testing—as distinct from general software testing—that could be given to any new game tester. At the time, there were only a few white papers or articles about testing games, or the occasional QA roundtable at conferences. The traditional software quality assurance (SQA) process assumption that a product should function as expected was a good foundation, but many adjustments had to be made in order to work in the world of game and "multimedia" testing.

I wasn't alone. The authors, Charles Schultz and Robert Bryant, wrote *Game Testing All In One* to analyze, document, and provide a training framework for the best practices in game testing. So when I became Director of Quality Assurance for 2K Games, one of the first things I did to promote a better understanding of the best practices of game testing was to distribute the first edition of their book to my team.

Since that time, so many things have changed in game development technology, and with that, game complexity. We also face the challenge of larger games being created to play online using Flash, 3D Flash, Unity, Android, iOS, and other technologies. Just as there have been changes in game development, we have had to adapt how to do QA. This is why the latest edition of this book is so important. Think of it as an upgrade or patch to help you test better.

Lawrence Durham

Redondo Beach, California

Lawrence Durham began his game testing career at VeriTest, and went on to co-found 20/20 Labs, one of the leading external game testing companies in the U.S. He later served as Director of Quality Assurance for 2K Games, a division of Take Two Interactive Software, Inc., where his credits included *The Darkness* and *BioShock*. He is currently Manager of Quality Assurance for Disney Interactive Media Group.

PREFACE

So much has happened in the six short years since we wrote the first edition of this book. Video games have exploded. There exist so many more dimensions of audience, platform, business models, and even input devices than there were in late 2004. Neither of us had ever imagined testing a game with *plastic guitars* when we first sat down to write the first edition. It now seems not only natural, but old hat.

New to the world of games in the last six years are (in no particular order): iOS and the App Store; Nintendo's wiggle sticks; Facebook and "social" games; indie game hits like *Braid*, *Limbo*, and *Super Meat Boy*; games rendered in the cloud and streamed via broadband; achievements; stereoscopic games and game systems; *Club Penguin* and a host of other free-to-play and "freemium" online games; body-sensing input devices; *League of Legends*; Android; and the ubiquitous and inevitable *Angry Birds*.

We felt the time was right to revisit our work. We wanted to revise and update it for today's video game industry—arguably now a series of industries (social, mobile, casual, triple-A, etc.). But although the technology has advanced in unforeseen ways and creators have innovated many new types of gameplay, in its purest form the game production process—and the centrality and importance of Quality Assurance to that process—remains unchanged. Programmers will make mistakes; designers will leave holes; artists will fail to close vertices. It is still up to the game tester to advocate for the player by breaking the game before the player sees it.

From the most complex triple-A console game to the simplest mobile game, it is up to the tester to fall on the (virtual) grenades in order to save the player from frustration, confusion, and lost time. We game testers are the unsung heroes—*Grandma's Boy* notwithstanding—of the entertainment software industry. Our hope is that the material presented herein will help you hone your skills as a tester, or a test manager. The players, though they may not know it, are most grateful for your hard work.

Charles P. Schultz

Robert D. Bryant

ACKNOWLEDGMENTS

The authors would like to thank and recognize the following people:

Heather Maxwell Chandler, for her role in bringing the authors and publisher together for this new edition of the book;

Eileen Worthley, for making this book better by way of her thorough and thoughtful copyediting;

Tim Langdell, for his contribution to the first edition of this book.

CHAPTER 1

TWO RULES OF GAME TESTING

In This Chapter

- The two most important rules every tester and test team needs to know:
  - ○ Rule 1: Don't Panic
  - ○ Rule 2: Trust No One

DON'T PANIC

In a game project, panic is a bad thing. The person panicking did not choose to panic, and may not realize it is happening. It is an irrational reaction to a set of circumstances, and it can lead a tester to cause harm to the project. When a tester is reacting inappropriately to some unreasonable request, remind him not to panic by asking "What's rule number one?"

Scuba divers put themselves in situations similar to what game testers might face: limited resources (the equipment you bring with you), time constraints (air supply), rules to follow (rate of descent/ascent), and other surprises (unexpected sea visitors). According to Dr. William Morgan, episodes of panic or near-panic may explain many recreational diving accidents and deaths. The panic attack was often spurred by something that a non-diver would deem serious: entanglement, an equipment malfunction, or the sight of a shark. But the attacks don't make things better, Morgan says. They can lead to irrational and dangerous behavior. Even scuba divers with many years of experience sometimes experience panic for no apparent reason [SCUBADOC].

Testing the wrong build, failing to notice an important defect, or sending developers on an avoidable search for a nonexistent bug shouldn't get you physically hurt, but there will be a price to pay in extra time, extra money spent, and/or loss of sales and reputation.

Game project panic happens when you are:

- Unfamiliar

- Unprepared

- Under pressure

- Unrested

- Nearsighted

Unfamiliar

As a member of a game team, you might be asked to do something you've never had to do before. You might be given someone else's tests to run, be thrown into the middle of a different game project, or be told to take someone else's place at the last minute to do a customer demo. In situations like these, rely on what you know, stick to basics, and pick up any new or different ways of doing things by watching the people who have already been doing them.

You might even be asked to accomplish something you've never done before, such as achieving 100% automation of the installation tests, or writing a tool to verify the foreign language text in the game. Maybe *no one* has ever done this before. Don't make a commitment right away, don't invent scenarios, and don't try to be a hero. If you are unfamiliar with a situation, you might act on your best judgment, but it still might not be right. It requires having good radar to know when to get help, and also a dose of humility so you don't feel like you have to take on everything yourself or say "yes" to every request. You don't need to lose any authority or credibility. Find someone who's "been there, done that" and who can steer you toward some working solutions. Stay away from responses that are known to fail. You can even search the Internet to see if anyone else has been through it and is willing to share their experiences.

NOTE

Chapter 6, "The Test Process," shows you how to define and follow a set of activities that will give you consistent test throughput and results, even when you're in unfamiliar territory.

Unprepared

A number of unexpected things will happen on your project. Expect the unexpected! Many parts of the game need to be tested at various points in the game's life cycle. Behind the scenes, many different technologies are at work—3D graphics, audio, user interfaces, multithreading, and file systems, to name a few. If you are not ready for a variety of test assignments and you don't have the skills needed to perform them successfully, then you will stumble rather than be a star.

Study, practice, and experience are ingredients for good preparation. During the course of the project, try to get to know more about the game code. Keep up with the industry so you are also aware of what the next generation of games and technologies will be like. Become an expert in the requirements and designs for the parts of the game you are responsible for testing, and then get familiar with the ones you *aren't* responsible for. When you least expect it, you might need to take on a different position, fill in for another tester, or grow into more responsibility. Be ready when it happens.

NOTE

The information in Chapter 5, "Test Phases," gives you information on preparing yourself to succeed as a game tester, as well as what kinds of test environments, projects, roles, and jobs you might find yourself in someday.

Under Pressure

Pressure can come from any of three directions:

- Schedule (calendar time to complete the project)

- Budget (money to spend on the project)

- Headcount (the quantity and types of people assigned to work on the game)

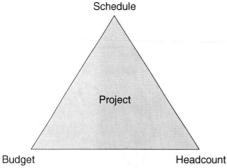

FIGURE 1.1 Resources balanced with project scope.

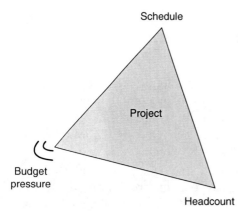

FIGURE 1.2 Budget reduction causes pressure.

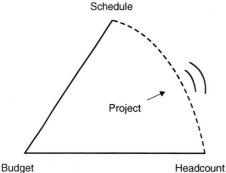

FIGURE 1.3 Budget and headcount pressure caused by project scope increase.

There's nothing to prevent one or more of these resources from shrinking at any time during the project. These factors won't be under your control as a tester. Usually they are determined by business conditions or project managers. In any case, you will be impacted. Figure 1.1 shows the resources in balance with the scope of the project.

Moving in any one of these points on the triangle squeezes the project, creating pressure. Sometimes a game project starts out with one of these factors being too small, or they can get smaller anytime after the project has launched. For example, money can be diverted to another game, developers might leave to start their own company, or the schedule gets pushed up to release ahead of a newly announced game that competes with yours. Figure 1.2 shows how a budget reduction can cause pressure on the game project's schedule and headcount.

Another way to cause pressure within this triangle is to try to add more to it than was originally planned for. This demand could be internally driven, such as adding more levels or characters, or scrapping the old graphics engine for a new one to take advantage of some newly announced hardware. Other unplanned changes might be made to support more game platforms than originally planned or to keep up with newly announced games in terms of number of levels, characters, online players supported, and so on. Figure 1.3 illustrates how increasing the scope of a project can put pressure on the budget and headcount if they are not also increased.

When there is pressure on the project, you can expect it to get passed on. Someone demands something from you, and uses phrases like the following:

- I/we need… immediately

- I don't care…

- That was then, this is now

- Figure out how to do it

- Make it happen

- Deal with it

- We can't afford to…

- Nothing else matters but…

It's likely that you will get more than one demand at a time, and from different people. Examine the schedule, budget, and headcount available to you. Achieve the request by then scaling down what you would normally do so that it fits in your new triangle. Do the things that will have the most impact on meeting the request to the greatest extent possible. Then, in the next release, take care of the issues that didn't fit this time around.

NOTE

Chapter 2, "Being a Game Tester," introduces you to what's expected of you in your role as a tester, and how to make an impact on the quality of the game.

Chapter 14, "Regression Testing and Test Reuse," provides techniques for being efficient when more tests or more testing is needed quickly and unexpectedly, and when more games need to be tested.

Unrested

Running long tests after staying up for 30 hours straight or working 100+ hours a week is not the best approach to finding defects. It is, however, a good way to introduce them! When developers do this, they keep testers in business, but it doesn't help get the game released. It's just as bad for the project when testers make mistakes.

Reporting a problem that doesn't really exist (for example, tested the wrong build, didn't do the setup or install properly, and so on) will cause the developers unnecessary reevaluations and will waste precious time. If you absolutely have to do testing late at night or at the end of a long week, make a checklist to use before and after the testing. If there's another tester around, have her check your work and you can check hers when she does her testing. Also, by writing down some of the information as you go along, you won't be prone to mistakes later on if you have to rely on your tired memory. It's kind of like a prelaunch checklist for the space shuttle. If something is wrong, stop the countdown. Go back and make it right—as it says in the test instructions. After testing is done, record pertinent results and facts. Here's an example checklist that you can start with and expand on to fit your own game projects:

Late Night Testing Checklist

PRE-TEST

Do you have the right version of the test?
Test version: _____

Are you using the right version of the build?
Build version: _____

Are you using the right hardware configuration/settings?
Describe: _____

Are you using the right game controller and settings?
Describe: _____

Which installation options did you use (if any)?
Describe: _____

Is the game in the right initial state before running the test case?
Describe: _____

POST-TEST

Did you complete all of the test steps in order?

Did you document the completion of the tests and the test results?

Did you record all of the problems you found?

If you reported a problem, did you fill in all of the required fields?

In addition to putting practices into place for checking mistakes, look for ways to prevent mistakes in the first place. Depending on your game platform and test environment, automation may be a viable option to make your work repeatable at any time of the day. Automated tasks can even go to work while you're at home resting.

NOTE *Chapter 8, "Combinatorial Testing," and Chapter 15, "Capture/ Playback Testing," describe techniques and tools you can use to make efficient use of your testing and resting time.*

Nearsighted

Panic symptoms can include too much focus on the near term. Many game projects take months, so make that a factor in deciding what to work on today and how to do it. A question I will ask a tester to put him back in the right frame of mind is "Will this be our last chance to test this?" If the answer is "no," then we discuss how to approach the present situation in the context of an overall strategy of repeated testing, feedback from test results, budgeting resources, and so on.

Successful sports teams know how to avoid panic. When they are losing, they're confident that they can come back from behind and win the game because they are a) familiar with the situation, b) prepared to deal with it from practice, film study, and in-game experience, c) rested, and d) don't feel pressure to make up the deficit immediately. Teams that have a losing record often lack one or more of these ingredients.

NOTE *Chapter 5, "Test Phases," shows you what kinds of testing should be done along the way as the game code matures. This helps you test appropriately for a particular situation and allows you to know that you can rely on the additional testing you will do later in the game.*

TRUST NO ONE

On the surface this sounds like a cynical approach, but the very fact that testing is built into the project means that something can't be trusted. You'll read more about this in Chapter 3, "Why Testing Is Important." The very existence of testers on a game project is a result of trust issues, such as the following:

- The publisher doesn't trust that your game will release on time and with the promised features, so they write contracts that pay your team incrementally based on demonstrations and milestones.

- The press and public don't trust that your game will be as good and fun and exciting as you promise, so they demand to see screen shots and demos, write critiques, and discuss your work in progress on bulletin boards.

- Project managers don't trust that the game code can be developed without defects, so testing is planned, funded, and staffed. This can include testers from a third-party QA house and/or the team's own internal test department.

- The publisher can't trust the development house testers to find every defect, so they may employ their own testers or issue a beta release for the public to try it out and report the defects they find.

Don't take it personally. It's a matter of business, technology, and competition. A great deal of money is on the line, and investors don't want to lose it on your project. The technologies required to produce the game may not even have been available at the time development started, giving your team the opportunity to create the kind of game no one has ever done before. By trying to break the game, and failing, you establish confidence that it will work. Games that don't come out right fall victim to rants and complaints posted on the Internet. Don't let this happen to you!

Balancing Act

Evaluate the basis of your testing plans and decisions. Hearsay, opinions, and emotions are elements that can distract you from what you should really be doing. Using test methods and documenting both your work and your results will contribute to an objective game testing environment.

Measuring and analyzing test results—even from past games—will give you data about your game's strengths and weaknesses. The parts that you trust the least—the weak ones—will need the most attention in terms of testing, retesting, and analysis. This relationship is illustrated in Figure 1.4.

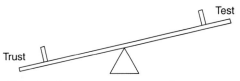

FIGURE 1.4 Low trust means more testing.

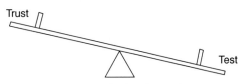

FIGURE 1.5 More trust leads to less testing.

The parts you can trust the most—the strong ones—will require the least attention from you, as illustrated in Figure 1.5. These should still be retested from time to time to reestablish your trust.

> **NOTE**
>
> *Chapter 4, "Software Quality," introduces you to some basic principles for evaluating the trustworthiness of your game code. Chapter 7, "Testing by the Numbers," describes measurements that you can make from the test data you normally collect and recommends how to analyze those measurements to zoom in on specific problem areas.*

Word Games

It's useful to be wary of advice you get from outside the test team. Well-meaning people will suggest shortcuts so the game development can make better progress, but you won't remove bugs from the game by simply not finding them. Don't trust what these people are telling you. At the same time, don't cross the boundary from being distrustful to turning hostile. The whole team is working to deliver the best game it can, even when it doesn't seem that way to a tester.

A general form of statements to watch out for is "X happened, so (only/don't) do Y." Here are some examples:

- "Only a few lines of code have changed, so don't inspect any other lines."

- "The new audio subsystem works the same as the old one, so you only need to run your old tests."

- "We added foreign language strings for the dialogs, so just check a few of them in one of the languages and the rest should be okay too."

And some variants:

- "We only made small changes so don't worry about testing <insert feature name here>."

- "You can just run one or two tests on this and let me know if it works."

- "We've gotta get this out today so just…"

You'll be surprised how many bugs you will find by behaving opposite from the advice you get from other people about what should and should not be tested.

Don't equate a "trust no one" attitude with a "don't do anything you're asked to do" attitude. If a test lead or the project manager needs you to meet goals for certain kinds of testing to be done, be sure you fulfill your obligation to them before going off and working on the issues you don't trust. The difference is between being a hero ("I finished the tests you wanted, and also managed to start looking at the tournament mode and found some problems there. We should do more testing on that next time around") or a zero ("I didn't have time to do the tests you wanted because I was getting some new tests to work for the tournament mode").

Last Chance

Examine your own tests and look for ways you can improve so you gain more trust in your own skills in finding defects. Just never let that trust turn into arrogance or the belief that you are perfect. Leave room to mistrust yourself just a little bit. Remain open to suggestions from managers, developers, other testers, and yourself. For example, if you're in the middle of running a test and you're not sure you are testing the right version—check it! You may have to go back and start over, but that's better than reporting the wrong results and wasting other people's time too.

As game development progresses, management and developers want to feel comfortable about the quality of the game and its readiness for the next milestone and, ultimately, final release. As a tester, you should not be lulled into complacency. I often reenergize my team by instructing them to "Treat this release like it's our last chance to find problems." Conflicts will arise about whether or not to introduce new tests, and you'll hear complaints about why important problems are found so late in the project. There are many reasons for late defects showing up that have nothing to do with incompetent testing. Here are some you will run into:

- The defects were introduced late, just before you found them.

- Bugs from earlier rounds of testing kept you from getting to the part of the game where the late defect was hiding.

- As you spend more time testing the game, you become more familiar with where the defects are coming from, so it is perfectly natural that especially subtle problems might not be found until late in the project.

In any case, even if the bugs were there from the very first release, they were not put there by the testers.

NOTE *Chapter 10, "Cleanroom Testing," and Chapter 12, "Play Testing and Ad Hoc Testing," give you methods to use for testing the game based on your testing intuition and insight.*

Trust Fund

You can get a head start on knowing what not to trust in a couple of ways. Sometimes the developers will tell you, if you just ask…

> **Tester:** "Hey Bill, is there anything you're particularly concerned about that I should focus on in my testing?"

> **Bill:** "Well we just redid the logic for the Fuzzy Sword quest, so we definitely want that looked at."

You can get more clues by mentioning parts of the system and seeing how people react. Rolling eyes and pauses in response are giveaways that there is some doubt as to how good that new weapon will work or if multiplayer will work as well as it did before the latest changes.

NOTE *In Chapter 3 you will find out why testing is important to the health of the game. It covers many factors that contribute to making things go wrong and how you, the game tester, should deal with them.*

GIVE AND TAKE

If you've been paying close attention up to this point—and you should have, as an aspiring or working game tester—you would have noticed an apparent contradiction between the testing approach to counteract panic ("don't treat this release like it's the last one"), and the "trust no one" approach of treating each release like it *is* the last one. A sports analogy might illustrate how these concepts can co-exist.

In baseball one batter can't step up to the plate with bases empty and put six runs on the board. Instead, batter by batter and inning by inning, the team members bat according to the situation, producing the most runs they can. The batters and base runners succeed by being patient, skilled, and committed to their manager's strategy. If every batter tries to hit a home run, the team will strike out often and leave the opposing pitcher fresh for the next inning.

At the same time, when each player is at bat or on base, he is aggressively trying to achieve the best possible outcome. He is fully analyzing the type and location of each pitch, executing his swing properly, and running as fast as he can once the ball is hit. He knows that it contributes to the team's comeback and that his one run or RBI could mean the difference between a win and a loss for the team.

So, as a tester, you can do *both at once* by following this advice:

- Know your role on the team based on what responsibilities have been assigned to you
- Execute your tasks aggressively and accurately
- Do the most important tests first
- Do the tests most likely to find defects often
- Make emotion-free and objective decisions to the extent possible

NOTE

Chapter 13, "Defect Triggers," describes how testing causes defects to appear so you can cover those possibilities in your testing. These also help you decide which tests will be the most important ones to run, and which ones should be run the most often.

THE REST OF THE STORY

The rest of this book equips you to apply the two rules to your game testing. Don't feel like you have to incorporate everything at once to be successful. You may already consider yourself an effective tester. Use new insights from this book to refine your existing skills and add the techniques you learn in Chapters 8 through 14 where it makes the most sense for your projects.

Apply the Two Rules to what you read in this book. Don't trust that what you read here will work every time for everything you do. If you get results that don't make sense, find out why. Try something, then measure or evaluate it to decide whether to go on using it and refining it, whether to try something new or whether to go back to what you were doing in the first place. But do try it before passing judgment. A word of caution: don't trust yourself too much before you make sure you are applying the technique properly. Then you can decide if it works for you. You will discover that the methods suggested in this book are good.

Remember, as a game tester, everyone is trusting in you to find problems before the game ships. Don't give them cause to panic!

NOTE *Chapter 8, "Combinatorial Testing," Chapter 9, "Test Flow Diagrams," and Chapter 11, "Test Trees," introduce you to three important game testing methods. Use them to understand the game software early in development and systematically explore the game's features and functions throughout the project.*

Summary

In this chapter you learned two important rules for game testing and how they relate to the remaining chapters of this book. Panic and trust are counterproductive to game testing. You can achieve the best results by remembering and applying the two rules.

Panic results in:

- Poor judgment and decision making

- Unreliable test results

- Too much emphasis on the short-term

Panic costs the project in:

- Unnecessary rework
- Wasted effort
- Loss of confidence and credibility

Avoid panic by:

- Recognizing when you need help, and getting it
- Preparing for the unexpected
- Relying on procedures
- Getting sufficient rest

Don't trust:

- Hearsay
- Opinions
- Emotions

Rely on:

- Facts
- Results
- Experience

Test each game release as if:

- It's not the last one
- It *is* the last one

Exercises

1. What is Rule 1?

2. Give two or three examples where you could have applied this rule but did not, and describe how results might have been different if you had applied it in one of those situations.

3. What is Rule 2?

4. Give two or three examples where you could have applied this rule but did not, and describe how results might have been different if you had applied it in one of those situations.

5. Which of the following puts pressure on a game project?

   a. New funding

   b. Taking people away to have them work on another game

   c. A requirement to add more levels to be comparable to a competitor's recently announced title

   d. b and c

6. EXTRA CREDIT: Name two science fiction video games that feature the phrases "Don't Panic" and "Trust No One."

CHAPTER 2

BEING A GAME TESTER

In This Chapter

- Testing versus playing
- Identifying bugs
- Reporting bugs
- Handling fixes

B eing a game tester starts with being a game player. This is the part that seems to attract most people to the profession. Just imagine— getting paid to play games! For the most part you don't get to test (play) whatever you feel like on any given day. You are given assignments that you're expected to complete thoroughly and on time, even if it means you have to stay late to get them done. The tests and the hours will pile up anytime you get close to a major release.

Just playing the game isn't enough to be a good tester, however. Sure, you need to have a knack for finding problems, but you also need to do a good job at other things, such as documenting and reporting bugs, reporting test progress, and helping developers find and fix your bugs. These tasks are done over and over again until the game ships. Think of the acronym "PIANo TV"—**P**lay, **I**dentify, **A**mplify, **N**otify, and **o**ptionally **T**estify and **V**erify.

PLAYING GAMES

At home, you play games to have fun. You get to choose what to play, when to play, and how to play it. Testing games can still be fun, but you have fewer choices about what, when, and how to play. Everything you do when you play is for a purpose—either to explore some area of the game, check that a specific rule is being enforced, or look for a particular kind of problem.

Your job begins by running a series of tests that are assigned to you. Some of the tests are very specific and consist of step-by-step instructions. These rely on your keen observations and attention to details. This is a good format for user interface (UI) testing.

Here's a short example for testing the character selection portion of the Edit Trooper UI in the *Song Summoner: The Unsung Heroes – Encore"* RPG (the character gallery is pictured in Figure 2.1):

1. Enter a town and tap the "Edit Trooper" icon to enter the Edit Trooper screen.

☐ Check that the main character's picture appears first in the list, with his name (Ziggy) above his image. Also check that the image frame and background reflect his current status in the game (in this case, "Gold").

☐ Check that the circular control within the slider bar is positioned to the far left, the number 1 appears to the left of the bar, and the number at the right of the slider bar equals the number of characters you have acquired during the game (83 in this example).

☐ Check that Ziggy's character class "Capable Conductor" appears in the upper left of the box in the lower left corner of the screen.

☐ Check that Ziggy's stats for Movement, Range, HP, and SP are correct.

☐ Check that a miniature version of Ziggy's avatar appears to the right of his stats, with a small musical note at his right.

FIGURE 2.1 *Song Summoner* Edit Trooper selection screen showing the initial state of the character gallery.

2. Scroll one character over by swiping the screen from right to left.

☐ Check that the second character's picture appears first in the list, with his name above his image. Also check that the image frame and background reflect his current status in the game.

☐ Check that the circular control within the slider bar moved slightly to the right and that the numbering on the ends of the bar has not changed.

☐ Check that the newly selected character's class appears in the upper left of the box in the lower left corner of the screen.

☐ Check that the newly selected character's stats for Movement, Range, HP, and SP are correct.

☐ Check that a miniature version of the new character's avatar appears to the right of his or her stats, with a small musical note to the right.

3. Scroll one character to the right by holding your finger on the circular control within the slider bar and dragging it slightly to the right until the third character's image is in the center of the screen.

☐ Perform the same checks that you made in step 2, but this time for the proper display of the third character's information.

4. Scroll one character to the left by swiping the screen from left to right.

☐ Perform the same checks that you made in step 2.

5. Scroll one character to the left by holding your finger on the circular control within the slider bar and dragging it slightly to the right until the first character's image is in focus.

☐ Perform the same checks that you made in step 1.

6. Scroll all the way to the end of the trooper list (see Figure 2.2) by swiping from right to left (multiple times if necessary).

FIGURE 2.2 *Song Summoner* Edit Trooper selection screen showing the end of the character gallery.

☐ Check that the last character's picture appears first in the list, with his name above his image. Also check that the image frame and background reflect the character's current status in the game.

☐ Check that the circular control within the slider bar is positioned to the far right and that the number 1 appears to the left of the bar and the number at the right of the slider bar equals the number of characters you have acquired during the game.

☐ Check that the last character's class appears in the upper left of the box in the lower left corner of the screen.

☐ Check that the last character's stats for Movement, Range, HP, and SP are correct.

☐ Check that a miniature version of the last character's avatar appears to the right of his or her stats, with a small musical note to the right.

7. Scroll all the way back to the beginning of the list by holding your finger on the circular control within the slider bar and dragging it all the way to the left until the first character's image is in focus.

☐ Perform the same checks that you made in step 1.

8. Scroll all the way to the end of the list by holding your finger on the circular control within the slider bar and dragging it all the way to the right until the last character's image is in focus.

☐ Perform the same checks that you made in step 6.

9. Scroll all the way to the beginning of the trooper list by swiping from left to right (multiple times if necessary).

☐ Perform the same checks that you made in step 1.

So, you see, you are given specific operations to perform and details to check at each step. This can become tedious over the course of a long test case, especially when doing many of these tests one after the other. To keep subtle problems from slipping past you, maintain concentration and treat each item as if it's the first time you've seen it.

Other test assignments involve more open-ended directives, and might be in checklist or outline form. These tests rely more on your own individual game knowledge, experience, and skills.

Testing special moves in a fighting game is a typical situation where you might run into a checklist. For example, use the following checklist from 2Dmoveset.com, "Indomitable Detective Chun-Li," [2DMOVESET 10] to test Chun Li's special attacks in *Super Street Fighter IV*. To successfully and efficiently complete this testing, you must be able to perform the game controller stick motions and button presses with the right timing and in the right fight situation for each move including:

- Lightning Legs
- Kikouken (Fireball)

- Hazan Shuu (Overhead Flip Kick)

- Spinning Bird Kick

- Air Throw

- Senretsu Kyaku (Hyper Lightning Legs)

- Housenka (Ultra 1)

- Kikoshou (Ultra 2)

- Kouhou Kaiten Kyaku (Flip Cross Up Kick)

- Yousou Kyaku (Head Stomp)

- Rear Spin Kick

- Hop Kick

Whereas a checklist tends to focus on verifying a narrow set of game behaviors, an outline can be used to test a broader range of results without worrying about the detailed steps to take to reach that goal. As of June, 2011, there were 123 Achievements possible in the Mafia Wars™ (Zynga®) game played on Facebook®. Imagine having to define or follow a button-by-button series of steps to complete jobs, fight in different locations, earn enough money, and reach the levels necessary to unlock and complete each achievement! You, the tester, need to know the game well enough to pick the right strategies and spend your points wisely. Additionally, you must play the game well enough to reach the goals for each achievement. Table 2.1 is a compact outline format that can be used for this purpose. For the sake of brevity, only the 17 New York Achievements are shown here. For a full list, go to your Mafia Wars profile and click the Achievements tab.

TABLE 2.1 Mafia Wars Achievements—New York

Achievement	Requirement
One Down	Master at least one stage in New York
What else you got?	Master all New York job tiers
Armed & Dangerous	Own 10 Tommy guns
Personal Fleet	Own 500 town cars

(Continued)

TABLE 2.1 Continued

Achievement	Requirement
The First is the Hardest	Make a $1,000,000 deposit (after bank fee)
Personal Bailout	Make a $1,000,000,000 deposit (after bank fee)
That's with a "T"	Make a $1,000,000,000,000 deposit (after bank fee)
Nest Egg	Make a $10,000,000,000,000 deposit (after bank fee)
What's After Trillion?	Deposit 999 Trillion Dollars
Collector	Vault any collection set
Curator	Vault at least nine New York collection sets
Slum Lord	Own a level 30 Tenement property
Knife Thrower	Loot 10 Butterfly Knives
Uncle Sam	Own 50 Federal Agents
Land Holder	Own 1 of each NY property
Land Baron	Upgrade all New York properties to level 25 or higher
Real Estate Tycoon	Upgrade all New York properties to level 100 or higher

In addition to writing and running your own tests, you could also find yourself writing tests for other testers to run. Later in this book you learn some formal methods for designing tests, but that option might not always be available to you. In an informal testing situation, choose from step-by-step, checklist, or outline form to describe the testing you want done, or to record any informal testing you might have completed.

IDENTIFYING BUGS

Game testing has two purposes. The first is to find defects that are in the game code or design. The second is to demonstrate which parts of the game are working properly. When the test doesn't find any problems, it "Passes." When a test finds a problem, it "Fails."

Another possible outcome of a test is "Blocked," which means an existing problem keeps you from getting to other parts of the test. One such example is when the PC version of *BioShock 2* crashes when you try to accept a friend invite on the Multiplayer Menu. This blocks you from doing any further testing in multiplayer mode after an invite [BIOSHOCK 10].

The test could also be "Not Available," meaning the part you are supposed to test has not been included in the version of the game you were given to test. It might be because the developers are still in the process of getting all the game elements put together, so a level, item, function, or character is intentionally left out of the test release. It could also be that the game version for the platform you are testing does not include what you need to test, such as the five additional *UFC Undisputed 2010* Ultimate Fight Mode events and three exclusive fighters, which are only available for the PS3 [UFC 10].

Here Comes the Judge

Not every tester will notice the same defects when testing the same part of a game. Likewise, not every tester will run the same test in the same way. Psychology can have an explanation as to why this happens, in the form of the Myers-Briggs Type Indicator (MBTI). One of the categories in this indicator rates a person as either a Judger or a Perceiver, as follows:

Judger Defined

Judgers require a very structured, ordered, and predictable environment to be happy. If Judgers are working in an unorganized environment, Judgers will either try to organize it or they will constantly complain that things are a mess, nothing is in its place or that the disorganized workplace environment affects their productivity. Judgers thrive in union or highly regulated environments. Judgers work first and play later.

Perceiver Defined

Perceivers like a more laid back approach. Perceivers focus on the experience and so perceivers prefer things to unfold as they will. Perceivers do not like to limit options and thrive in dynamic, ever-changing workplace environments. Perceivers can work in a mess; in fact, they prefer to work in chaos as it stimulates creative thinking when predictability is removed. Perceivers seek employers that offer flexible working arrangements. Perceivers love to play, therefore if work is playful and unconventional, they are happy [SUITE101 10].

NOTE

Not sure if you are more of a Judger or Perceiver? You can take a quick, informal temperament test at the Personality Test Center [PERSON 01] to find out.

Read more about Judgers and Perceivers at Suite101®.com, Judgers and Perceivers at Work: MBTI or Myers Briggs Type and Preferred Working Environments [SUITE101 10].

The tendency toward one of these behaviors versus the others will manifest itself in the way you approach testing, and the kinds of defects you tend to find. For example, a Judger is good at following step-by-step instructions, running through a number of tests, and finding problems in game text, the user manual, and anywhere the game is inconsistent with historical facts. The Perceiver tends to wander around the game, come up with unusual situations to test, report problems with playability, and comment on the overall game experience. Assign Judgers to verify the game's "authenticity" and Perceivers to verify its "fun-ticity."

Conversely, there are things Judgers and Perceivers might not be good at. A Judger would perhaps not do steps or notice problems that aren't in the written tests. A Perceiver could miss seeing problems when running a series of repetitive tests. Although testing without written tests provides more freedom, Perceivers might not always have good documentation of how they got a bug to show up.

You are probably not 100% of one type, but you most likely have a tendency toward one or the other. Don't treat that as a limitation. Use that knowledge to become more aware of areas you can improve so you can find more bugs in the games you test. Your goal should be to use both sets of qualities at the appropriate times and for the right purpose. When you see a bug that someone else found and it makes you think "Wow! I never would have tried that," then go and talk to that person and ask her what made her think of doing that. Do this often and you can start to find those same kinds of bugs by asking yourself "How would Linda test this?" Make sure you share your own bug stories too. *Computer Related Risks* [NEUMANN 94] and *Fatal Defect* [PETERSON 96] are two books that will give you some more insight, with real-world examples and analysis from outside of the video game industry.

Table 2.2 shows some of the ways that each personality type affects the kinds of bugs testers will find and what kinds of testing are best used to find them.

TABLE 2.2 Tester Personality Comparison

Judger	Perceiver
Run the tests for...	Find a way to...
Conventional game playing	Unconventional game playing
Repetitive testing	Testing variety
User manual, script testing	Gameplay, usability testing
Factual accuracy of game	Realistic experience of game
Step-by-step or checklist-based testing	Open-ended or outline-based testing
May rely too much on test details to see defects	May stray from the original test purpose
Concerned about game contents	Concerned about game context

AMPLIFYING PROBLEMS

Normally the word "amplify" makes you think of something getting bigger or louder. In this case, "amplifying" your defect will narrow it down for the developers, make it more likely the defect will be fixed right the first time, and reduce the overall time and cost spent on the problem.

If you found a way to crash the game by performing basic operations, there's not much else you need to do to draw attention to your defect in order to get it fixed. If the way to cause the crash is obscure, or you find it late in the project, or it seems difficult to pinpoint and repair, your defect will likely take a back seat to other ones. In both cases, there are some specific ways that you can amplify the defects to maximize their "fixability."

Early Bird

Find defects *early* by testing the following items as soon as they become available. If you don't know how to get the information you need, ask the development team or build engineer for some kind of report of the changes put into each build.

- New levels, characters, items, cut scenes, and so on as soon as they are introduced

- New animations, lighting, physics, particle effects, and so on

- New code that adds functionality or fixes defects

- New subsystems, middleware, engines, drivers, and so on

- New dialog, text, translations, and so on

- New music, sound effects, voice-overs, audio accessories, and so on

Places Everyone

Once you have found a defect in some deep, dark corner of the game, that might not be the only place it shows up. If you stop looking there and hurry to log your bug and move on to the next test, you might overlook a more common place or scenario in the game where the same bug shows up. It would be nice if all game bugs were fixed before the product shipped, but there are reasons why that's not done. A defect that only happens in an obscure place can get left in the game that ends up on the store shelves.

Find defects in *more places* within the game by looking for the following:

- All of the places in the game where the same faulty behavior can be activated

- All of the places in the code that call the defective class, function, or subroutine

- All of the game functions that use the same defective item, scene, and so on

- All of the items, levels, characters, and so on that have a shared attribute with the faulty one (for example, character race, weapon type, levels with snow, and so on)

Then, use this two-step process to increase the frequency of the defect:

1. Eliminate unnecessary steps to get the defect to appear.

2. Find more frequent and/or more common scenarios that could include the remaining essential steps.

NOTIFYING THE TEAM

Once you've found the problem and can describe all the ways in which it affects the game, you need to record that information and notify the developers about it. Typically, project teams will use software tools to help with this. DevTrack™ is a defect management tool that has been used by many game companies including Activision®, Electronic Arts™, Vivendi Universal™, and Sony Online Entertainment®. Although you don't have to be concerned about the installation and management of the tool itself, you need to become familiar with how to best use it to record your defects and get them closed. This section is not meant to be a full-blown tutorial, but provides an initial exposure and discussion of the following:

- Using a defect tracking system

- Information that is essential to good defect reports

- Avoiding typical mistakes and omissions

- Extra things you can do to help get your bug looked at and fixed

Figure 2.3 shows the new defect entry window of the DevTrack tool. The main elements of this window are the function selection along the top,

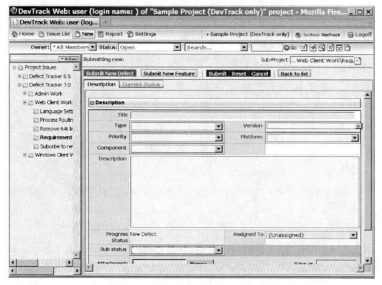

FIGURE 2.3 DevTrack New Defect window. (Permission from Colleen Grisley, TechExcel.)

the folder browser at the left, and the data viewing/entry screen on the right. Field names with red text provide a visual cue that these fields are mandatory. You must provide information in each of these fields before your defect can be submitted.

In general, this function and the view selection choices are very similar to using an email program like Microsoft® Outlook®. You can see which things need your attention, browse through them, and add information to them if you need to.

The data entry screen is where you make your contribution, so the following sections explore some of the key fields you need to work with. To learn more about using other functions of DevTrack, you can explore the demo at TechExcel's "Try DevSuite Live" Web page [TECHEXCEL 10].

Describe

Start your entry with a descriptive title. Generic or broad descriptions like "Had to restart game" or "Problem in multiplayer lobby" do not sufficiently describe the problem to get the attention of the people who need to go after the problem to fix it. Imagine picking up a newspaper and reading headlines like "Some Crime Happened" or "A Team Won"—you might be left wondering. Instead, provide one or two details that help narrow down the problem.

Take a cue from the Sports page. If a team beats another under no special circumstances, you might see a headline like "Yankees Beat Red Sox." If something else noteworthy happens, however, there might be more detail, such as "Marlins Shut Out Yankees to Win Series." Think of your bug as a noteworthy event that will be competing for the reader's attention.

Figure 2.4 shows Title and Description fields for a problem found while playing the free version of *Doodle Bowling* for iPhone® and iPod touch®. In this case, the Title mentions *what* happened and *where* it happened. Always include the "what" and then add one or two of the distinctive "who," "where," "when," or "how" factors.

In the Description, be sure to include all of these details: who (player—as opposed to a computer opponent or NPC), what (pin in gutter gets replaced), where (in "realistic" themed bowling alley), when (in second half of frame), how (pin is upright). Then, describe how you were able to remedy or avoid the situation, if at all, and add any things that you tried to do that would not reverse or undo the effects of the problem. This serves two purposes: First, it helps the project leaders evaluate the importance of fixing the bug. Second, it gives the developers clues about how the problem happened and how they might go about fixing it. It also establishes the minimum criteria for testing later on when you need to verify that this bug was properly fixed.

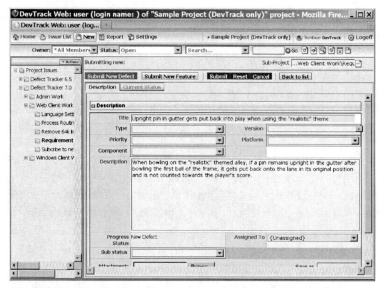

FIGURE 2.4 Defect Title and Description. (Permission from Colleen Grisley, TechExcel.)

Another way to describe your defect in detail would be to provide a step-by-step description of how you found it. Don't start from when you turned the computer on, but include the steps that are relevant to reproducing the problem. An alternative description for the "pin in the gutter" bug would be:

Select the "realistic" *Doodle Bowling* theme. Continue to play until you leave a pin upright in the gutter. When the pins are reset, the pin in the gutter has been placed back onto the lane in its original position.

You should also include information about any additional places you looked for the problem where it *didn't* show up. For example, does an upright pin in the gutter after rolling the second ball in the frame get counted?

Pick a Type

The defect Type field is also important for the routing and handling of your defect. Use your best judgment to provide a Type, even if the field is not mandatory. This helps the team understand how urgent it might be and who is best equipped to handle the issue. What we have here is a good old-fashioned "Bug." Figure 2.5 shows a list provided by DevTrack.

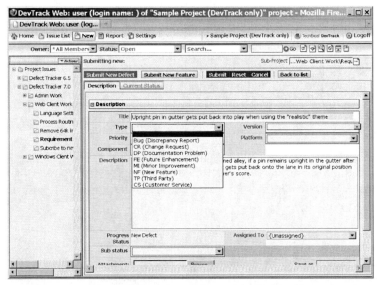

FIGURE 2.5 Defect Type selection. (Permission from Colleen Grisley, TechExcel.)

Not everything you find as a tester is a bug in the sense that something doesn't work as planned. You will find things that could be improved or added to the game to make it better. These kinds of issues would be classified as "Minor Improvement" or "New Feature," respectively.

Likewise, you can enter a "Future Enhancement" for such things as:

- An idea for the sequel

- An optimization to make for the next platform you port the game to

- Adding support for a brand new type of controller

- A feature or item to make available for download after the game ships

Another function of the game tester is to check the documentation. You could be looking for consistency with how the actual game functions, important things that are left out, or production errors such as missing pages, mislabeled diagrams, and so on. These would fall into the "Documentation Problem" type.

The "Third Party" type could be problems introduced by software or hardware that your team does not produce. For example, a particular brand of steering wheel controller doesn't give force feedback to the user, whereas three other brands work fine.

For the kinds of defects in which the game is simply not working the way it is supposed to, the "Bug" type would be specified, while the "CR" (Change Request) choice might be used for something that has a larger scope, such as redoing the collision detection mechanism in the game.

Prioritize

Depending on the "rules of engagement" for your project, you might also be required to classify the defect priority (or "severity") and/or type. Figure 2.6 shows a pull-down menu of choices for assigning an initial priority to this defect.

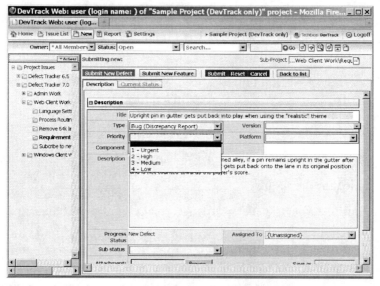

FIGURE 2.6 Defect Priority selection. (Permission from Colleen Grisley, TechExcel.)

The names and meanings of the priority choices could be different for your project, but the concept is the same. Rank the defect according to its importance, as defined for each choice. For example, "Urgent" can be defined as a defect that stops or aborts the game in progress without any way to recover and continue the game. An Urgent bug might also have side effects, such as causing the player's recent progress to be lost, as well as the loss of newly won or discovered items. If your character was frozen in a multiplayer game, this could also result in player death and its associated penalties after the evil horde you were fighting continued happily pummeling you until your health reached 0.

A "High" priority bug could be a problem that causes some severe consequence to the player, such as not getting a quest item after successfully completing the quest. This priority could also be used for an "Urgent" type of defect that happens under obscure circumstances. You should be stingy about making that kind of a downgrade when you first log the bug, especially in a multiplayer game, because nefarious players might be able exploit that bug to their advantage or your disadvantage if the obscure circumstances are discovered in the released game and subsequently publicized. An example of this kind of misuse happened in the *Asheron's Call* PC-based online game where players would kill their character and then intentionally crash the game server. Once the server was back up, they were able to retrieve a duplicate of a rare item from their corpse. See "A Note on the Hotfix" sidebar for the developers' response to this defect when it occurred in January of 2001.

A Note on the Hotfix

January 23, 2001

We wanted to thoroughly explain the cause of today's hotfix, and what impact it will have on you, the players.

Late Monday night, a bug was discovered that allowed players to intentionally crash the server their characters were on. Additionally, a person could use this bug and the resulting time warp (reverting back to the last time your character was saved to the database), to duplicate items. By intentionally crashing the servers, this also caused every other player on that server to crash and time warp, thus losing progress.

We were able to track down this bug and we turned off the servers to prevent additional people from crashing the servers and/or duplicating items.

The good news is that we were able to track down all the players who were exploiting this bug and crashing the servers. As we have stated in the past: Since *Asheron's Call* was commercially released, it has been our policy that if players make use of a bug that we did not catch or did not have time to fix before releasing the game, we would not punish them for our mistake, instead directing our efforts toward fixing those bugs as soon as possible. *The exceptions to this are with those bugs that significantly affect the performance or stability of the game.*

The players who were discovered repeatedly abusing this bug to bring down the servers are being removed from the game. While we dislike taking this type of action, we feel it is important that other players know that it is unacceptable to disrupt another player's game in such a fashion.

We deeply regret this bug, and sincerely apologize for the consequences this has had on our players.

The *Asheron's Call* Team [ASHERON 01]

"Medium" defects cause noticeable problems but probably do not impact the player in terms of rewards or progress. The difference between "High" and "Medium" could be the difference between getting your bug looked at and fixed, put aside to be fixed in a post-release patch, or left in the game as it is. When in doubt, unless otherwise directed by your project leads, assign the "High" priority so it will be fairly evaluated before being downgraded. Be careful not to abuse this tactic, or the defects you find will not be taken as seriously as they should.

The "Low" priority is normally for very minute defects that don't affect gameplay, those that occur under impossible conditions, or those that are a matter of personal taste. For example, in *Madden 2008*, many long player names are cutoff or abbreviated on their jerseys and stat displays, including prominent players Ben Roethlisberger and T. J. Houshmanzadeh. Even if this is intentional, it should be pointed out by the tester as something that detracts from the game experience. Figures 2.7 and 2.8 show two of the scenarios in which the altered names are revealed during gameplay.

FIGURE 2.7 Roethlisberger misspelling.

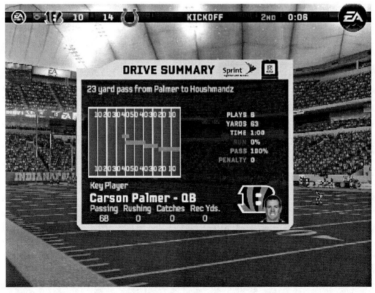

FIGURE 2.8 Houshmandzadeh name truncation.

In many game companies, an additional "severity" rating is used in conjunction with a "priority." In these cases, the severity field describes the potential impact of the bug on the player, while the priority field is used by the team to establish which defects are determined to be the most important to fix. These categories can differ when a low impact (severity) defect is very conspicuous, such as misspelling the game's name on the main menu, or when a very severe defect is not expected to occur in a player's lifetime, such as a crash that is triggered when the console's date rolls over to the year 3000. The ability of a player to recover from a defect, and the risk or difficulty associated with fixing a defect, are also factors in determining the priority, apart from the severity. In this arrangement, severities are typically assigned by the person who logs the defect and the priority gets assigned by the CCB or the project manager.

Be Helpful

Finally, make sure you fill in any remaining required fields and include any other artifacts or information that might be of help to anyone trying to assess or repair the problem, such as the fact that the *Doodle Bowling* bug was first introduced in version 1.6 of the game.

In addition to adding more details to the description, with DevTrack you can use the Attachment function to add helpful files to the defect record. Attach or provide links to any of the following items you can get your hands on:

- Server logs
- Screen shots
- Transcripts from the character's journal
- Sound files
- Saved character file
- A digital recording (including audio) of the events leading up to and including the appearance of the bug
- Traces of code in a debugger
- Log files kept by the game platform, middleware, or hardware
- Operating system pop-ups and error codes

■ Data captured by simulators for mobile development environments, such as Eclipse for BlackBerry ™ or Android ™, Apple's XCode IDE, and Microsoft's Windows® Mobile SDK

Figures 2.9 and 2.10 show two screen shots to attach to the *Doodle Bowling* bug report. These provide before and after the error event occurred (the pin in the gutter was put back into play), and also show the impact on the player's score at the bottom of the screen.

FIGURE 2.9 Pin remains upright in the gutter after rolling the first ball. (Permission Marc Andreoli, GameResort LLC.)

FIGURE 2.10 Pin appears back on the lane in the second half of the frame. (Permission Marc Andreoli, GameResort LLC.)

Not all defect tracking systems you use will have the same kind of structure or user interface as DevTrack. Pay attention to getting the basics right and ask the other testers or your test lead what else is expected of you when reporting a bug. For example, you might be expected to send an email to a special mailing list if the defect tracking system you are using does not do that automatically, or you could be using a shared spreadsheet instead of a tool specifically designed for defect tracking.

!
TIP
For an online list of more defect tracking tool options, see "Bug and Defect Tracking Tools" [APTEST 10].

Pass or Fail?

Tests that fail are good from your perspective, but it's also important for the project to know which tests passed. You will probably be expected to record the completion and results of your tests by indicating which passed and which failed. Other status types might include "Blocked" or "Not Available," where "Blocked" indicates that an existing problem is preventing you from executing one or more steps in the tests, and "Not Available" indicates that a feature or capability that is part of the test is not available in the version of the game you are testing. For example, a multiplayer scenario test is "Blocked" if a defect in the game prevents you from connecting to the multiplayer server. A test that can't be run because the level hasn't been added to the game yet would be classified as "Not Available."

Usually this information goes to the test lead and it's important to provide it in a timely manner. It might just be a physical sheet of paper you fill out and put on a pile, or an electronic spreadsheet or form you send in. This information can affect planning which tests get run for the next release, as well as the day-to-day assignments of each tester.

!
TIP
In the course of testing, keep track of what version of the game you are running, what machine settings to use, peripherals, and so on. It's also a good idea to make and keep various "save" files for the game so you can go back later to rerun old tests, or try new ones without having to play through the game again. You should also keep your own list of the bugs you have found so that you can follow up on them during the project. It's not uncommon to become the victim of bug reports that were "lost" or "moved," even though the bugs themselves were still in the software. Just make sure you have a way to identify each saved file with the game version it was made for. Otherwise, you can get false test results by using old files with new releases or vice versa.

TESTIFY TO OTHERS

As much as you might become attached to the defects you find, you could have very little to say directly about whether or not they get fixed. Your precious defects will likely be in the hands of a merciless Change Control Board (CCB). This might go by some other name in your company or project team, but the purpose of this group is to prioritize, supervise, and drive the completion of the most necessary defects to create the best shipping game possible when the project deadline arrives. This implies that defects are easier to get fixed when they are found early in the project than when they are found later. The threat of messing up the rest of the game and missing the shipping deadline will scare many teams away from fixing difficult defects near the end of the project. This is why you want to find the most significant issues early!

The CCB generally includes representatives from development, testing, and project management. On a small game team, everyone might get together to go over the bugs. On larger productions, the leads from various groups within the project will meet, along with the project manager and the configuration manager—the person responsible for doing the builds and making sure the game code files are labeled and stored properly in the project folder or other form of code repository. Your defects will be competing with others for the attention of the CCB. The defect type and priority play an important role in this competition. Also, if you were diligent in providing details about how to reproduce the bug and why it is important to fix, your bugs will get more attention.

Different strategies for determining the "final" priority of a defect can produce different results for the same defect. If only a single individual, like the head of the CCB, gets to decide on the priority, then the tendency will be for defects to have a lower average priority (meaning less "severe") than if people with different perspectives, such as producers, designers, developers, and testers, each give a score and the average score is used.

Also keep in mind that if your project has a particular goal or threshold for which kinds of defects are allowed to be released in the game, then anything you submit will be under pressure to get de-prioritized below that threshold. This is where amplifying the defect helps you make a stronger case for why something should be considered high priority versus medium, for example.

One of the difficulties some testers have is balancing "ownership" of the defect with knowing when to "let go." You are expected to find problems and report them. Other people on the project are usually designated to take responsibility for properly processing and repairing the defects. Don't take it personally if your defect doesn't get fixed first, or other people don't get as excited about it as you do.

VERIFY THE FIX

As a tester, your involvement doesn't end after the bug is found and reported. You can expect to help developers reproduce the bug, run experiments for them, and re-test after they think the bug is fixed. Sometimes you will run the test on a special build that the developer makes and then you will need to re-run it after the fix is put into the main version of the game release.

Summary

Use your knowledge of your Judger/Perceiver traits to get better at finding a wider variety of defects and to get more testing done. This includes reading and thoroughly knowing the rules of the game. At the same time, take on positions, assignments, or roles that make the most of your tendencies.

Once you've seen a bug, identify it and try to make it show up in more places, and more frequently. Then you're ready to document the bug in the defect tracking system. Use a specific title and provide a detailed description. Include files that provide evidence of the problem and could help reproduce and track down the defect. A poorly documented bug costs the CCB time to figure out the proper severity to assign to the problem, developers' time to reproduce and root cause the problem so it can be fixed, and *your* time in reprocessing the same defect instead of moving on to find more bugs.

While you're testing, have the tape running, so to speak, so that when the defect happens you have all the evidence to include in the bug report. Screen shots and log files really help!

Over the course of any project, expect to spend a portion of your time writing up defects, reporting your results, going back over your issues with developers, and re-running your tests on one or two experimental builds before a good fix makes it into a general release.

Exercises

1. What is Rule 2?

2. Identify each of the following as Judger (J) or Perceiver (P) behaviors:

a. Noticed a misspelling in the user manual

b. Created a character with all skills set to 0 just to see what would happen

c. Reported that the AK-47 doesn't fire at the correct rate

d. Found a way to get his skater off the map

3. Which of the following is an appropriately detailed defect title?

a. Game crashes

b. Found a bug in multiplayer mode

c. Can't drive Fastkat vehicle into the hallway south of the main chamber

d. Character dies unexpectedly

4. Which of the following should be in the defect description?

a. Where the defect happened

b. How the defect happened

c. Who in the game caused the problem

d. What the defect did to the game

e. All of the above

5. Your first assignment for Gamecorp is testing a first-person shooter game. Your character, a cyborg wearing heavy armor, is on the second level carrying a knife and ammo for the megazooka weapon. You find an empty megazooka, pick it up and try to fire it, but it doesn't shoot because it's reading 0 ammo. You know from your project meetings that the weapon is supposed to automatically load any ammo you are carrying for it. What are some things you should do to "amplify" this defect?

6. What are some of the kinds of problems you might find by running the step-by-step test example from the "Playing Games" section of this chapter?

7. Rewrite the step-by-step test in outline form. What are some advantages of doing this? What are some disadvantages?

CHAPTER 3

WHY TESTING IS IMPORTANT

In This Chapter

- Types of defects to look for
- Looking at source code to find bugs
- Other sources of problems

W riting this chapter led to a lengthy list of answers to the question of "Why is testing important?", including:

- It's easy for game software to go wrong.
- There are many opportunities to make a mistake.
- Game software is complex.
- People write game software and people make mistakes.
- Software tools are used to produce games and these tools are not perfect.
- There is a great deal of money at stake for games that succeed.

- Games must work on multiple platforms with a variety of configurations and devices.

- People expect more out of every game you make.

- It better work right if over a million people will be playing at the same time online and paying a monthly fee for that privilege.

- Critics are standing by, ready to rate your game in print, in app stores, and on the Internet.

- Games have to be fun, meet expectations, and get released on time.

A short and simple answer, which summarizes everything in this list, is "Because games get made wrong." If you can identify mechanisms or patterns that describe how games get made wrong, you can relate that to what kinds of problems you should look out for and anticipate testing as you follow your path to becoming a top-notch game tester. Maybe the people who care the most about game testing can help you to understand.

WHO CARES?

Testing must be important to game publishers because of all the trouble they go through to staff and fund testers and then organize and manage the rounds of beta testing that precede the official game release. It's important to console providers because they require certain quality standards to be met before they will allow a title to ship for their box. Mobile game testing is required by handset manufacturers and wireless carriers in order for games to get approved for use on their devices and networks.

Testing is important to the development team. They rely on testers to find problems in the code. The testers bear the burden of getting blamed when serious defects escape their notice. If defects do escape, someone wonders why they paid all that money for testing.

Testing is important because of the contractual commitments and complex nature of the software required to deliver a top-notch game. Every time someone outside of your team or company gets a look at the game, it is going to be scrutinized and publicized. If all goes well, you might get canonized. If not, then your sales and profits could vaporize.

Despite all of the staffing, funding, and caring, games still get made wrong.

DEFECT TYPING

Let's leave the people behind for a minute and look at the software. Software can fail in a variety of ways. It is useful to classify defects into categories that reveal how the defect was introduced and how it can be found or, even better, avoided in the future. The Orthogonal Defect Classification (ODC) system, developed by IBM, was developed for this purpose. This system defines multiple categories of classification, depending on the development activity that is taking place. This chapter explores the eight Defect Type classifications, and examines their relevance to game defects. The Defect Type classifies the way the defect was introduced into the code. As we go along, keep in mind that each defect can be the result of either incorrect implementation or code that is simply missing. The following ODC Defect Types summarize the different categories of software elements that go into producing the game code:

- Function

- Assignment

- Checking

- Timing

- Build/Package/Merge

- Algorithm

- Documentation

- Interface

If you have trouble remembering this list, try remembering the acronym FACT BADI (pronounced "Fact Baddie").

Defect examples in this section are taken from the *Dark Age of Camelot* (DAOC) game Version 1.70i Release Notes, posted on July 1, 2004 [JEUX 04]. A predecessor to *World of Warcraft, Dark Age of Camelot* is also a Massive Multiplayer Online Role Playing Game (MMORPG) that is continually modified by design to continue to expand and enhance the players' game experience. As a result, it is patched frequently with the dual purpose of fixing bugs and adding or modifying capabilities. This gives us the opportunity to examine it as it is being developed, as opposed to a game that has a single point of release to the public.

The defect description by itself doesn't tell us *how* the defect was introduced in the code—which is what the Defect Type classification describes. Because we don't have access to the development team's defect tracking system in order to know exactly how this bug occurred, let's take one specific bug and look at how it *could* have been caused by any of the defect types.

Here is a fix released in a patch for *Dark Age of Camelot,* which will be referenced throughout the examples in this chapter:

"The Vanish realm ability now reports how many seconds of super stealth you have when used."

If that's how it's supposed to work, then you can imagine that the bug was logged with a description that went something like this:

"The Vanish realm ability fails to report how many seconds of super stealth you have when it's used."

Details of the Vanish ability are as follows:

Provides the stealther with super stealth, which cannot be broken. Also will purge DoTs and Bleeds and provides immunity to crowd control. This ability lasts for one to five seconds depending on the level of Vanish. The stealther also receives an increase in movement speed as listed. A stealther cannot attack for 30 seconds after using this ability.

Effect:

L1 - Normal Speed, 1 second immunity

L2 - Speed 1, 2 second immunity

L3 - Speed 5, 5 second immunity

Type: Active

Re-use: 10 minutes.

Classes that can use Vanish: Infiltrator, Shadowblade [ZAM 11].

Functions

A *Function* error is one that affects a game capability or the way the user experiences the game. The code providing this function is missing or incorrect in some or all instances where it is required.

Here's an imaginary code snippet that illustrates code that could be used to set up and initiate the Vanish ability. The player's Vanish ability level is passed to a handler routine specific to the Vanish ability. This routine is required to make all of the function calls necessary to activate this ability. The g_vanishSpeed and g_vanishTime arrays store values for each of the three levels of this ability, plus a value of 0 for level 0. These arrays are named with the "g_" prefix to indicate that they are global, because the same results apply for all characters that have this ability. Values appearing in all uppercase letters indicate that these are constants.

Missing a call to a routine that displays the time of the effect is an example of a Function type defect for this code. Maybe this block of code was copied from some other ability and the "vanish" globals were added but without the accompanying display code. Alternatively, there could have been a miscommunication about how this ability works and the programmer didn't know that the timer should be displayed.

```
void HandleVanish(level)
{
    if (level == 0)
        return; // player does not have this ability so
leave
    PurgeEffects(damageOverTime);
    IncreaseSpeed(g_vanishSpeed[level]);
    SetAttack(SUSPEND, 30SECONDS);
    StartTimer(g_vanishTime[level]);
    return;
} // oops! Did not report seconds remaining to user -
hope they don't notice
```

Alternatively, the function to show the duration to the user could have been included, but called with one or more incorrect values:

```
ShowDuration(FALSE, g_vanishTime[level]);
```

Assignments

A defect is classified as an *Assignment* type when it is the result of incorrectly setting or initializing a value used by the program or when a required value assignment is missing. Many of the assignments take place at the start of a game, a new level, or a game mode. Here are some examples for various game genres:

Sports

- Team schedule
- Initialize score for each game
- Initial team lineups
- Court, field, rink, etc., where game is being played
- Weather conditions and time of day

Role Playing Game (RPG), Adventure

- Starting location on map
- Starting attributes, skills, items, and abilities
- Initialize data for current map
- Initialize journal

Racing

- Initialize track/circuit data
- Initial amount of fuel or energy at start of race
- Placement of power-ups and obstacles
- Weather conditions and time of day

Casino Games, Collectible Card Games, Board Games

- Initial amount of points or money to start with
- Initial deal of cards or placement of pieces
- Initial ranking/seeding in tournaments
- Position at the game table and turn order

Fighting

- Initial health, energy
- Initial position in ring or arena
- Initial ranking/seeding in tournaments
- Ring, arena, etc., where fight is taking place

Strategy

- Initial allocation of units
- Initial allocation of resources
- Starting location and placement of units and resources
- Goals for current scenario

First Person Shooters (FPS)

- Initial health, energy
- Starting equipment and ammunition
- Starting location of players
- Number and strength of CPU opponents

Puzzle Games

- Starting configuration of puzzle
- Time allocated and criteria to complete puzzle
- Puzzle piece or goal point values
- Speed at which puzzle proceeds

You can see from these lists that any changes could tilt the outcome in favor of the player or the CPU. Game programmers pay a lot of attention to balancing all of the elements of the game. Initial value assignments are important for providing that game balance.

Even the Vanish defect could have been the result of an Assignment problem. In the imaginary implementation that follows, the Vanish ability is activated by setting up a data structure and passing it to a generic ability handling routine.

```
ABILITY_STRUCT        realmAbility;
realmAbility.ability = VANISH_ABILITY;
reamAbility.purge = DAMAGE_OVER_TIME_PURGE;
realmAbility.level = g_currentCharacterLevel[VANISH_
ABILITY];
reamAbility.speed = g_vanishSpeed[realmAbility.level]
```

```
realmAbility.attackDelay = 30SECONDS;
realmAbility.duration = g_vanishTime[realmAbility.level];
realmAbility.displayDuration = FALSE;   // wrong flag value
HandleAbility(realmAbility);
```

Alternatively, the assignment of the `displayDuration` flag could be missing altogether. Again, cut and paste could be how the fault was introduced, or it could have been wrong or left out as a mistake on the part of the programmer, or there could have been a misunderstanding about the requirements.

Checking

A *Checking* defect type occurs when the code fails to properly validate data before it is used. This could be that a check for a condition is missing or improperly defined. Some examples of improper checks in C code would be the following:

- "=" instead of "==" used for comparison of two values

- Incorrect assumptions about operator precedence when a series of comparisons are not parenthesized

- "Off by one" comparisons, such as using "<=" instead of "<"

- A value (`*pointer`) compared to NULL instead of an address (`pointer`)—either directly from a stored variable or as a returned value from a function call

- Ignored (not checked) values returned by C library function calls such as `strcpy`

Back to our friend the Vanish bug. The following shows a Checking defect scenario where the ability handler doesn't check the flag for displaying the effect duration or checks the wrong flag to determine the effect duration.

```
HandleAbility (ABILITY_STRUCT ability)
{
    PurgeEffect(ability.purge);
    if (ability.attackDelay > 0)
        StartAttackDelayTimer(ability.attackDelay);
    if (ability.immunityDuration == TRUE)
    // should be checking ability.displayImmunityDuration!
        DisplayAbilityDuration(ability.immunityDuration);
}
```

Timing

Timing defects have to do with the management of shared and real-time resources. Some processes could require time to start or finish, such as saving game information to a hard disk. Operations that depend on that data shouldn't be prevented until completion of the dependent process. A user-friendly way of handling this is to present a transition such as an animated cut scene or a "splash" screen with a progress bar that shows the player that the information is being saved. Once the save operation is complete, the game resumes. Other Timing-sensitive game operations include preloading audio and graphics so that they are immediately available when the game needs them. Many of these functions are now handled in the gaming hardware, but the software still might need to wait for some kind of notification, such as a flag that gets set, an event that gets sent to an event handler, or a routine that gets called once the data is ready for use.

NOTE
The FMOD multiplatform audio engine [GAMEDEV 04] illustrates how an audio event notification scheme is set up and utilized. To play a song, the developer starts by initializing FMOD, loading a song which returns a handle, and passing that handle to the PlaySong function. When an event is eventually detected that should stop the song—such as when the game environment changes to a new setting (city, arena, planet, etc.)—StopSong will do just what its name suggests and the handle can be freed using FreeSong.

User inputs can also require special timing considerations. Double-clicks or repeated presses of a button could cause special actions in the game. There could be mechanisms in the game platform operating system to handle this or the game team might put its own into the code.

In MMORPG and multiplayer mobile games, information is flying around between players and the game server(s). This information has to be reconciled and handled in the proper order or the game behavior will be incorrect. Sometimes the game software tries to predict and fill in what is going on while it is waiting for updated game information. When your character is running around, this can result in jittery movement or even a "rubber band" effect, where you see your avatar run a certain distance and, all of a sudden, you see your character being attacked way back from where you thought you were.

Getting back to the familiar Vanish bug, let's look at a Timing-defect scenario. In this case, pretend that one function starts up an animation for casting the Vanish ability, and a global variable g_animationDone is set when the animation has finished playing. Once g_animationDone is TRUE, the duration should be displayed. A Timing defect can occur if the ShowDuration function is called without waiting for an indication that the Vanish animation has completed. The animation will overwrite anything that gets put on the screen. Here's what the defective portion of code might look like:

```
StartAnimation(VANISH_ABILITY);
ShowDuration(TRUE, g_vanishImmunityTime[level]);
```

This would be the correct code:

```
StartAnimation(VANISH_ABILITY);
while(g_animationDone == FALSE)
    ; // wait for TRUE
ShowDuration(TRUE, g_vanishImmunityTime[level]);
```

Build/Package/Merge

Build/package/merge or, simply, *Build* defects are the result of mistakes in using the game source code library system, managing changes to game files, or identifying and controlling which versions get built.

Building is the act of compiling and linking source code and game assets such as graphics, text, and sound files in order to create an executable game. Configuration management software is often used to help manage and control the use of the game files. Each file might contain more than one asset or code module. Each unique instance of a file is identified by a unique version identifier.

The specification of which versions of each file to build is done in a configuration specification—or "config spec." Trying to specify the individual version of each file to build can be time consuming and error prone, so many configuration management systems provide the ability to label each version. A group of specific file versions can be identified by a single label in the config spec.

Table 3.1 shows some typical uses for labels. Your team perhaps will not use the exact label names shown here, but they will likely have similarly named labels that perform the same functions.

TABLE 3.1 Typical Labels and Uses

Label	Usage
[DevBuild]	Identifies files that programmers are using to try out new ideas or bug fix attempts
[PcOnly]	Developing games for multiple platforms might require a different version of the same file that is built for only one of the supported platforms
[TestRelease]	Identifies a particular set of files to use for a release to the testers. Implies that the programmer is somewhat certain the changes will work. If testing is successful, the next step might be to change the label to an "official" release number
[Release1.1]	After successful building and testing, a release label can be used to "remember" which files were used. This is especially helpful if something breaks badly later on and the team needs to backtrack either to debug the new problem or revert to previous functionality

Each file has a special evolutionary path called the *mainline.* A *version tree* provides a graphical view of all versions of a file and their relationship to one another with respect to the mainline. Figure 3.1 shows how a new version added to the mainline is represented on the version tree.

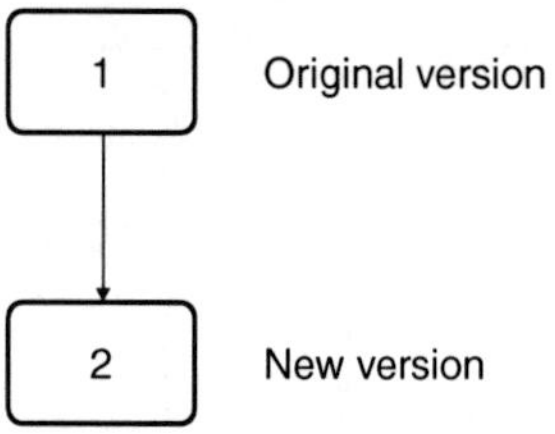

FIGURE 3.1 Mainline of a simple version tree.

Any new versions of files that are derived from one already on the mainline are called *branches*. Files on branches can also have new branches that evolve separately from the first branch. Figure 3.2 shows how a branch is numbered and represented graphically with respect to the mainline.

The changes made on one or more branches can be combined with other changes made in parallel by a process called a *merge*. Merging can be done manually, automatically, or with some assistance from the configuration

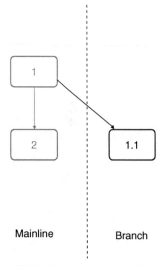

FIGURE 3.2 A version tree with a branch.

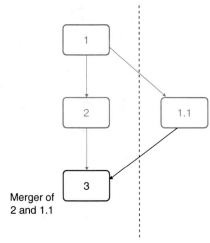

FIGURE 3.3 Merging back to the mainline.

management system, such as highlighting which specific lines of code differ between the two versions being merged together. See Figure 3.3 for an example of how a version tree can evolve as a result of branching and merging.

When a programmer wants to make a change to a file using a configuration management system, the file gets checked out. Then, once the programmer is satisfied with the changes and wants to return the new file as a new version of the original one, the filed is checked in. If at some point in time the programmer changes his mind, the file check out can be cancelled and no changes are made to the original version of the file.

With that background, let's explore some of the ways a mistake can be made.

Specifying a wrong version or label in the configuration specification might still result in successfully generating a game executable, but it will not work as intended. It could be that only one file is wrong, and it has a feature used by only one type of character in one particular scenario. Mistakes like this keep game testers in business.

It's also possible that the configuration specification is correct, but one or more programmers did not properly label the version that needed to be built. The label can be left off, left behind on an earlier version, or typed incorrectly so that it doesn't exactly match the label in the config spec.

Another problem can occur as a result of merging. If a common portion of code is changed in each version being merged, it will take skill to merge the files and preserve the functionality in both changes. The complexity of the merge increases when one version of a file has deleted the portion of code that was updated by the version it is being merged with. If a real live person is doing the merges, these problems will perhaps be easier to spot than if the build computer is making these decisions and changes it entirely on its own.

Sometimes the code will give clues that something is wrong with the build. Comments in the code like *// TAKE THIS OUT BEFORE SHIPPING!* could be an indication that a programmer forgot to move a label or check a newer version of the file back into the system before the build process started.

Referring back to Figure 3.3, assume the following for the Vanish code:

1. Versions 1 and 2 do not display the Vanish duration.

2. Version 1.1 introduced the duration display code.

3. Merging versions 2 and 1.1 produces version 3, but deletes the part of the code in version 1.1 that displays the duration.

For the Vanish display bug, here are some possible Build defect type scenarios:

- The merge that produced version 3 deleted the part of the code in version 1.1 that displays the duration. Version 3 gets built but we get no duration display.

- Versions 1.1 and 2 were properly merged, so the code in version 3 will display the duration. The label used by build specification has not been moved up from version 2 to version 3, however, so version 2 gets built and we get no duration display.

- Versions 1.1 and 2 were properly merged, so the code in version 3 will display the duration. The build label was also moved up from version 2 to version 3. However, the build specification was hard-coded to build version 2 of this file instead of using the label, so we get no duration display.

Algorithms

Algorithm defects include efficiency or correctness problems that result from some calculation or decision process. Think of an algorithm as a process for arriving at a result (for example, the answer is 42) or an outcome (for example, the door opens). Each game is packed with algorithms that you might not even notice if they are working correctly. Improper algorithm design is often at the root of the ways people find to gain an unexpected advantage in a game. Here are some places where you can find algorithms and Algorithm defects in games from various genres:

Sports

- CPU opponent play, formation, and substitution choices
- CPU trade decisions
- Modeling the play calling and decision making of an actual coach or opponent
- The individual AI behavior for all positions for both teams in the game
- Determining camera angle changes as the action moves to various parts of the field/court/ice, etc.
- Determining penalties and referee decisions
- Determining player injuries
- Player stat development during the course of the season
- Enabling special power-ups, awards, or modes

Role Playing Game (RPG), Adventure

- Opposing and friendly character dialog responses
- Opposing and friendly character combat decisions and actions
- Damage calculations based on skills, armor, weapon type and strength, etc.
- Saving throw calculations
- Determining the result of using a skill; for example, stealth, crafting, persuading, etc.
- Experience point calculations and bonuses
- Ability costs, duration, and effects
- Resources and conditions needed to acquire and use abilities and items
- Weapon and ability targeting, area of effect, and damage over time

Racing

- CPU driver characteristics, decisions, and behaviors—when to pit stop, use power-ups, etc.

- Damage and wear calculations for cars, and damaged car behavior

- Rendering car damage

- Automatic shifting

- Factoring effects of environment such as track surface, banking, weather

- CPU driver taunts

Casino Games, Collectible Card Games, Board Games

- Opposing player styles and degree of skill

- Applying the rules of the game

- House rules, such as when dealer must stay in Blackjack

- Betting options and payouts/rewards

- Fair distribution of results; for example, no particular outcome (card, dice roll, roulette number, etc.) is favored

Fighting

- CPU opponent strike (offensive) and block (defense) selection

- CPU team selection and switching in and out during combat

- Damage/point calculation, including environmental effects

- Calculating and rendering combat effects on the environment

- Calculating and factoring fatigue

- Enabling special moves, chains, etc.

Strategy

- CPU opponent movement and combat decisions

- CPU unit creation and deployment decisions

- Resource and unit building rules (pre-conditions, resources needed, etc.)
- Damage and effect calculations
- Enabling the use of new units, weapons, technologies, devices, etc.

First Person Shooters (FPS)

- CPU opponent and teammate AI
- Opposing and friendly character combat decisions and actions
- Damage calculations based on skills, armor, weapon type and strength, etc.
- Weapon targeting, area of effect, and damage over time
- Environmental effects on speed, damage to player, deflection or concentration of weapons (for example, *Unreal Tournament* Flak Cannon rounds will deflect off of walls)

Puzzle Games

- Points, bonus activation, and calculations
- Determining criteria for completing a round or moving to the next level
- Determining success of puzzle goals, such as forming a special word or matching a certain number of blocks
- Enabling special power-ups, awards, or modes

To complicate matters further, some game titles incorporate more than one genre, each with a different set of algorithms. For example, the *Pokémon Soul Silver* and *Heart Gold* titles for the Nintendo® DS™ mainly focus on following a storyline while training up your Pokémon to higher levels, but they also include beauty and athletic competitions, as well as a Minesweeper-style mini-game. *Unreal Tournament 3* is typically considered an FPS, but it also incorporates adventure and sports elements at various stages of the tournament. FIFA 09 introduced a FIFA Ultimate Team mode where teams are created by purchasing trading cards using virtual currency earned from winning games and tournaments.

 NOTE *You can find out more about the Ultimate Team mode in FIFA 09 by watching the video on YouTube.com [FIFAULTIMATE 09].*

Some other areas where Algorithm type defects can appear in the game code are graphics rendering engines and routines, mesh overlay code, z-buffer ordering, collision detection, and attempts to minimize the processing steps to render new screens.

For the Vanish bug, consider an Algorithm-defect scenario where the duration value is calculated rather than taken from an array or a file. Also suppose that a duration of 0 or less will not get displayed on the screen. If the calculation (algorithm) fails by always producing a 0 or negative number result, or the calculation is missing altogether, then the duration will not get displayed.

The immunity duration granted by Vanish is one second at Level 1, two seconds at Level 2, and five seconds at Level 3. This relationship can be expressed by the equation

```
vanishDuration = (2 << level) - level;
```

So at Level 1, this becomes 2 – 1 = 1. For Level 2, 4 – 2 = 2, and at Level 3, 8 – 3 = 5. These are the results we want, according to the specification.

Now, what if by accident the modulus (%) operator was used instead of the left shift (<<) operator? This would give a result of 0 – 1 = –1 for Level 1, 0 – 2 = –2 for Level 2, and 2 – 5 = –3 for Level 3. The immunity duration would not get displayed, despite the good code that is in place to display this duration to the user. An Algorithm defect has struck!

Documentation

Documentation defects occur in the fixed data assets that go into the game. This includes text, audio, and graphics file content, as listed here:

Text

- Dialogs

- User interface elements (labels, warnings, prompts, etc.)

- Help text

- Instructions

- Quest journals

Audio

- Sound effects
- Background music
- Dialog (human, alien, animal)
- Ambient sounds (running water, birds chirping, etc.)
- Celebration songs

Video

- Cinematic introductions
- Cut scenes
- Environment objects
- Level definitions
- Body part and clothing choices
- Items (weapons, vehicles, etc.)

This special type of defect is not the result of improper code. The errors themselves are in the bytes of data retrieved from files or defined as constants. This data is subsequently used by statements or function calls that print or draw text on the screen, play audio, or write data to files. Defects of this type are detectable by reading the text, listening to the audio, checking the files, and paying careful attention to the graphics.

String constants in the source code that get displayed or written to a file are also potential sources of Documentation type errors. When the game has options for multiple languages, putting string constants directly in the code can cause a defect. Even though it might be the proper string to display in one language, there will be no way to provide a translated version if the user selects an alternate language.

The examples in this section take a brief detour from the Vanish bug and examine some other bugs fixed in the *Dark Age of Camelot* 1.70i release, which appear at the end of the "New Things and Bug Fixes" list:

- If something damages you with a DoT and then dies, you see "A now dead enemy hits you for X damage" instead of garbage.

This could be a Documentation type defect where a NULL string, or no string, was provided for this particular message, instead of the message text that is correctly displayed in the new release. There could be other causes in the code, however. Note that this problem has the condition "… and then dies" so maybe there is a Checking step that had to be added to retrieve the special text string. A point to remember here is that the description of the defect is usually not sufficient to determine the specific defect type, although it might help to narrow it down. Someone has to get into the bad code to determine how the defect got put in there.

- Grammatical fixes made to bug report submissions messages, autotrain messages, and grave error messages.

  This one is almost certainly a Documentation type defect. No mention is made of any particular condition under which these are incorrect. The error is grammatical, so text was provided and displayed, but the text itself was faulty.

- Sabotage ML delve no longer incorrectly refers to siege equipment.

  This description refers to doing a /delve command in the game for the Sabotage Master Level ability. The quick conclusion is that this was a Documentation defect fixed by correcting the text. Another less likely possibility is that the delve text was retrieved for some other ability similar to Sabotage due to a faulty pointer array index—perhaps due to an Assignment or Function defect.

Interfaces

The last ODC Defect Type that needs to be discussed is the *Interface* type. An interface occurs at any point where information is being transferred or exchanged. Inside the game code, Interface defects occur when something is wrong in the way one module makes a call to another. If the parameters passed on somehow don't match what the calling routine intended, then undesired results occur. Interface defects can be introduced in a variety of ways. Fortunately, these, too, fall into logical categories:

1. Calling a function with the wrong value of one or more arguments

2. Calling a function with arguments passed in the wrong order

3. Calling a function with a missing argument

4. Calling a function with a negated parameter value

5. Calling a function with a bitwise inverted parameter value

6. Calling a function with an argument incremented from its intended value

7. Calling a function with an argument decremented from its intended value

Here is how each of these could be the cause of the Vanish problem. Let's use the ShowDuration, which was introduced earlier in this chapter, and give it the following function prototype:

```
void ShowDuration(BOOLEAN_T bShow, int duration);
```

This routine does not return any value, and takes a project-defined Boolean type to determine whether or not to show the value, plus a duration value, which is to be displayed if it is greater than 0. So, here are the Interface type defect examples for each of the seven causes:

1. ShowDuration(TRUE, g_vanishSpeed[level]);

In this case, the wrong global array is used to get the duration (speed instead of duration). This could result in the display of the wrong value or no display at all if a 0 is passed.

2. ShowDuration(g_vanishDuration[level], TRUE);

Let's say a #define statement causes the BOOLEAN_T data type to be an int, so inside ShowDuration the duration value (first parameter) will be compared to TRUE, and the TRUE value (second parameter) will be used as the number to display. If the duration value does not match the #define for TRUE, then no value will be displayed. Also, if a #define assigns TRUE a value of 0 or some negative number, then no value will be displayed because of our rule for ShowDuration that a duration less than or equal to zero does not get displayed.

3. ShowDuration(TRUE);

No duration value is provided. If it defaults to 0 as a result of a local variable being declared within the ShowDuration routine, then no value will be displayed.

4. `ShowDuration(TRUE, g_vanishDuration[level] | 0x8000);`

Here's a case where the code is unnecessarily fancy and causes trouble. An assumption was made that the high-order bit in the duration value acts as a flag that must be set to cause the value to be displayed. This could be left over from an older implementation of this function or a mistake made by trying to reuse code from some other function. Instead of the intended result, it changes the sign bit of the duration value and negates it. Because the value used inside of `ShowDuration` will be less than zero, it will not be displayed.

5. `ShowDuration(TRUE, g_vanishDuration[level] ^ TRUE);`

More imaginary complexity here has led to an Exclusive OR operation performed on the duration value. Once again, this is a possible attempt to use some particular bit in the duration value as an indicator for whether or not to display the value. In the case where `TRUE` is `0xFFFF`, this will invert all of the bits in the duration, causing it to be passed in as a negative number, thus altering its value and preventing it from being displayed.

6. `ShowDuration(FALSE, g_vanishDuration[level+1]);`

This can happen when an incorrect assumption is made that the level value needs to be incremented to start with array element 1 for the first duration. When `level` is 3, this could result in a 0 duration, because `g_vanishDuration[4]` is not defined. That would prevent the value from being displayed.

7. `ShowDuration(FALSE, g_vanishDuration[level-1]);`

Here the wrong assumption is made that the level value needs to be decremented to start with array element 0 for the first duration. When `level` is 1, this could return a 0 value and prevent the value from being displayed.

Some of these examples are far-fetched, but they illustrate the variety of ways every single parameter of every single function call can be a ticking time bomb. One wrong move can cause a subtle, undetected, or severe Interface defect.

Summary

Testing happens.

Anytime someone plays a game, it is being tested. When someone finds a problem with the game, it makes an impression. A beta release is published for the express purpose of being tested. Hasn't the game already been extensively tested prior to the beta release? Why are problems still found by the Beta Testers? Even after the game is released to the general public, it's still being tested. Game companies scramble to get patches out to fix bugs in PC and online games, but unfortunate console game publishers have to live with the bugs that were burned onto the game cartridge or CD-ROM. Mobile developers have an easier time of it, but when they spend their time fixing old problems, that's time they're not spending on building their next popular mobile hit. Even patches can miss issues or create new problems that have to be fixed in yet another patch. All of those bugs escaped the watchful eyes of the game company's paid and volunteer testers.

Despite the best efforts of everyone on the game team, games get made incorrectly. When games go wrong it's because of defects described by the eight ODC Defect Types covered in this chapter: Function, Assignment, Checking, Timing, Build/Package/Merge, Algorithm, Documentation, and Interface.

In *Memoirs of Constant, Volume III*, Chapter IX, it is written "… there is much in common between smugglers and policemen, the great art of a smuggler being to know how to hide, and that of the detective to know how to find." (Accessible at *http://www.napoleonic-literature.com/Book_11/ V3C9.html.*) This chapter has shown you the ways of the smuggler in the hope that it will make you a better game testing policeman.

Exercises

1. Is game testing important?

2. Which of the Defect Types do you think is the hardest for testers to find? Explain why.

3. List five situations where *assignments* are likely to occur in the code for a simulation game, such games in the *The SIMS*™ or *Zoo Tycoon*® series.

4. List five type of *algorithms* that you might find in a simulation game.

5. From the following code example from the publicly available source code for *Castle Wolfenstein: Enemy Territory* [WOLFENSTEIN 04], identify line numbers (added in parentheses) that might be a source of a defect for each of the ODC Defect Types.

```
/*
===============
RespawnItem
===============
*/
(0) void RespawnItem( gentity_t *ent ) {
(1)     // randomly select from teamed entities
(2)     if (ent->team) {
(3)         gentity_t        *master;
(4)         int count;
(5)         int choice;

(6)         if ( !ent->teammaster ) {
(7)             G_Error( "RespawnItem: bad teammaster");
(8)         }
(9)         master = ent->teammaster;

(10)        for ( count = 0, ent = master;
(11)            ent;
(12)            ent = ent->teamchain, count++)
(13)            ;

(14)        choice = rand() % count;

(15)        for ( count = 0, ent = master;
(16)            count < choice;
(17)            ent = ent->teamchain, count++)
(18)            ;
(19)    }

(20)    ent->r.contents = CONTENTS_TRIGGER;
(21)    //ent->s.eFlags &= ~EF_NODRAW;
(22)    ent->flags &= ~FL_NODRAW;
```

```
(23)   ent->r.svFlags &= ~SVF_NOCLIENT;
(24)   trap_LinkEntity (ent);

(25)   // play the normal respawn sound only to nearby
clients
(26)   G_AddEvent( ent, EV_ITEM_RESPAWN, 0 );

(27)   ent->nextthink = 0;
}
```

6. That was fun! Let's do it again with another *Wolfenstein* example:

```
/*
============
G_SpawnItem

Sets the clipping size and plants the object on the
floor.

Items can't be immediately dropped to floor, because they
might be on an entity that hasn't spawned yet.
============
*/
(0) void G_SpawnItem (gentity_t *ent, gitem_t *item) {
(1)    char      *noise;

(2)    G_SpawnFloat( "random", "0", &ent->random );
(3)    G_SpawnFloat( "wait", "0", &ent->wait );

(4)    ent->item = item;
(5)    // some movers spawn on the second frame, so delay
item
(6)    // spawns until the third frame so they can ride
trains
(7)    ent->nextthink = level.time + FRAMETIME * 2;
(8)    ent->think = FinishSpawningItem;

(9)    if(G_SpawnString("noise", 0, &noise))
(10)       ent->noise_index = G_SoundIndex(noise);
```

```
(11)    ent->physicsBounce = 0.50;       // items are bouncy

(12)    if(ent->model) {
(13)        ent->s.modelindex2 = G_ModelIndex(ent->model);
(14)    }

(15)    if ( item->giType == IT_TEAM ) {
(16)        G_SpawnInt( "count", "1", &ent->s.density );
(17)        G_SpawnInt( "speedscale", "100",
&ent->splashDamage );
(18)        if( !ent->splashDamage ) {
(19)                ent->splashDamage = 100;
(20)        }
(21)    }
}
```

CHAPTER 4

SOFTWARE QUALITY

In This Chapter

- Game quality factors
- Game quality appraisal
- Game quality standards
- Software Quality Assurance

S oftware quality can be determined by how well the product performs the functions for which it was intended. For game software, this includes the quality of the player's experience plus how well the game features are implemented. Various activities can be performed to evaluate, measure, and improve game quality.

In the book *Quality is Free,* Philip Crosby states that, well, "Quality is free" [CROSBY 80]. This should be the high concept of your quality program. If the cost of performing some quality function is not expected to produce eventual savings, find a way to do it less expensively or more efficiently. If you can't, then stop doing it.

GAME QUALITY FACTORS

Different gamers might have different criteria for what makes a game "good" for them. Some qualities are likely to be important to many game customers:

- Quality of the story

- Quality of the game mechanics

- Quality (for example, style, realism) of in-game audio and visual effects

- Quality of the download and update experience

- Appeal and/or realism of the visual style

- Use of humor and exaggeration

- "Human-like" nonplayer character Artificial Intelligence (AI)

Additionally, games should have an interface that is easy to use and clear to understand. This includes both the graphical user interface elements presented on the screen during gameplay and the game control(s) provided for the player to operate and affect the game. The user interface can consist of multiple elements such as on-screen displays and menus. The game control includes the way players control and operate their characters (or teams, cars, armies, and so on) during the game, as well as the way they can control their experience through point-of-view and lighting settings. The game should also support a variety of controllers that are especially suited for the game's genre, such as joysticks for air combat, guitars for making music, and steering wheels for driving.

Another factor in providing a quality experience for the user is to ensure that game code and assets are compatible with the memory constraints of the target platform. This includes the available working memory required for the game to run properly as well as the size, quantity, and types of target media supported, such as cartridges, CD-ROMs, DVDs, or digital downloads.

Higher memory requirements could affect game performance while time is spent switching game assets in and out of memory during play. The impact is magnified when the assets are sent from a remote server to the console, PC, or mobile gaming device.

If the game code and assets don't fit within the memory footprint of the least expensive device, the market for the game and profit potential are reduced.

Handheld device and console memory is not as upgradeable as PCs are. Games have to fit within the memory constraints of the onboard chips, removable memory, and/or hard-drive devices that are supported. Mobile games are the most constrained in terms of available fixed and removable memory and tend to use up more and more memory as fixes and updates are made during the life of the game. Both mobile and console gamers are likely to reach a point where memory consumption reaches the limitations of their device, and they have to make a decision about deleting a less frequently used game for the new, shiny download that caught their eye.

Any efforts at "code crunching" get more and more expensive the later they happen in the game development cycle. The cost isn't just in the labor to do the reduction work; shrinking game code or reformatting assets to fit on the target media or memory footprint can introduce new, hard-to-find bugs late in the project. This creates an extra burden on development, project management, defect tracking, version control, and testing.

GAME QUALITY APPRAISAL

The actual quality of the game is established by its design and subsequent implementation in code. Appraisal activities are necessary, however, in order to identify the difference between what was produced and what should have been produced. Once identified, these differences can be repaired before—and sometimes after—releasing the game.

Testing is considered an appraisal activity. It establishes whether the game code performs the functions for which it was intended. Testing, however, is not the most economical way to find game defects; it's best to catch problems at the point where they are introduced.

Having peers review game deliverables as they are being produced provides immediate feedback and the opportunity to repair problems before they are introduced and commingled with the rest of the game. It will be much more difficult and more expensive to find and repair these problems at later phases of the project.

> *Peer reviews come in different "flavors." In each case, there are times when you, the tester, will be required to participate. If you don't put in the necessary time and effort to contribute to the review, you and your team will be less likely to be asked to participate in the future. Make sure you take this responsibility seriously when your number gets called.*

Walkthroughs

Walkthroughs are one form of peer review. A general outline of a walkthrough is as follows:

1. Leader (for example, the designer) secures a room and schedules the walkthrough.

2. Leader begins the meeting with an overview of work including scope, purpose, and special considerations.

3. Leader displays and presents document text and diagrams.

4. Participants ask questions and raise issues.

5. New issues raised during the walkthrough are recorded during the meeting.

The room should comfortably fit the number of people attending and should have a projector for presentations. A whiteboard or paper easel pad can be used by the leader or participants to elaborate on questions or answers. Limit attendance to 6–8 people at most. This should not turn into a team meeting. Only include a representative from each project role that is potentially affected by the work you are walking through. For example, someone from the art team does not have to be in most code design walkthroughs, but an experienced game artist should be involved when graphics subsystem designs are being presented. Don't invite the test lead to every single walkthrough that affects the test team. If you do, then game knowledge and walkthrough experience won't get passed on to other testers. This also keeps the test lead from spending too much time on walkthroughs and not enough time on test leading. Work with the test lead to find other capable representatives on her team. If you are the test lead, send someone capable from your team in your place when you can.

Be sure to invite one or more developers to your test walkthroughs. It's a great way to find out if what you intend to test is really what the game is going to do once it's developed. Conversely, get yourself invited to design and code walkthroughs. Brush up on the design techniques and programming language your team is using. Even if you don't have any comments to improve the author's work, you can use what you learn there to make your tests better.

It's also not a bad idea to use some walkthroughs as mentoring or growth opportunities for people on your team. The "guests" should limit their own questions and comments during the meeting to the material being presented and should have a follow-up time with their "host" to go over any other questions about procedures, the design methodology being used, and so on. This probably should not be done for every walkthrough, but it works in situations where someone already has a background in the topic and/or is expected to grow into a lead role for some portion of the project.

Here's a list of representatives to consider inviting to walkthroughs of various project artifacts:

- **Technical Design Document (TDD)**: tech lead, art director, producer, project manager
- **Story board**: producer, development lead, artists
- **Software Quality Assurance Plan (SQAP)**: project manager, producer, development lead, test lead, QA (Quality Assurance) lead, and engineer(s)
- **Code designs, graphics**: key developers, art representative, test representative
- **Code designs, other**: key developers, test representative
- **Code**: key developers, key testers
- **Test plan**: project manager, producer, development lead, key testers
- **Tests**: feature developer, key testers

Relevant topics to cover in walkthroughs include:

- Possible implementations
- Interactions

- Appropriate scope
- Traceability to earlier work products
- Completeness

Issues raised during the walkthrough are also recorded during the meeting. Sometimes the presenter will realize a mistake simply by talking about his work. The walkthrough provides an outlet for that. One participant acts as a recorder, recording issues and presentation points that are essential in order to understand the material. Other participants could use the information for downstream activities, such as coding or testing. The leader is responsible for promptly closing each issue and distributing the meeting notes to the team within one week of the walkthrough. QA is expected to follow up by checking that the issues were indeed closed before any work was done based on the material that was walked through and that the notes were distributed to the participants.

Reviews

Reviews are a little more intimate than walkthroughs. Fewer people are involved—typically 4 to 6—and the bulk of time is spent on the reviewers' comments.

Reviewers are expected to prepare their comments prior to the review meeting and submit them to the review leader so that they can be consolidated prior to the actual meeting. Comments sent electronically are easier to compile and understand. Be sure to let the review leader know when you are going to submit a pen-and-paper markup instead of an electronic file. The review leader could perhaps be the author of the material being reviewed.

The review itself can be an in-person meeting between the author and reviewers or simply a review of the comments by the author alone who contacts individual reviewers if he has any questions about their issues. An in-between approach is for the author to look over the reviewer comments prior to the review meeting and to limit the meeting time to discussions over the few issues that the author disagrees with or has questions about.

Review meetings can also take place virtually, using network meeting software and phone headsets. That is especially useful for projects distributed across studios that are separated by space and time.

During the meeting, someone—usually the review leader—must take notes and publish the resolution of each item to the team. If the opinions of a reviewer differ from what the author believes should be done, decisions on technical matters are left to the author, whereas procedural matters can be resolved by QA.

Checklist-Based Reviews

Another form of review takes place between only two people: the author and a reviewer. In this case, the reviewer follows a checklist to look for mistakes or omissions in the author's work. The checklist should be thorough and should be based on specific mistakes that are common for the type of work being reviewed. Requirements, code, and test reviews of this type would each use different checklists. At times it would even be appropriate to have checklists specific to a game project. These checklists should constantly evolve to include new types of mistakes that start to appear. Mistakes found during the checklist review that were not on the checklist should be recorded and considered for use in the next version. Technology, personnel, and methodology changes could all lead to new items being added to the checklist.

Inspections

Inspections are more structured than reviews. Fagan Inspections are one particular inspection methodology from which many others have been derived. They were defined by Michael Fagan in the 1970s, based on his work at IBM, and are now part of the Fagan Defect-Free Process™. The reference list at the end of this chapter provides information for learning more about this process [FAGAN 11].

A Fagan Inspection follows these steps:

1. Planning

2. Overview

3. Preparation

4. Meeting

5. Rework

6. Follow-Up

7. Causal Analysis

The inspection meeting is limited to four people, with each session taking no longer than two hours. Larger work should be broken up into multiple sessions. These guidelines are based on data that shows a decline in the effectiveness of the inspection if these limits are exceeded. If you don't know your inspection rates, such as pages per hour or lines of code per hour, measure them for the first 10 or so inspections you do. Then use those results to calculate how many sessions are needed for any future inspections.

In the Fagan Inspection method, each participant plays a specific role in the inspection of the material. The Moderator, who is not the Author, organizes the inspection and checks that the materials to be inspected satisfy predefined criteria. As with the checklist reviews, you will need to establish these criteria for different items that you will be inspecting. Once the criteria are met, the Moderator schedules the review meeting, plus an "overview" session that takes place prior to the review. This is to discuss the scope and intent of the inspection with the participants. Participants might also have questions that can be answered then or soon after the meeting. Typically there should be two working days between the overview and the inspection meeting. This is to give reviewers adequate preparation time.

Each of the inspectors is assigned a role to play in the inspection meeting. The Reader is expected to paraphrase the material being inspected. The idea is to communicate any implied information or behavior that the Reader interprets in order to see if it matches the Author's intended function. For example, here is a line of code to read:

```
LoadLevel(level[17], highRes, 0);
```

You could just say "Call LoadLevel with level seventeen, high res and zero." A better reading for inspection purposes would be to say "Call LoadLevel without checking the return value. Pass the level information using a constant index of seventeen, the stored value of highRes and a hard-coded zero." This second reading raises the following potential issues:

1. The return value of LoadLevel is not checked. Should it return a value to indicate success, or a level number to verify that the level you intended to load did in fact get loaded?

2. Using a constant index for the level number is perhaps not a good practice. Should the level number come from a value passed to the routine that this code belongs to or should the number 17 be referenced by a more descriptive defined constant such as HAIKUDUNGEON, in case something in the future causes the level numbering to be re-ordered?

3. The value of 0 provides no explanation about its function or the parameter it is being assigned to.

You can get similar results from reading test cases. Having another person try to literally understand your test steps word for word will perhaps not turn out as you intended.

The Tester does not have to be the person from the test team. This is a role where the person questions things like whether the material being inspected is internally consistent or consistent with any project documents it is based on. It is also good if the Tester can foresee how this material will fit in with the rest of the project and how it would potentially be tested.

A Recorder takes detailed notes about the issues raised in the inspection. The Recorder is a second role that can be taken on by any of the four people involved. The Reader is probably not the best choice for Recorder and you might find that it works best if the Moderator accepts the Recorder role. The Moderator also helps keep the meeting on track by limiting discussions to the material at hand.

Throughout the meeting the participants should not feel confined by their roles. They need to become engaged in discussions of potential issues or how to interpret the material.

NOTE

A successful inspection is one that invites the "Phantom Inspector." This is neither an actual person nor a supernatural manifestation. Rather, it is a term to explain the source of extra issues that are raised by the inspection team coming together and feeding off of each other's roles.

Once the meeting has concluded, the Moderator determines whether any rework is required, before the material can be accepted. He continues to work with the Author to follow up on issues until they are closed. An additional inspection could be necessary, based on the volume or complexity of the changes.

The final step of this process involves causal analysis of the product (inspected item) faults and any inspection process (overview, preparation, meeting, and so on) problems. Issues can be discussed, such as how the overview could have been more helpful, or requiring stricter compiler flags to be set that could flag certain code defects prior to submitting the code for inspection.

GAME STANDARDS

Among its many responsibilities, the QA team should establish that the project work products follow the right formats. This includes assuring that the game complies with any standards that apply. User interface standards and coding standards are two kinds of standards applicable to game software.

User Interface Standards

User interface (UI) standards help players identify with your game title.

Following are some examples of user interface standards, which are derived from Rob Caminos' 2004 GDC presentation, "Cross-Platform User Interface Development" [CAMINOS 04]. As part of your Quality Assurance function, you would examine relevant screens to confirm they had the properties and characteristics called for in the standards.

1. Text should be large and thick, even at the expense of creating an extra page of text.

2. Make all letter characters the same size.

3. Avoid using lowercase letters. Instead, user smaller versions of upper-case letters.

4. Use an outline for the font where possible.

5. On-screen keyboards should resemble the look of an actual keyboard.

6. On-screen keyboards should have the letters arranged alphabetically. Do not use the QWERTY arrangement.

7. Split alphabet, symbol, and accent characters into three separate on-screen keyboards.

8. Common functions, such as Done, Space, Backspace, Caps Lock, and switching between character sets should be mapped to available buttons on the game controller.

9. Assign Space and Backspace keyboard functions to the left and right shoulder buttons.

10. Each menu should fit on one screen.

11. The cursor should blatantly draw attention to the currently selected menu item.

12. Avoid horizontal menus.

13. Vertical menus should consist of no more than 6–8 items, each with its own button.

14. Menus should by cyclic, allowing the player to loop through the menu choices.

15. Leave breathing room for text localization. (Some languages, such as German, might require more letters per word than your game's native language.)

16. Place button icons next to their functions instead of using lines to connect the functions to the buttons.

17. Point button icons to their location on the controller.

18. Separate thumb-stick movement functions from button functions.

Additional standards could apply to consistent keyboard assignments ("F1 should always be the Help button") or the flexibility of game controller options ("There shall always be an option to enable or disable vibration").

Your list of standards can be used as a checklist that gets filled out for each screen. The checklist should include other information such as the QA person's name, the date of the appraisal, the name of the software build and/or identifier being checked, and the name of the screen.

Don't wait until the UI is coded and put into a release before you check it. Work with developers to verify that the standard is being followed in their UI design.

Some checking should also take place after code is released in order to verify that the implementation matches the intent. This could include a suite of tests that specifically check that each UI standard is met.

You might find that some of the items listed above make perfect sense for your game, while some don't. Use what's right for you and your customers. The important thing is to have some standards, have a reason for including each item in the standard, and have a way to periodically check that the team uses the standard.

Coding Standards

Coding standards can prevent the introduction of defects when the game code is written. Some of the topics typically addressed by coding standards include:

- File-naming conventions

- Header files

- Comment and indentation styles

- Use of macros and constants

- Use of global variables

NOTE

To many critics, coding standards pay too much attention to the format of the code rather than its substance. On the other hand, there must be some reason why development tool companies continue to provide more and more coding assistance using visual means such as colors and graphs. Both have the same goal in mind: to help the developer get the code right the first time.

Coding standards aren't just about formatting. Many of the rules are designed to address important issues such as portability, clarity, modularity, and reusability. The importance of these standards is magnified in a project that is distributed across different teams, sites, and countries. There are few things less fun than tracking down a defect caused by one team defining SUCCESS as 0 and another team defining SUCCESS as 1.

Here are some excerpts from the C Coding Standards for the Computer Associates Ingres® project:

- Do not use constants to check for machine-dependent ranges or values. Use the symbolics instead (for example: UINT_MAX, not 4294967295).

- Constants must be properly typed to match their usage. For example, a constant 1 that will be passed to a procedure expecting a long must be defined as ((long)1).

- Do not use the literal zero as a NULL pointer value.

- Use TYPEDEF, not #define, to declare new types.

As a tester, you should be aware that these standards also give clues as to how code will fail under certain situations. For example, if machine-dependent ranges are hard-coded, you will see the resulting failure on one type of machine but not on another. So, features that depend on values that could be machine dependent should be tested on different machines.

In a QA role, your responsibility is to check that the programmers have coding standards which they apply to their code. This is typically done by sampling files from the game code and doing a manual or automated check against the appropriate standards. If you are doing QA on behalf of a publisher or third-party QA group, you can still do this by gaining access to the programmer's standards, tools, and files. Alternatively, you could require the programming team to submit evidence, such as printouts, that they did this checking themselves.

GAME QUALITY MEASUREMENTS

How good is "good" game software? Certainly the number of defects in the code has something to do with goodness. The team's ability to find defects in its product is another factor to consider. A "sigma level" establishes the defectiveness of game code relative to its size, while "phase containment" provides an indicator of how successful the team is at finding defects at their source, leaving fewer to escape to your customers.

Six Sigma Software

A "sigma level" is one way to establish a goal for the outgoing quality of your game. For software, this measure is based on defects per million lines of code, excluding comments (also referred to as "non-commented source lines" or NCSL). The "lines of code" measure is often normalized to Assembly-equivalent lines of code (AELOC) in order to balance the different levels of abstraction across the variety of languages in use, such as C, C++, Java, Visual Basic, and so on. The level of abstraction of each language is reflected in its multiplier. For example, each line of C code is typically regarded as the equivalent of three to four AELOC, whereas each line of Perl code is treated as about 15 AELOC. It's best to measure this factor based on your specific development environment and use that factor for any estimates or projections you need to make in the future. If you are using different languages for different parts of your game, multiply the lines of code for each portion by the corresponding language factor.

Assembly code is the low-level instructions that are understood by the microprocessors running in your PC, game console, portable game device, or mobile phone. "Assembly-equivalance" refers to the number of Assembly language lines of code that are generated by compiling your game code in whatever language you wrote it in.

Table 4.1 shows defect rates required to achieve a software quality measure anywhere between three and six sigma. Six sigma—only 3.6 defects per million lines of code—is typically regarded as an outstanding result, and getting in the 5.5 sigma range is very good. In case you think it's silly to worry about 1 million lines of code unless you're writing software for NASA, keep in mind that even mobile games can chew up a hundred thousand lines of code or more.

TABLE 4.1 Sigma Table for Various Sizes of Delivered Software

Released Defects per (AELOC)				Sigma Value
20,000	100,000	250,000	1,000,000	
124	621	1552	6210	4.0
93	466	1165	4660	4.1
69	347	867	3470	4.2
51	256	640	2560	4.3
37	187	467	1870	4.4
27	135	337	1350	4.5
19	96	242	968	4.6
13	68	171	687	4.7
9	48	120	483	4.8
6	33	84	337	4.9
4	23	58	233	5.0
3	15	39	159	5.1
2	10	27	108	5.2

(Continued)

TABLE 4.1 Continued

Released Defects per (AELOC)				Sigma Value
20,000	100,000	250,000	1,000,000	
1	7	18	72	5.3
	4	12	48	5.4
	3	8	32	5.5
	2	5	21	5.6
	1	3	13	5.7
		2	9	5.8
		1	5	5.9
0	0	0	3	>6.0

Don't fool yourself by measuring your sigma on the sole basis of the open defects you know about in the product. This might reward poor testing that did not find many defects that still remain in the game, but wouldn't reflect the experience your customers will have. The defects being counted must include both the game defects you know about that have not been fixed, whatever defects your customers have already found, and your projection of defects that remain in the software that haven't been discovered yet.

It's best to wait anywhere from 6 to 18 months after shipping to calculate your sigma. If you still have a good result after that, continue to operate your projects in a similar manner by repeating what went "right" but also fix what went "wrong." If you have poor results, take a good hard look at what changes you can make to avoid a repeat performance. You can start by going through the list of nonconformances that QA found during the project.

Phase Containment

Phase containment is the ability to detect faults in the project phase in which they were introduced. Phase Containment Effectiveness (PCE) is a measure of how well that is being done.

Faults that are found in the phase in which they are introduced are known as in-phase faults or "errors." Faults that don't get caught in the same phase in which they are introduced are said to escape and become "defects." The principle is that if any subsequent work is derived from the faulty item, then a defect has occurred. Think of the 18-inch high Stonehenge descending from the ceiling in the movie *Spinal Tap*. That could have been avoided (but not as funny!) if someone had noticed that the size had been given in inches instead of feet on the drawing given to the artist.

Errors are typically found by reviews, walkthroughs, or inspections. Defects are most noticeably found by testing and unhappy customers, but they can also be found in reviews of downstream work products. For example, a code inspection issue might actually be the result of incorrect design or requirements. Because other work has already been done based on the fault, this is a defect.

PCE is typically tracked and reported by showing the faults found in each development phase. The faults are organized into columns for each phase in which they might be found. A coding fault can't be detected in the requirements phase because the code does not exist at that point. Calculate PCE by dividing the number of in-phase faults by the sum of faults found in all phases to come up with the PCE for that phase. From the data shown in Figure 4.1, the design phase PCE is calculated by dividing the number of faults found in the coding phase, 93, by the sum of all faults introduced by coding, which is 93 + 6 + 24 = 123. The result is 93/123 = 0.76.

Phase where faults are found

Phase created	REQMTS	DESIGN	CODING	TEST	PCE
REQMTS	114	27	4	15	0.71
DESIGN		93	6	24	0.76
CODING			213	105	0.67
Totals	114	120	223	144	

FIGURE 4.1 Game code phase containment data.

Figure 4.2 shows a graph summarizing the code PCEs for each phase.

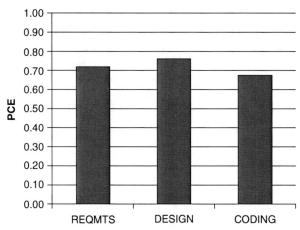

FIGURE 4.2 Game code phase containment graph.

Alternatively, test results could be broken out into separate catego-ries, as shown in Figure 4.3. These extra categories do not affect the PCE numbers or graphs, but this could be more convenient for data collection if different systems or categories are used for different release types. This data also helps the team understand whether there will be addi-tional testing activities that could further reduce the PCE numbers as more defects are found. In Figure 4.3, no Beta testing results are avail-able to add to the table. So, the PCE numbers for requirements, design, and coding represent only the maximum possible value. New defects found in Beta testing will be sourced to these phases and will reduce the corresponding PCEs.

Phase where faults are found

Phase created	REQMTS	DESIGN	CODING	TESTING				PCE
				DEV TEST	DEMOS	ALPHA	BETA	
REQMTS	114	27	4	11	3	1		0.71
DESIGN		93	6	19	5	0		0.76
CODING			213	90	10	5		0.67
Totals	114	120	223	120	18	6	0	

FIGURE 4.3 Game code phase containment data with expanded test categories.

If this practice is useful for understanding how well the team is capturing defects in the game code, it should also be applied to the work produced by the testers. Figure 4.4 shows example PCE data for testing deliverables.

Phase where faults are found

Phase created	DESIGN	SCRIPTING	CODING	EXECUTION	PCE
DESIGN	211	56	23	7	0.71
SCRIPTING		403	37	16	0.88
CODING			123	24	0.84
Totals	211	459	183	47	

FIGURE 4.4 Game test phase containment data.

Figure 4.5 shows a graph that corresponds to the PCE data example depicted in Figure 4.4.

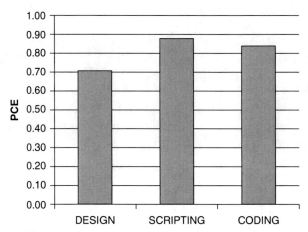

FIGURE 4.5 Game test phase containment graph.

As the test PCE data shows, some faults in the tests don't get noticed until the test is executed on the game code. The problem might have been recognized as a test defect by the tester running the test, or it might have started out as a code defect before analysis and retesting uncovered the fact that the test was wrong, not the code. You can imagine how much more time consuming that is, versus finding the defect before releasing the test.

Remember, this is not a measure of how well the executed tests perform. This is a measure of how well faults were captured in the test designs, scripts, and/or code. Any mistakes made in one of these activities will need to be repaired when they are eventually discovered. Test mistakes that don't get discovered could impact the quality of the game itself. A missing test, or a test that checks for the wrong result and passes, can send game bugs on their merry way to the paying public.

As with the sigma value, look for ways to improve your PCE. If you had 100% containment in all of your phases, you would have to run each test only once and they would all pass. Your customers wouldn't find any problems and you'd never have to issue a patch. Think of the time and money that would save! Because the PCE is a function of the faults produced and the faults found, you can attack a low PCE at both ends. Programmers can improve their ability to prevent the introduction of faults. Testers and QA can improve their ability to detect faults. In both cases, some basic strategies to address low PCE areas are:

- Improve knowledge of the subject matter and provide relevant training

- Have successful team members provide mentoring to less-successful members

- Document methods used by successful individuals and deploy them throughout the team

- Increase compliance with existing methods and standards

- Add standards which, by design, help prevent faults

- Add checking tools that run during the creation process, such as color-coded and syntax-aware editors

- Add checking tools that run after the creation process, such as stronger compilers and memory leak checkers

QUALITY PLANS

Each game project should establish its own plan for how quality will be monitored and tracked during the project. This is typically defined in a document called the Software Quality Assurance Plan (SQAP). The SQAP contains *no* information about testing the game. That is covered in the game's Software Test Plan. An SQAP is strictly concerned with the independent monitoring and correction of product quality and process quality issues. It should address the following topics, most of which are covered in more detail in this section:

- QA personnel
- Standards to be used in the product
- Reviews and audits that will be conducted
- QA records and reports that will be generated
- QA problem reporting and corrective actions
- QA tools, techniques, and methods
- QA metrics
- Supplier control
- QA records collection, maintenance, and retention
- QA training required
- QA risk management

 The companion DVD contains an SQAP template document [SQAP 03] that includes the elements in this outline.

QA Personnel

Begin this section of the SQAP by describing the organizational structure of the QA team. Show who the front-line QA engineers work for and who the head of QA reports to. Identify at which level the QA reporting chain is independent from the person in charge of the game development staff. This helps establish a path for escalating QA issues and identifies which key relationships should be nurtured and maintained during the project. A good rapport between the QA manager and the development director will have a positive effect on both the QA staff and the development staff.

Describe the primary role of each person on the QA team for this project. List what kinds of activities each of them will be involved in. Be as specific as possible. If a person is going to be responsible for auditing the user interface screens against the company's UI standards, then indicate that. If another person is going to take samples of code and check them with a static code analysis tool, then include that. Use a list or a table to record this information.

Strictly speaking, QA and testing are separate, distinct functions. QA is more concerned with auditing, tracking, and reporting, whereas testing is about the development and execution of tests in the relentless pursuit of finding operational defects in the game. Depending on the size and skills of your game project team, however , you might not have separate QA and test teams. It's still best to keep those two plans separate even if some or all of the same people are involved in both kinds of work.

Standards

Two types of standards should be addressed in this section: product standards and process standards. Product standards apply to the functions of things that are produced as part of the game project. These include code, graphics, printed materials, and so on. Process standards apply to the way things are produced. These include file naming standards, code formatting standards, and maintenance of evolving project documents, such as the technical design document. Document all of the standards that apply as well as which items they apply to. Then describe how the QA staff will monitor them, and how they will follow up on any discrepancies.

Reviews and Audits

The kinds of reviews performed by QA are not the same as developers or testers would do for code or test designs. A QA review is usually done by a single QA engineer who evaluates a work product or ongoing process against some kind of reference such as a checklist or standard. QA reviews and audits span all phases and groups within the game project.

Project documents, project plans, code, tests, test results, designs, and user documentation are all candidates for QA review. QA should also audit work procedures used by the team. These can include the code inspection process, file backup procedures, and the use of tools to measure game performance over a network.

Reviews and audits can be performed on the results of the process, such as checking that all required fields in a form are filled in with the right type of data, and that required signatures have been obtained. Another way to audit is to observe the process in action. This is a good way to audit peer reviews, testing procedures, and weekly backups. Procedures that occur very infrequently, such as restoring project files from backup, can be initiated by QA to make sure that the capability is available when it is needed.

QA itself should be subject to independent review (Rule #2: Trust No One). If you have multiple game projects going on, each project's QA team can review the work of the other in order to provide feedback and suggestions to ensure that they are doing what they documented in the SQAP. If no other QA team exists, you could have someone from another function such as testing, art, or development use a checklist to review your QA work.

The QA activities identified in this section of the SQAP should be placed on a schedule to ensure that the QA people will have the time to do all of the activities assigned to them. These activities should also be coordinated with the overall project schedule and milestones so you can count on the work products or activities that are being audited to be available at the time you are planning to audit them.

Planned QA activities that will disrupt other people's work, such as restoring backups or sitting down with someone to review a month's worth of TDD updates, should be incorporated into the overall project schedule so the people affected will be able to set aside the appropriate amount of time for preparing and participating in the audit or review. This is not necessary for activities such as sitting in on a code review, because the code review is going to take place whether or not you are there.

Feedback and Reports

The SQAP should document what kinds of reports will be generated by SQA activities and how they will be communicated. Reporting should also include the progress and status of SQA activities against the plan. These get recorded in the SQAP along with how frequently the QA team's results will be reported and in what fashion. Items that require frequent attention should be reported on regularly. Infrequent audits and reviews can be summarized at longer intervals. For example, the QA team might produce weekly reports on test result audits, but produce quarterly reports on backup and restoration procedure audits. Test result audits would begin shortly after testing starts and continue through the remainder of the project. Backup and restoration audits could start earlier, once development begins.

NOTE

SQA reporting can be formal or informal. Some reports can be sent to the team via email, while others will perhaps aggregate into quarterly results for presentation to company management at a quarterly project-quality review meeting.

Problem Reporting and Corrective Action

SQA is not simply done for the satisfaction of the QA engineers. The point of SQA is to provide a feedback loop to the project team so that they are more conscientious about the importance of doing things the right way. This includes keeping important records and documents complete and up to date. It's up to QA to guide the team or the game company in determining which procedures and work products benefit the most from this compliance. Once an SQA activity finds something to be noncompliant, a problem report is generated.

Problem reports can be very similar to the bug reports you write when testing finds a defect in the software. They should identify which organization or individual will be responsible and describe a timeframe for resolving the issue. The SQAP should define what data and statistics on noncompliant issues should be reported, as well as how and when they are to be reviewed with the project team.

History has shown, unfortunately, that some project members might be more reluctant to spend time closing SQA problems because they have their "real job" to do—development, testing, artwork, and so on. As a consequence, it's a good idea to define the criteria and process for escalating unresolved issues. Similarly, there should be a defined way for resolving issues with products that can't be fixed within the game team, such as software tools or user manuals.

In addition to addressing compliance issues one at a time, SQA should also look for the causes of negative trends or patterns and suggest ways to reverse them. This includes process issues such as schedule slippages and product issues such as game asset memory requirements going over budget. The SQAP should document how the QA team will detect and treat the causes of such problems.

Tools, Techniques, and Methods

Just like the development and testing teams, the QA team can benefit from tools. Because QA project planning and tracking needs to be coordinated with the rest of the project, it's best if the people responsible for QA use the same project management tools as the rest of the game team. Likewise, tracking issues found in QA audits and reviews should be done under the same system used for code and test defects. Different templates or schemas might be needed for QA issue entry and processing, but this will keep the team software licensing and operation costs down and make it easy for the rest of the team to access and update QA issues.

Some statistical methods might be useful for QA analysis of project and process results. Many of these methods are supported by tools. Such tools and methods should be identified in the SQAP. For example, Pareto Charts graph a list of results in descending order. The bars furthest to the left represent the most frequently occurring items. These are the issues you should spend your time on first. If you are successful at fixing them, the numbers will go down and other issues will replace them on the left of the chart. You can go on forever addressing the issue at the left of the chart because there will always be one. This is kind of like trying to clean out your garage. At some point in time, you can decide the results are "good enough" and move on to some entirely different result to improve.

Figure 4.6 shows an example Pareto Chart of the number of defects found per thousand lines of code (KLOC) in each major game subsystem. The purpose of such a chart could be to identify which portion of the code would benefit the most from using a new automated checking tool. Because there are costs associated with new technologies—purchasing, training, extra effort to use the tool, and so on—it should be introduced where it would have the greatest impact. In this case, start with the rendering code.

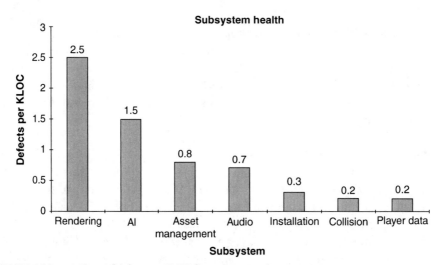

FIGURE 4.6 Pareto Chart of defects per KLOC for each game subsystem.

Another useful software QA method is to plot control charts of product or process results. The control chart shows the average result to expect and the "control limit" boundary lines for the set of data provided. Any items outside of the control limits fall beyond the range of values that would indicate they came from the same process as the rest of the data. This is like having a machine that stamps metal squares a certain way, but every once in a while, one comes out very different from the others. If you have the right amount of curiosity to be a QA person, you would want to know why the square comes out incorrectly some of the time. The same is true for software results that come out "funny." The control chart reveals results that should be investigated in order to understand their cause. It might simply be a result of someone entering the wrong data (date, time, size, defects, and so on). Figure 4.7 shows an example control chart for new lines of delta (added or deleted) code changes in the game each week. The numbers are in KLOC.

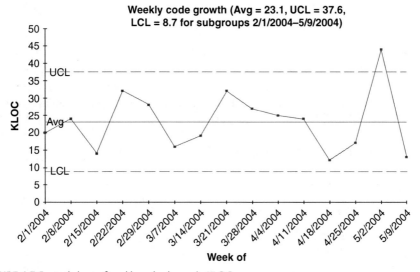

FIGURE 4.7 Control chart of weekly code change in KLOC.

The solid line running across the middle of the chart is the average value for the data set. The two dashed lines labeled UCL and LCL represent the Upper Control Limit and the Lower Control Limit, respectively. These values are calculated from the data set as well. The data point for the week of 5/2/2004 lies above the UCL. This is a point that should be investigated.

NOTE

The Pareto Chart and control chart in Figures 4.6 and 4.7, respectively, were created using SPC for Excel [SPC 11]. A downloadable demo version is available from their site. See the reference list for this chapter in Appendix F for more information.

The SQAP can include tools and techniques that will account for both positive and negative test data. These tools are good for measuring, but it's the people who drive the results. See the Sidebar titled "Bud's Vacation," about a case of one person's impact on the team's testing results.

Bud's Vacation

During one project, there was a noticeable dip in the number of defects submitted one week. This was a good result for the developers but bad for the testers. A quick investigation revealed that "Bud," an especially productive tester, had been on vacation that week. The test data for the rest of the team was within the normal range. Legitimately bad results should be understood and subsequently prevented from happening in the future. Especially good results are just as important to understand so they can be imitated. Additional tools and techniques can be identified in the SQAP for those purposes. The data could be reported in a different way, such as defects per tester, to account for inevitable fluctuations in staffing. This could replace the original chart or be used in addition to it.

Supplier Control

Your game is not just software. It's a customer experience. The advertisements in the store, the game packaging, the user's manual, and the game media are all part of that experience. In many cases these items come from sources outside the game team. These are some of your "suppliers." Their work is subject to the same kinds of mistakes you are capable of producing on your own. You could also have software or game assets supplied to you that you use within the game, such as game engines, middleware, art, and audio files.

In both of the cases above, QA should play a role in determining that the supplied items are "fit for use." This can be done in the same way internal deliverables are evaluated. Additionally, the QA team can determine the supplier's capability to deliver a quality product by conducting on-site visits to evaluate the supplier's processes. When you go to the deli, it's nice to see that the food is laid out nicely in the display case. You also appreciate the fact that a food inspector has checked out the plant where the food originates from to see that it is uncontaminated, and that it is produced in a clean and healthy environment. The same should be true for game-related software and materials that are supplied to you from other companies.

Training

If new tools, techniques, and/or equipment are going to be used in the development of the project, it might be necessary for one or more QA personnel to become acquainted with them so they can properly audit the affected deliverables and activities. The impact of the new technologies could affect QA preparation as well, such as requiring new audit checklists to be created or new record types to be defined in the audit entry and reporting system.

The QA training should be planned and delivered in time for QA to conduct any activities related to work products or processes using the new technology. If the team is already having an in-house course delivered, then add some seats for QA. If the team is inventing something internally, try to get a briefing from one of the inventors. Some tools and development environments come with their own tutorials, so get some QA licenses and allocate time to go through the tutorial.

New tools or techniques identified for QA-specific functions should be accompanied with appropriate training. Identify these, document them in the SQAP, and get your training funded.

Risk Management

Risk management is a science all unto itself. In addition to all of the risks involved with developing a game, there are also risks that could hamper your team's QA efforts. Some typical SQA risks are:

- Project deliverables go out of sync with planned audits

- QA personnel diverted to other activities such as testing

- Lack of independent QA reporting structure

- Lack of organization commitment to take corrective actions and/or close out issues raised by QA

- Insufficient funding for new QA technologies

- Insufficient funding for training in new development and/or QA technologies

It's not enough to list your risks in the SQAP. You also need to identify the potential impact of each risk and describe how you would proceed if the risk occurs and/or persists.

Summary

Software quality is certainly affected by testing, but there are other activities that can impact quality earlier in the project and less expensively. Various forms of peer reviews can find faults before they escape to other phases of the project. Standards can be defined and enforced as a way to prevent defects from being introduced into the game, many of which are difficult to detect by testing. Measures such as sigma value and phase containment provide stakes in the ground from which you can set improvement goals. The Software Quality Assurance organization carries out a plan of activities that monitor and promote the use of these techniques and measures. Their cost must be weighed against the consequences and costs of releasing a poor quality game.

NOTE *For more information and resources on software quality, check out the Web site of the American Society for Quality at http://www.asq.org.*

Exercises

1. Your game code size is 200,000 AELOC. It had 35 defects you knew about when you released it. The people who bought it have reported 17 more. What sigma level is your code at?

2. Describe the differences between the leader role in a walkthrough and the moderator role in a Fagan Inspection.

3. Add the following defects found in Beta testing to the data in Figure 4.3: Requirements – 5, Design – 4, Coding – 3. What are the updated code PCEs for the requirements, design, and coding phases?

4. Using the SPC Tool demo, create a control chart of the following test case review rates, measured in pages per hour:

Review 1: 8.5

Review 2: 6.1

Review 3: 7.3

Review 4: 4.5

Review 5: 13.2

Review 6: 9.1

Which reviews, if any, fall above or below the control limits? Describe which are "good" and which are "bad." How might a high or low review rate impact the number of faults found in those reviews?

CHAPTER 5

TEST PHASES

In This Chapter

- Pre-production
- Test kickoffs
- Alpha testing
- Beta testing
- Gold testing
- Post-release testing

Video games can range in size from tiny, downloadable, mobile phone games that take a few weeks to produce, to epic, massively-multiplayer, online, role-playing games developed over four or five years. No matter what size the game or how long the production schedule, the testing of the game should always follow the same basic structure:

1. Pre-Production

2. Alpha

3. Beta

4. Gold

5. Post-Release

Like the plot of a suspense thriller, each sequence occurs more rapidly, and with much more heightened excitement—and stress—than the previous one. Figure 5.1 illustrates a very rough timeline for a hypothetical mid-budget, hand-held racing game.

FIGURE 5.1 Hypothetical hand-held racing game timeline.

The following sections examine each phase in order to understand why it is vital to the project and distinct from the other phases.

PRE-PRODUCTION

Depending on your role on the team and when you were brought into the project, you might think that testing begins sometime after a good portion of the game is developed. In reality, testing begins when the project begins. There might not be people called "testers" involved at the beginning, but code, scripts, and assets are being produced from the start, which need to be evaluated, critiqued, and corrected.

Much of what happens at the early stages of the project will set the tone for how well testing will go later on. This includes both how good the game stands up to testing, and how well the tests themselves are organized and executed. The bottom line is that both the QA team and the development team (or "dev team") can go home earlier at night if more effort and skill is applied to testing activities at the beginning of the project. It is profoundly more difficult and expensive to try to make up for a lack of early testing by throwing more testers (and more overtime work) on the game in the later stages of development.

You can't test quality into a game. The quality of the game is established by the code, the art, the audio, and the feedback loop between the game and the player—the "fun factor"—that is compiled into the software. All testing can do is to tell the development team what is wrong with the software. Testing better, and testing earlier, can get problems fixed sooner and less expensively.

If you received a coupon in the mail at the beginning of your project that said "mail back this coupon to save 20% or more on your game budget," would you send it in? When you delay testing until the end of a project, it is the same as having that coupon but not mailing it in because you didn't want to pay for the postage stamp.

Planning Tasks

Almost as soon as a project is conceived, planning for test begins. Test planning includes the tasks outlined in the following sections.

Determine the Scope of Testing the Project Will Require

The game design document (GDD), technical design document (TDD), and the project schedule are reviewed by the test manager in order to formulate a "scope of test" document that outlines the amount of testing resources—that is, time, people, and money—he will need to get the game tested thoroughly for release.

The following sidebar, "Expansion Plans," is a brief scope-of-test memo written by a small publisher planning to develop an expansion pack to a real-time strategy (RTS) game released earlier that same year.

Expansion Plans

MEMORANDUM

To: **Executive Producer**
From: **Manager of Quality Assurance**
RE: **RTS EXPANSION TEST PLAN SUMMARY**

Summary

I have evaluated the GDD you forwarded last week. Assuming no changes to the game scope outlined in the document, it will take 1,760 hours to test the expansion pack, based on the following assumptions:

- 50-day production schedule,

- Four-person test team,

- 10% allowance for overtime, and

- No post-release patch testing.

Single Player (900 hours)

A significant amount of QA time will be spent testing the new campaign. Because the story mode of these missions will be highly script-dependent, testers will be tasked with breaking those scripts to ensure the user will have a seamless, immersive gameplay experience.

Because the developer has not designed cheats into the game, and because our experience with the base game was such that saved games could not reliably be brought forward from prior builds, campaign mode will take up the majority of test time.

Multiplayer (650 hours)

The thrust of multiplayer testing will be to:

1. Ensure correct implementation of new units and the new tile set,

2. Debug new maps,

3. Debug "interface streamlining" (new functionality described in the design doc),

4. Stress test game size,

5. Stress test army size,

6. Stress test game length, and (as time permits)

7. Balance testing.

Because the expansion pack introduces 12 new units, we will be concerned only with the high-level balance testing—if one of the new units gives its clan an overwhelming advantage (or disadvantage), we would bug it out. We do not have the resources available to re-evaluate each of the more-than-50 existing units against the new units. We will count on the developer's design team (and user feedback compiled since the release of the base game) to fine tune the balance of the expansion pack.

Test Matrices (210 hours)

Because this is a product for the PC and not consoles, there will not be a first-party TRC component to the testing. However, we will provide a similar standards-based level of final release testing based on a number of PC standards developed from our own experience as well as standards used at other PC game publishers.

We will run the following standard matrices on the game:

1. Install/uninstall matrix (with an emphasis on interoperability with the previous product)

2. Windows 9x "gotchas" matrix

3. Publisher standards matrix

4. Multiplayer connectivity matrix

We will also produce and run the unit matrix developed while testing the original game on each new unit in the expansion pack.

Compatibility Testing (0 hours)

Because the minimum system requirements will not change from the original game, we do not anticipate needing the services of a third-party hardware compatibility lab for compatibility testing. If any machine-specific bugs on the varied hardware in our internal lab crop up during the normal course of testing, we will evaluate at that point whether a full compatibility sweep is warranted, along with an estimated additional budget.

Overtime (tbd)

Because this product has only a modest upside for the company, QA will work with Production to make best efforts to contain overtime costs. At this point we anticipate working overtime only on such occasions that failure to do so will make the product late.

Assign a Lead Tester

This is no trivial matter. The lead tester's experience, temperament, and skill set will have a tremendous influence over the conduct of the testing cycle. This might be the single most important decision the test manager makes on the project. A lead tester must be

- A **leader** able to motivate the test team and keep them focused and productive.

- A **team player** able to recognize the role testing plays as part of the larger production process.

- A **communicator** able to gather and to present information clearly and concisely.

- A **diplomat** able to manage conflicts as they arise (and they will arise).

The test manager, or the lead tester, should then appoint a "vice lead tester," often called a *primary tester*. On very large teams it is not uncommon to have more than one primary tester, each leading specific subteams (e.g., multiplayer, franchise mode, tutorial, map editor, etc.).

Determine Phase Acceptance Criteria

In an ideal world, you will be working from a contract, design spec, or product plan that defines very specific criteria for each phase of testing. The world is seldom ideal, however.

The lead tester should take whatever materials are available and write a specification for the Alpha, Beta, and Gold (release) versions of the game. By establishing clear and unambiguous entry acceptance criteria for each phase of testing, conflicts can be avoided later in the project when pressure might be felt from various parts of the organization to begin, say, Beta testing on a build that isn't truly Beta. Once the test manager has approved these criteria, they should be distributed to all senior members of the project team.

Three elements are required in the certification planning for each test phase:

1. **Entry criteria:** The set of tests that a build must pass before entering a given test phase. The game won't be considered "at Alpha" until the code passes the Alpha Entry test, for example.

2. **Exit criteria:** The set of tests that a build must pass before completing a test phase.

3. **Target date:** The date both the development and test teams are working toward for a specific phase to launch.

Participate in Game Design Reviews

As mentioned in earlier chapters, all stakeholders benefit from the test team playing an active role from the beginning of a project. The lead tester or primary tester should participate regularly in design reviews. Their role is not to design the game, but rather to stay abreast of the latest design changes, as well as to advise the project manager of any technical challenges or testing complications that might arise from any anticipated feature revision. Changes in the scope of the game will dictate changes in the flow of the testing. The sooner the lead tester knows of a design change, the easier it is for her to change the test plan to accommodate those changes.

Set Up the Defect Tracking Database

This is a critical step, in that a poorly designed database can waste precious minutes every time someone uses it, and those minutes quickly add up to man-hours toward the end of a project—man-hours you will wish you had back! Figure 5.2 shows a typical entry in a bug database—note that the bug type "Unexpected Result" is too general. Aren't all bugs unexpected?

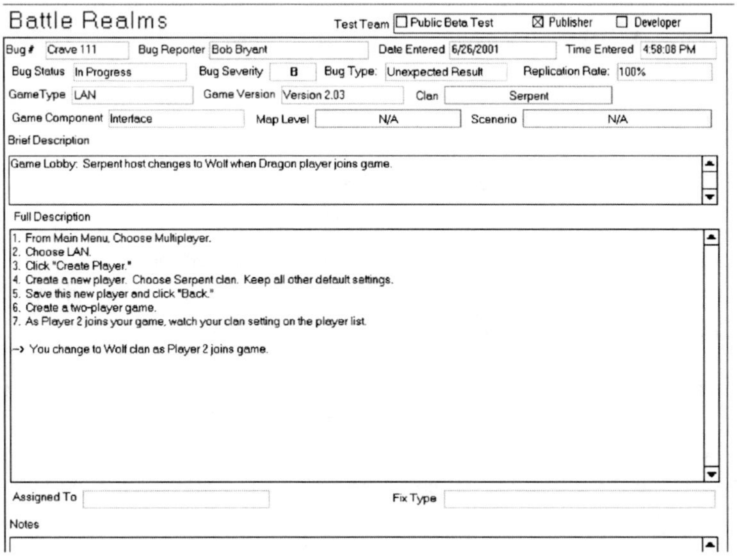

FIGURE 5.2 Typical entry in a bug database.

The lead tester and project manager should mutually agree on appropriate permissions—that is, those team members in each department who have edit rights to specific fields. The lead tester should also ask the project manager for a list of development team members to whom bugs will be assigned. The "assigned to" field allows the lead tester, project manager, or anyone else so entrusted to review new bugs and assign them to the right member of the development team. Programmers, artists, and other dev team members then search the database for the bugs assigned to them and, presumably, fix their own defects. They can then assign the bug back to the lead tester so that the fix can be verified in the next build.

Whether the bug database is going to exist on an internal server or be accessible over the Internet, it's a good idea at this point to populate the bug database with a few dummy records and double-check all passwords and permissions, both locally and remotely. Every person who will have access to the *"bug base"* should be assigned an individual password, and the lead tester can allow or block edit rights to individual fields based on the role that person will play on the project team. Learn more about bug bases in the sidebar, "Bug Base Tips."

Bug Base Tips

A bug database that is editable by only the lead tester is not very useful—these tend to be very static and incapable of conveying current information about the state of the project. Neither is a bug base in which every member of the team can edit every field—these are chaotic and ultimately useless.

In designing the bug base, the lead tester must balance the need for team members to communicate with each other about a particular defect with the equally important need to control the flow of information in order to manage task priorities. Programmers need to be able to comment on or to ask questions about a defect in the Developer Comments or Notes field, but they can't be allowed to close a bug arbitrarily by changing the Status field to "closed." Testers need to be able to describe the bug in the Brief Description and Full Description fields, but they might not be qualified to judge who should own the bug in the Assigned To field.

Here are some recommendations:

- **Status** should be editable by the lead tester only. The default value for this field should be "New," so that as testers enter bugs, they can be reviewed and re-fined by the lead tester before the status is changed to "Open" and is assigned to a member of the development team.

- **Severity** should be editable by the lead tester or primary testers. *Remember that the severity of a defect is not the same as its fix priority.* Testers, rightly, tend to be passionate about the defects they find. It is the job of the test team leaders to check against this and assign a severity in an objective manner.

- **Priority** should be editable by the project manager and senior members of the development team. This field is primarily a tool to help the project manager prioritize the flow of work to members of the development team. With agile development methodologies becoming more and more popular in the games industry, project managers want maximum flexibility in assigning day-to-day or hour-to-hour priorities. Leave the priority field to them.

- **Category Fields** should be input by the testers and editable by the lead or primary tester. These fields include such specifics as Game Type, Number of Players, Level, Bug Type, Reproduction Rate, and any other field that includes specific information about the bug.

- **Brief/Full Description** should be input by the testers and editable by the lead or primary tester. This is the meat of the bug description, including the steps to reproduce. It should not become a message board about the bug. Leave that to the comments field.

- **Assigned To** is a field that should be editable by the lead tester and any member of the development team. The lead tester will typically assign new bugs to the project manager, who will then review the bug and assign it to a specific programmer or artist to be fixed. Once the bug is fixed, that person can either assign it back to the project manager for further review, or back to the lead tester so that the fix can be verified in the next build and the bug can be closed.

- **Developer Comments** should be editable by the project manager and any member of the development team.

- **QA Comments** should be editable by testers, the lead tester, and the primary tester.

Draft Test Plans and Design Tests

Having current and detailed knowledge of the game design is critical as the lead tester begins to draft the test documents. An overall test plan document defines what types of tests will be done and what the individual test suites and matrices will look like (see Chapter 6, "The Game Testing Process"). This is the point in the project where you can put the methods described in Part IV of this book to good use. Remember: *Prior planning prevents poor performance.*

Test Plan

A *test plan* acts as the playbook for the QA team. It identifies the team's goals along with the resources (staff, time, tools, and equipment) and methods necessary to achieve them. Test goals are typically defined in terms of time and scope. The testing timeline often includes intermediate goals for one or more milestones that occur prior to the final release of the game. Any risks that could affect the test team's ability to meet the test goals are identified in the test plan, along with information about how to manage those risks if they occur. The scope of a test plan can be limited to a single subsystem of the game, or it can span many game features and releases. If the game is being developed at multiple sites, the test plan helps to define what test responsibilities are assigned to each team. Appendix B contains a basic template for a test plan, and the book's DVD provides a link to a template for a test plan document you can fill in for your own project.

Test Case

A *test case* describes an individual test that is to be performed by a tester or testers. Each test case has a distinct objective, which is part of the test case description. A test case also describes what operations to perform in order to meet its objective. Each individual operation within a test case is a *test step*. The level of detail in the test case can vary based on the standards of a particular test organization. Test cases are conceived and documented by each tester who is assigned a set of responsibilities in the test plan. The total set of test cases produced by a tester should fully cover his or her assigned responsibilities.

Test Suite

A *test suite* is a collection of related rest cases that are described in further detail. The test suite gives step-by-step instructions about what operations to perform on the game and what details to check for as a result of each step. These instructions should be sufficient for manual execution of the test or for writing code to automate the test. Depending upon how the tests cases are written, they might or might not depend on the steps that were taken in a previous test case. Ideally, each test in the suite can be individually identified and executed independently of the other tests in the suite. Think of the test cases as individual chapters, while the test suite is a book that puts the test cases together into a detailed, cohesive story.

Testing Before Testing Begins

You might soon begin to get proto-builds in bits and pieces, with requests from the development team to do very narrowly focused testing of certain specific features in order to give them confidence that these bits of code are working as intended before writing more and more code on top of them. This is sometimes called *modular testing*, because you're testing individual "modules" of code, not a complete build of the game.

At this stage in development, it is entirely likely that as code becomes functional and modules are tested, the design of the game might be revised significantly "on the fly." Patience is required as you revise, and re-revise, your test documents accordingly. Just as game design is often an iterative process, game test materials must iterate as well.

During modular testing, it is premature to begin writing bugs beyond the narrow scope of the module's test case. True defect testing of the game won't begin until the dev team submits the first Alpha candidate.

Finally, the lead tester should begin to recruit or hire additional team members as necessary, according to her resource plan. Once the team is in place, test kickoffs can begin.

TEST KICKOFFS

Kickoffs have a positive impact on game development, leading to better process definition, better problem solving, and schedule reduction. On a team in which testers have various levels of testing and game project experience, individual needs are not likely to be addressed at the project kickoff. Rather, it benefits the team to have kickoffs at the next-lowest level: a test kickoff for each "test" that is being created or executed by individual testers. The test kickoff illustrates the principle that increasing an organization's speed results from an iterative process of identifying obstacles, designing a new process that eliminates them, and ensuring that the new method is implemented.

Test kickoff activities are broken into two parts: tester preparation and the kickoff meeting, which is conducted according to the kickoff agenda. The tester's preparation steps and the kickoff agenda are documented in a test kickoff checklist, as shown in Figure 5.3.

From the test kickoff checklist, the tester should prepare in the following ways:

1. Read the requirements and/or documentation for the game feature being tested.

2. Gather equipment, files, and programs needed for the test.

3. Read through the tests, making certain everything is clear and able to be performed.

The tester should consult with a "test expert" if there seem to be any roadblocks or questions regarding the completion of any preparation activities. The test expert can be the original author of the test, a tester who already has a lot of experience with the game feature, or the test lead. The expert should also be familiar with the recent defect history of the game or

TEST KICKOFF CHECKLIST

version 01.00

Game/Feature _____

Tester _____ **Date** _____

Tester preparation

    □ Read the requirements for the feature being tested

    □ Gather equipment needed per the test equipment list

       Game platform(s) hardware

       Monitor

       Cables

       Controllers

       Save files

       Updates/patches/mods

       Test instruments

    □ Read the test script/report

Kickoff Agenda

Kickoff Leader

- Gives feature overview

- Addresses feature questions

- Brings up special instructions

- Brings up and solicits relevant improvement suggestions

- Addresses test execution questions/issues

FIGURE 5.3 Test kickoff checklist.

feature(s) to be tested. Experienced testers should not be exempt from this preparation process; just as "familiarity breeds contempt," overconfidence breeds carelessness, and this process should be completed fully before conducting the kickoff meeting.

Once the tester has completed the preparation activities, the test lead conducts the kickoff meeting by doing the following:

1. Giving a feature overview

2. Addressing feature questions

3. Bringing up any special test instructions

4. Bringing up and soliciting any relevant test improvement suggestions

5. Addressing any test execution questions or issues

6. Recording important issues on the kickoff form and providing a copy to the tester after the meeting is completed

Following the preparation steps listed on the checklist and participating in the meeting, per the kickoff agenda, benefits testing in the following ways:

- **Prepares and equips** the tester to run through the entire test without stopping for equipment or questions

- **Familiarizes** the tester with the *expected behavior* of the game or module during testing to increase tester awareness of "right" from "wrong"

- **Resolves any conflicts** in test instruction prior to executing the test in order to eliminate retesting because of test ambiguities or errors

- **Provides a forum** for test improvement at the grassroots level, improving tester involvement in and ownership of the test process

Each test kickoff is an opportunity to improve test understanding, test quality, and test execution. These opportunities would have been missed or identified much later in the test phase if the kickoff process was not used. The net result is that the test kickoff acts as a "pre-mortem" that identifies important issues prior to performing the test, rather than waiting to identify them in a postmortem after testing has already been done. As kickoff records are collected, systemic issues can be identified and addressed in the *current* test phase. Checklists, group meetings, and email are all means of communicating the lessons learned from the kickoffs and suggesting remedies to implement on the *current* project, rather than the next project.

By collecting and evaluating the results of kickoffs for each project, actions can be taken to prevent repeating any problems in future test efforts. The careful analysis of test kickoff results and the time savings achieved by using kickoffs can improve the way hundreds of other tests will be conducted going forward. The across-the-board use of test kickoffs will translate into further improvements in the test schedule and uncover more defects, leading to better game quality.

The following behaviors, which are driven by the use of test kickoffs, can reduce the length of the testing critical path:

- **Make fewer mistakes:** The test kickoff steps are designed to ensure that testing does not begin until the tester is fully equipped to test and understands the details and goals of the specific test. Among other things, this results in quicker and more accurate measurement of results.

- **Wasting less time:** As part of preparation, the tester reviews the test and requirements in their entirety. This reduces misunderstood and improperly performed steps, resulting in much less test effort spent on backing up and redoing test sections.

- **All effort results in something that will be used:** Metrics show that the use of test kickoffs *reduces* the testing cycle time, even when you add in the time it takes to plan and hold the kickoffs.

- **Truth-telling is encouraged:** The one-on-one setting of a test kickoff is less intimidating than the group setting of a phase or release kickoff. The kickoff leader should make the tester comfortable and remind the tester of the kickoff goals. When testers see that their feedback results in improvements, they are more open about voicing their opinions and ideas.

- **Produce constructive discussions rather than destructive debates:** The test kickoff meeting gets every tester involved in process improvement. It also gives the tester and kickoff leader shared responsibility to address the issues raised and recorded in the meeting. Sticking to the kickoff agenda keeps the meeting focused on test-related issues.

NOTE
The idea that having a meeting would actually save time is counter intuitive to most people. We have held test kickoffs for tests side-by-side with testing conducted without kickoffs. Our metrics show that the "kicked-off" tests were executed at 1.4 times the rate of the "non-kicked-off" tests. Putting it another way, testers who benefitted from a kickoff meeting completed 40% more tests than those who did not have a kickoff.

Test kickoffs can provide the same benefits for test creation as they can for test execution. Whether it's test flow diagrams (TFDs) and combinatorial tables (both discussed later in the book), test trees, matrices or checklists, the process of creating test tools is made more efficient by using a kickoff process. All it takes is a slightly different agenda and checklist, as shown in Figure 5.4.

GAME TEST CREATION KICKOFF CHECKLIST
version 01.00

Game/Feature _____

Tester _____ Date _____

Test creator preparation

□ Read the requirements for the feature being tested

□ Read existing test scripts from similar features and/or games

Kickoff Agenda

Kickoff Leader

• Gives feature overview

• Addresses feature questions

• Brings up special instructions

• Brings up and solicits relevant improvement suggestions

• Addresses test case questions/issues

FIGURE 5.4 Test creation kickoff checklist.

Both of the test kickoff checklists shown in this chapter are available on the book's DVD.

ALPHA TESTING

Now it's time to get busy. The project manager delivers you an Alpha candidate. You certify it against the Alpha criteria you established in the planning phase. Full-bore testing can begin at last.

Over the course of Alpha testing, the game design is fine tuned. Features are play tested and revised (or scrapped). Missing assets are integrated. Systems developed by different programmers are linked together. It's an exciting time.

As each member of the code and art teams checks new work into the build, they're also checking in new defects. This means that the game at this phase is a "target-rich environment" for a tester. It can also seem very overwhelming (remember Rule #1: Don't Panic). It is critical at this stage that the test suites are strictly adhered to. They will provide a structure for bringing order to what might seem like chaos.

Over the course of Alpha testing, all modules of the game should be tested at least once, and performance baselines should be established (frame rate, load times, and so on). These baselines will help the development team determine how far they have to go to get each performance standard up to the target for release. For example, a frame rate of 30 (or even 15) frames of video per second (fps) might be acceptable in the early stages of developing a 3D action game, but the release target might be a solid 60 fps with no prolonged dips when there are a greater-than-usual number of animations and effects on the screen.

Alpha Phase Entry Criteria

The following are Alpha entry criteria for a typical console game:

1. **All major game features exist and can be tested.** Some might still be in separate modules for testing purposes.

2. **A tester can navigate the game along some path from start to finish.** This assumes the game is linear, or has some linear component (for example, career mode in a sports game). Because many games are nonlinear, the lead tester and project manager must agree ahead of

time on a content completion target for such games (for example, three of 12 mini-games).

3. **The code passes at least 50% of the platform TRC.** Each console game has a set of standards published and tested against by the manufacturer of that platform. When you produce a PlayStation®3 game, the Format QA team at Sony Computer Entertainment America (SCEA) will test it against the PlayStation *Technical Requirements Checklist* (TRC) to make certain that the game complies with platform conventions. These requirements are very exacting, such as specifying the precise wording of status or error messages a game must display during the save process.

4. **Basic interface is complete and preliminary documentation is available to QA.** The main menu, most submenus, and the in-game interface (sometimes called the Heads-Up Display, or HUD) should be functional, if not yet finalized and visually polished. *Preliminary documentation* in this context means any explanation of new functionality, changed controller maps, and cheat codes (if any).

5. **The game is compatible with most specified hardware and software configurations.** For a cross-platform console game, this means that the game will run on every targeted platform (Xbox® 360 or PlayStation® 3) slated for initial commercial release. For a PC game, this criterion dictates that the game must run on a variety of systems with varying specifications (a range of CPU speeds, a range of RAM caches, and so on).

6. **Level scripting is implemented.** This pertains primarily to single-player story mode. An Alpha candidate that requires the tester to load separate levels manually would fail this criterion.

7. **First-party controllers and other peripherals work.** Each platform manufacturer (e.g., SCEA, Microsoft, and Nintendo) either manufactures or licenses for manufacture its own line of peripherals. Because support of these first-party peripherals is required by the platform TRCs, and because the majority of testing will be done using first-party peripherals, they need to be supported by Alpha.

8. **Final or placeholder art is in for all areas of the game.** All the levels and characters must be textured and animated, though these textures, animations, and even the level geometry, might be refined as the game approaches Beta.

9. **Online multiplayer can be tested.** Enough networking code must be implemented so that at least two consoles can connect over a LAN and play a game.

10. **Placeholder audio is implemented.** Is it entirely possible that the voice recording and final mixing sessions have not yet taken place at Alpha. In this case, members of the development team should record "stub" dialog and sound effects and integrate them where needed.

BETA TESTING

By the end of Alpha, the development team should have a very clear idea of the game they're creating. The development team has, for the most part, stopped creating new code and new artwork, and will not shift their focus to perfecting what they've already created. It's time to identify and fix the remaining bugs.

Although the term "Beta testing" frequently refers to any outside testing, it is only at the early stages of the Beta phase that final gameplay testing should take place with people outside the design team. The majority of testing done by outside Beta testers during true Beta is bug reporting and load testing. Gameplay feedback and suggestions should continue to be recorded for possible post-release implementation in a patch or sequel.

Beta Phase Entry Criteria

The following criteria are typical for the Beta phase of a console game:

1. **All features and options are implemented.** The game is "feature complete."

2. **The code passes at least 100% of platform TRC.** Toward the end of Beta, the game should be ready for a "pre-certification" submission to the platform manufacturer. This process allows the platform manufacturer's QA team to test the game against the latest TRC and warn of any potential compliance issues.

3. **The game can be navigated on all paths.** Any bugs that might have closed off portions of the game are eliminated.

4. **The entire graphical user interface (GUI) is final.**

5. **The game is compatible with all specified hardware and software configurations.**

6. **The game logic and AI is final.** Programming is complete on the gameplay of the game. The game knows its own rules. All AI profiles are complete.

7. **All controllers work.** Those third-party peripherals that have been chosen by the development team (and the publisher) to be supported function with the game.

8. **Final artwork is implemented.** There should be no placeholder artwork left. Beta is the phase when most screenshots, trailers, and gameplay footage will be taken to use in the packaging and to market the game.

9. **Final audio is implemented.** All placeholder audio has been replaced with final assets of the voice talent. (There might be a few do-over or "pick-up" lines that have yet to be integrated, but these should not have an impact on in-game event timing or level scripting.)

10. **All online modes are complete and testable.**

11. **All language version text is implemented and ready for simultaneous release.** The game script (both written and spoken) is locked and can be sent forward for translation and integration into the foreign language versions of the game.

Design Lock

At some point during Beta testing, the project manager should declare the game to be in a state of *design lock* (sometimes called *feature lock*). The play testing has concluded. Questions of balance have been resolved as best they can. The focus of the test team at this point should be to continue to run the test cases against the builds in an iterative manner, because each defect fixed at this point might have introduced another defect elsewhere in the game.

Toward the end of Beta, many tough decisions must be made. The teams are tired, tempers are on edge, and time is running out. In this charged atmosphere, with very little sleep themselves, the project team leaders have to make such critical choices as:

- **Whether or not to implement that last-minute feature enhancement.** The designers might have had a great idea at the eleventh hour and are eager to introduce a new feature, character, or level. The project team leaders must weigh the risks of implementing the new feature (and possibly introducing new bugs and schedule slippage) against shipping a perhaps less compelling game on time.

- **Whether to cut that level that just doesn't seem to be much fun.** Occasionally it becomes clear during the course of testing that a level or other content component is a "problem child," and requires too much work relative to the time left in the schedule to redesign. Cutting it out entirely could be problematic, however, in that the game will require new tests to ensure that the remaining levels run seamlessly around the deleted content. Critical story or gameplay information might have been presented in the problem level, and other levels will have to be reworked (and retested) to accommodate this.

- **Which bugs to ship with.** In many ways, this is the toughest decision of all—which bugs to let go.

Letting Bugs Go

As a gamer, you might have encountered a defect in a game you've played. Your reaction might likely have been, "I wonder how the testers missed this one?" Chances are that they didn't miss the defect. It's highly likely that a game tester found the bug and wrote it into the bug database. Not all bugs get fixed.

There will be times, especially late in the project, when the development team determines that they can't (or won't) fix a bug. This can happen for a variety of reasons. Perhaps the technical risks involved in the fix outweigh the negative impact of the defect. Perhaps there is a workaround in place that the technical support team can supply to players who encounter the defect. Perhaps there simply isn't enough time.

NOTE

Whatever the reason, each project must have a quick and orderly process in place to determine which defects will be waived, that is, which will not be fixed by the development team. This designation has many different names. Waived bugs can be known as "as is," ISV (In Shipped Version), DWNF (Developer Will Not Fix), or CBP (Closed by Producer). The worst of all possible names for waived status is "featured," which institutionalizes the cynical joke, "It's not a bug; it's a feature." Not surprisingly, one studio that repeatedly used "featured" to describe waived defects is now defunct, having released too many buggy games.

Cynicism, defeatism, and defensiveness have no place in the bug waiving process. On the one hand, testers work very hard and want to feel as though their efforts matter to the project. On the other hand, developers work just as hard (and longer) and have a duty to ship the project on schedule. It is crucial that all parties involved maintain an understanding and respect for the role each plays in the overall project team.

Ideally, the senior members of the project team will meet regularly and often to discuss those bugs that the development team has requested to be waived. These can be flagged as "waive requested" or "request as is" in the Status or Developer Status fields of the bug database. The senior members of the project team (the producer, executive producer, lead tester, and QA manager) can meet to evaluate each bug and to discuss the costs and benefits of fixing it versus leaving it in the game. Other team members, such as programmers or testers, should be available for these meetings as needed. This decision-making body is sometimes called the CCB (Change Control Board) or the Bug Committee.

In some cases, where a post-release software update—or *patch*—is anticipated, a number of bugs will be designated for fixing after the game has been shipped (see "Post-release Testing," later in this chapter). Because most current game consoles are Internet-capable and have some on-board means of storing data, console developers are relying or patches more and more as a means of artificially extending their development schedule. Whereas in the last console generation (PlayStation 2, Xbox, Nintendo GameCube™) a game had to be ready to ship *before* it was manufactured, console developers can now fix bugs up until the game ships or goes live, as long as they have the patch tested and live by the street date.

Once a bug has been waived, it's important to remind both the bug author and the test team as a whole that merely because the bug was waived doesn't mean that it wasn't a legitimate bug. Nor does it mean that they shouldn't continue to find defects with the same level of diligence.

NOTE	*It is the duty of the test team to write up every bug, every time, no matter when in the production cycle they find it.*

They supply the lead tester, project manager, and the business unit heads (marketing, sales, product development) with the best information possible about the state of the game so that the best business decisions can be made.

GOLD TESTING

Once the Beta test phase winds down, the game should be ready for release or, in the case of a console title which must be tested and certified by a third party, final submission. The following entry criteria are typical for release testing:

1. All known Severity 1 bugs (crashes, hangs, major function failures) are fixed.

2. Greater than 90% of all known Severity 2 bugs are fixed.

3. Greater than 85% of all known Severity 3 bugs are fixed.

4. Any known open issues have a workaround that has been communicated to Technical Support (or documented in an FAQ or a readme.txt file).

5. Release-level performance has been achieved (for example, a 60 fps frame rate).

Upon meeting your release criteria, the game is declared at "code lock." A brief, intense period of testing is performed on what everyone on the team hopes will be (but which will probably not be) the final build. Because the version of the game that is sent to be manufactured is known as the *gold master*, the final few versions tested are known as *gold master candidates* (GMCs) or *release candidates* (RCs).

At this point the game looks and feels like a released, commercial game. It's up to the testers to serve as the last line of protection for both the players and the project team by sniffing out any remaining hidden defects that might have a significant impact on player satisfaction. This should be done by rerunning all of the test suites—or as many as time permits—one final time. In addition, a number of testers should be tasked with "breaking" the game one final time. Any remaining bug found during this final effort deemed too severe to be waived is called a *show stopper*, because it causes the GMC to be rejected. A new GMC must be prepared with a fix for the new defect, and Gold testing must start all over again from the beginning.

Last-Minute Defects

Because the final stages of the project are so intense and pressure-laden, people will react negatively to show stoppers. "Why are we [or you] just finding this now? Testing has been going on for months!" This refrain is frequently heard from stressed-out executives. It is best for the test team to take such emotional comments in stride and remember several inviolable truths of game development:

1. There is seldom enough time in any project to find every bug.

2. Every time a programmer touches the code, bugs might be introduced.

3. Code changes accumulate over time, so that several iterative changes to different parts of the game might result in a bug showing up downstream from those changes.

4. Programmers are much more tired and prone to mistakes toward the end of a project.

5. Testers are much more tired and prone to missing things toward the end of the project.

6. Bugs happen.

In the case of a PC game, Web games, and games for other "open" platforms, the game's publisher or financing entity is the sole arbiter of whether to release the product. In these cases, once the Gold testing phase has been concluded, the game is ready for manufacture. In the case of a console game, however, there is one final gatekeeper—the platform manufacturer (for example, Nintendo, Microsoft, Sony, or Apple®)—who must certify the code. This final release testing process is known as *certification testing*.

RELEASE CERTIFICATION

A clean GMC is sent to the platform manufacturer for final certification once the project team has finished gold testing. The platform manufacturer then conducts its own intensive testing on the GMC. This testing consists of two phases, which can happen concurrently or simultaneously. The *standards phase* tests the code against the Technical Requirements Checklist. The *functionality phase* tests the code for functionality and stability.

The certification testers generally play the game all the way through at least once per submission. They often find show-stopper bugs of their own.

At the end of certification testing, the platform manufacturer's QA team will issue a report of all the bugs they found in the GMC. Representatives of the publisher will discuss this bug list with the representatives at the platform manufacturer, and will (in theory) mutually agree upon which bugs on the list must be fixed.

The development team is well advised to fix only those bugs on the "must fix" list, and to avoid fixing each and every minor bug on the list in an effort to please the platform manufacturer. Fixing more bugs than is absolutely necessary to win final certification only puts the code at risk for more defects, and the schedule at risk for further delays.

Once the game has been resubmitted and certified by the platform manufacturer, it is "gold." The champagne should flow. The project is not over yet, however.

POST-RELEASE TESTING

Patches are a fact of life. Users don't like them, but want them if they're available. Publishers don't like them, because they potentially add to the overall cost of the project. Developers don't like them, because they can be perceived as a tacit admission of failure. However, if the game was shipped with even one or two bad defects, either intentionally or inadvertently, it's time for a patch.

The upside of developing and testing a patch is that it allows the development team to revisit the entire list of waived bugs and last-minute design tweaks to further polish the game. Each additional bug fix or feature polish means more testing, however, and should be planned for accordingly.

Sometimes the development team will release more than one patch. In that case, the testing becomes more complicated, because interoperability must be tested. Each new patch must be tested to see whether it functions with both the base retail game and earlier patched versions.

The significance of downloadable content (DLC) is discussed in the sidebar, "A Note on DLC."

A Note on DLC

DLC, or downloadable content, is growing more and more popular—even expected—with console gamers. Sometimes DLC is planned after a game's release; sometimes on the fly during its development. DLC can take many forms and sizes, from additional vehicles or outfits, to map packs or bonus levels, to completely new storylines and casts of characters. In social or mobile games, items or levels can be purchased *à la carte*, and are released regularly throughout the game's life cycle.

No matter what its size, *each DLC release should be treated as a new product* and subject to all the planning, test kickoffs, and phase entry criteria described in this chapter. DLC should not be marginalized or treated as less of a product—nor should it be tested with less diligence—merely because it is released after its parent game.

Summary

Structured game testing breaks the test activities into distinct phases, each of which has its own inputs, deliverables, and success criteria. These phases reflect the progressive completion and improvement of the game code until it is finally fit to be released to the playing public. Once test planning and preparation are completed, different types of testing are used in the remaining phases. Like pieces of a mosaic, they each reveal something different about the game code—in the right place and at the right time.

Exercises

1. What are the main responsibilities of a lead tester?

2. Which fields in the bug database should the primary tester be allowed to modify?

3. The Beta build is the version that will be sent to manufacturing. True or false?

4. Describe whether each of the following is an appropriate topic to discuss during a test execution kickoff, and why:

a. Possible contradictions in the feature requirements

b. Ideas for new tests

c. Company stock prices

d. Identical tests already being run in other test suits

e. How "buggy" a feature was in a previous release

f. Recent changes to the game data-file formats

g. Lack of detail in the test case documentation

5. Feature lock should happen at Alpha. True or false?

6. Online multiplayer features can be tested at Alpha. True or false?

7. Being a team player is not an important criterion for being a lead tester. True or false?

8. All bugs must be fixed before a build can be considered a GMC. True or false?

9. Explain the difference between a test case and a test plan.

CHAPTER 6

THE GAME TESTING PROCESS

In This Chapter

- "Black box" testing
- "White box" testing
- The life cycle of a build
- On writing bugs well

Developers don't fully test their own games. They don't have time to, and even if they did, it's not a good idea. Back at the dawn of the video game era, the programmer of a game was also its artist, designer, and tester. Even though games were very small—the size of email—the programmer spent most of his time designing and programming. Little of his time was spent testing. If he did any testing, it was based on his own assumptions about how players would play his game. The following sidebar illustrates the type of problem these assumptions could create.

The Player Will Always Surprise You

The programmer of *Astrosmash*, a space shooter released for the Intellivision® system in 1981, made an assumption when he designed the game that no player would ever score 10 million points. As a result, he didn't write a check for score overflowing. He read over his own code and—based on his own assumptions—it seemed to work fine. It was a fun game—its graphics were breathtaking (for the time) and the game went on to become one of the best sellers on the Intellivision platform.

Weeks after the game was released, however, a handful of customers began to call the game's publisher, Mattel Electronics, with an odd complaint: when they scored more than 9,999,999 points, the score displayed negative numbers, letters, and symbol characters. This in spite of the promise of "unlimited scoring potential" in the game's marketing materials. The problem was exacerbated by the fact that the Intellivision console had a feature that allowed players to play the game in slow motion, making it much easier to rack up high scores. John Sohl, the programmer, learned an early lesson about video games: *the player will always surprise you*.

The sidebar story demonstrates why video game testing is best done by testers who are: (a) professional, (b) objective, and (c) separated—either physically or functionally—from the game's development team. That removal and objectivity allows testers to think independently of the developers, to function as players, and to figure out new and interesting ways to break the game. This chapter discusses how, like the gears of a watch, the game *testing* process meshes into the game *development* process.

"BLACK BOX" TESTING

Almost all game testing is *black box* testing, testing done from outside the application. No knowledge of, or access to, the source code is granted to the tester. Game testers typically don't find defects by reading the game code. Rather, they try to find defects using the same input devices available to the average player, be it a mouse, a keyboard, a console gamepad, a motion sensor, or a plastic guitar. Black box testing is the most cost-effective way to test the extremely complex network of systems and modules that even the simplest video game represents.

Figure 6.1 illustrates some of the various inputs you can provide to a video game and the outputs you can receive back. The most basic of inputs are positional, and control data in the form of button presses and cursor movements, or vector inputs from accelerometers, or even full-body cameras. Audio input can come from microphones fitted in headsets or attached to a game controller. Input from other players can come from a second controller, a local network, or the Internet. Finally, stored data such as saved games and options settings can be called up as input from memory cards or a hard drive.

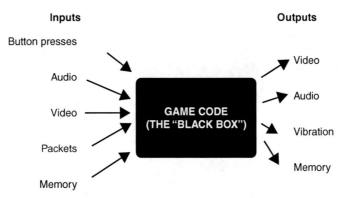

FIGURE 6.1 Black box testing: planning inputs and examining outputs.

Once some or all of these types of input are received by the game, it reacts in interesting ways and produces such output as video, audio, vibration (via force feedback devices), and data saved to memory cards or hard drives.

The input path of a video game is not one-way, however. It is a feedback loop, where the player and the game are constantly reacting to each other. Players don't receive output from a game and stop playing. They constantly alter and adjust their input "on the fly," based on what they see, feel, and hear in the game. The game, in turn, makes similar adjustments in its outputs based on the inputs it receives from the player. Figure 6.2 illustrates this loop.

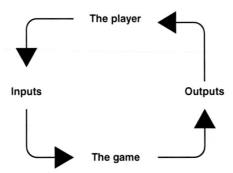

FIGURE 6.2 The player's feedback loop adjusts to the game's input, and vice versa.

If the feedback received by the player were entirely predictable all the time, the game would be no fun. Nor would it be fun if the feedback received by the player were entirely random all the time. Instead, feedback from games should be just random enough to be unpredictable. It is the unpredictability of the feedback loop that makes games fun. Because the code is designed to surprise the player and the player will always surprise the programmer, black box testing allows testers to think and behave like players.

"WHITE BOX" TESTING

In contrast to black box testing, *white box* testing gives the tester opportunities to exercise the source code directly in ways that no player ever could. It can be a daunting challenge for the white box tester to read a piece of game code and predict every single interaction it will have with every other bit of code, and whether the programmer has accounted for every combination and order of inputs possible. Testing a game using only white box methods is also extremely difficult because it is nearly impossible to account for the complexity of the player feedback loop. There are, however, situations in which white box testing is more practical and necessary than black box testing. These include the following:

- Tests performed by developers prior to submitting new code for integration with the rest of the game

- Testing code modules that will become part of a reusable library across multiple games or platforms

- Testing code methods or functions that are essential parts of a game engine or middleware product

- Testing code modules within your game that might be used by third-party developers or "modders" who, by design, could expand or modify the behavior of your game to their own liking

- Testing low-level routines that your game uses to support specific functions in the newest hardware devices, such as graphics cards or audio processors

In performing white box tests, you execute specific modules and the various paths that the code can follow when you use the module in various ways. Test inputs are determined by the types and values of data that can be passed to the code. Results are checked by examining values returned by the module, global variables that are affected by the module, and local variables as they are processed within the module. To get a taste of white box testing, consider the TeamName routine from *Castle Wolfenstein: Enemy Territory*:

```
const char *TeamName(int team)   {
    if (team==TEAM_AXIS)
        return "RED";
    else if (team==TEAM_ALLIES)
        return "BLUE";
    else if (team==TEAM_SPECTATOR)
        return "SPECTATOR";
    return "FREE";
}
```

Four white box tests are required for this module to test the proper behavior of each line of code within the module. The first test would be to call the TeamName function with the parameter TEAM_AXIS and then check that the string "RED" is returned. Second, pass the value of TEAM_ALLIES and check that "BLUE" is returned. Third, pass TEAM_SPECTATOR and check that "SPECTATOR" is returned. Finally, pass some other value such as TEAM_NONE, which makes sure that "FREE" is returned. Together these tests not only exercise each line of code at least once, they also test the behavior of both the "true" and "false" branches of each if statement.

This short exercise illustrates some of the key differences between a white box testing approach and a black box approach:

- Black box testing should test all of the different ways you could choose a test value from within the game, such as different menus and buttons. White box testing requires you to pass that value to the routine in one form—its actual symbolic value within the code.

- By looking into the module, white box testing reveals all of the possible values that can be provided to and processed by the module being tested. This information might not be obvious from the product requirements and feature descriptions that drive black box testing.

- Black box testing relies on a consistent configuration of the game and its operating environment in order to produce repeatable results. White box testing relies only on the interface to the module being tested and is concerned only about external files when processing streams, file systems, or global variables.

THE LIFE CYCLE OF A BUILD

Game testers are often frustrated that, like players, they must wait (and wait) for the work product of the development team before they can spring into action. Players wait for game releases; testers wait for code releases, or *builds*. The test results from each build is how all stakeholders in the project—from QA to the project manager to the publisher—measure the game's progress toward release.

A basic game testing process consists of the following steps:

1. **Plan and design the test.** Although much of this is done early in the planning phase, planning and design should be revisited with every build. What has changed in the design spec since the last build? What additional test cases have been added? What new configurations will the game support? What features have been cut? The scope of testing should ensure that no new issues were introduced in the process of fixing bugs prior to this release.

2. **Prepare for testing.** Code, tests, documents, and the test environment are updated by their respective owners and aligned with one another. By this time the development team should have marked the bugs fixed for

this build in the defect database so the QA team can subsequently verify those fixes and close the bugs.

3. **Perform the test.** Run the test suites against the new build. If you find a defect, test "around" the bug to make certain you have all the details necessary to write as specific and concise a bug report as possible. The more research you do in this step, the easier and more useful the bug report will be.

4. **Report the results.** Log the completed test suite and report any defects you found.

5. **Repair the bug.** The test team participates in this step by being available to discuss the bug with the development team and to provide any directed testing a programmer might require to track the defect down.

6. **Return to Step 1 and re-test.** With new bugs and new test results comes a new build.

These steps not only apply to black box testing, they also describe white box testing, configuration testing, compatibility testing, and any other type of QA. These steps are identical no matter what their scale. If you substitute the word "game" or "project" for the word "build" in the preceding steps, you will see that they can also apply to the entire game, a phase of development (Alpha, Beta, and so on), or an individual module or feature within a build. In this manner, the software testing process can be considered fractal—the smaller system is structurally identical to the larger system, and vice versa.

As illustrated in Figure 6.3, the testing process itself is a feedback loop between the tester and developer. The tester plans and executes tests on the code, then reports the bugs to the developer, who fixes them and compiles a new build, which the tester plans and executes, and so on.

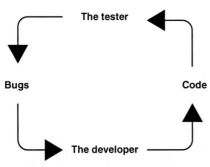

FIGURE 6.3 The testing process feedback loop.

A comfortable scale from which to examine this process is at the level of testing an individual build. Even a relatively small game project could consist of dozens of builds over its development cycle.

Test Cases and Test Suites

As discussed in the previous chapter, a single test performed to answer a single question is a test case; a collection of test cases is a test suite. The lead tester, primary tester, or any other tester tasked with test creation should draft these documents prior to the distribution of the build. Each tester will take his or her assigned test suites and perform them on the build. Any anomalies not already present in the database should be written up as new bugs.

In its simplest form, a test suite is a series of incremental steps that the tester can perform sequentially. Subsequent chapters in this book discuss in depth the skillful design of test cases and suites through such methods as combinatorial tables and test flow diagrams. For the purposes of this discussion, consider a short test suite you might execute on *Minesweeper*, a simple game available with most versions of Microsoft Windows®. A portion of this suite is shown in Figure 6.4.

Step	Pass	Fail	Comments
1. Launch Minesweeper			
2. Musical tone plays?			
3. Visible menu options are Game and Help?			
4. Right Number (time elapsed) displayed as 0?			
5. Left Number (bombs left) displayed is 10?			
6. Click Game on the menu and choose Exit.			
7. Game closes?			
8. Re-launch Minesweeper.			
9. Choose Game > Options > Custom			
10. Enter 0 in the Height box			
11. 0 accepted as input?			
12. Click OK.			
13. Error message appears?			
14. Click OK again.			
15. Game grid 9 rows high?			
16. Game grid 9 columns wide (unchanged)?			
17. Choose Game > Options > Custom			
18. Enter 999 in the Height box			
19. 999 accepted as input?			
20. Click OK.			
21. Playing grid 24 rows high?			
22. Playing grid 9 columns wide (unchanged)?			

FIGURE 6.4 A portion of a test suite for *Minesweeper*.

This is a very small portion of a very simple test suite for a very small and simple game. The first section (steps one through seven) tests launching the game, ensuring that the default display is correct, and exiting. Each step either gives the tester one incremental instruction or asks the tester one simple question. Ideally, these questions are binary and unambiguous. The tester performs each test case and records the result.

Because the testers will inevitably observe results that the test designer hadn't planned for, the Comments field allows the tester to elaborate on a Yes/No answer, if necessary. The lead or primary tester who receives the completed test suite can then scan the Comments field and make adjustments to the test suite as needed for the next build.

Where possible, the questions in the test suite should be written in such a way that a "yes" answer indicates a "pass" condition—the software is working as designed and no defect is observed. "No" answers, in turn, should indicate that there is a problem and a defect should be reported. There are several reasons for this: it's more intuitive, because we tend to group "yes" and "pass" (both positives) together in our minds the same way we group "no" and "fail." Further, by grouping all passes in the same column, the completed test suite can be easily scanned by both the tester and test managers to determine quickly whether there were any fails. A clean test suite will have all the checks in the Pass column.

For example, consider a test case covering the display of a tool tip—a small window with instructional text incorporated into many interfaces. A fundamental test case would be to determine whether the tool tip text contains any typographical errors. The most intuitive question to ask in the test case is:

```
Does the text contain any typographical errors?
```

The problem with this question is that a pass (no typos, hence no bugs) would be recorded as a "no." It would be very easy for a hurried (or tired) tester to mistakenly mark the Fail column. It is far better to express the question so that a "yes" answer indicates a "pass" condition:

```
Is the text free of typographical errors?
```

As you can see, directed testing is very structured and methodical. After the directed testing has concluded, or concurrently with directed testing, a less structured, more intuitive form of testing, known as *ad hoc* testing, takes place.

Entry Criteria

It's advisable to require that any code release meets some criteria for being fit to test before you risk wasting your time, or your team's time, testing it. This is similar to the checklists that astronauts and pilots use to evaluate the fitness of their vehicle systems before attempting flight. Builds submitted to testing that don't meet the basic entry criteria are likely to waste the time of both testers and programmers. The countdown to testing should stop until the test "launch" criteria are met.

The following is a list of suggestions for entry criteria. Don't keep these a secret from the rest of the development team. Make the team aware of the purpose—to prevent waste—and work with them to produce a set of criteria that the whole team can commit to.

- The game code should be built without compiler errors. Any new compiler warnings that occur are analyzed and discussed with the test team.

- The code release notes should be complete and should provide the detail that testers need to plan which tests to run or to re-run for this build.

- Defect records for any bugs closed in the new release should be updated so they can be used by testers to make decisions about how much to test in the new build.

- Tests and builds should be properly version-controlled, as described in the sidebar, "Version Control: Not Just for Developers."

- When you are sufficiently close to the end of the project, you also want to receive the game on the media on which it will ship. Check that the media provided contains all of the files that would be provided to your customer.

Version Control: Not Just for Developers

A fundamental principle of software development is that every build of an application should be treated as a separate and discrete version. Inadvertent blending of old code with new is one of the most common (and most preventable) causes of software defects. The process of tracking builds and ensuring that all members of a development team are checking current code and assets into the current version is known as *version control*.

Test teams must practice their own form of version control. There are few things more time wasting than for a test team to report a great number of bugs in an old build. This is not only a waste of time, but it can cause panic on the part of the programmer and the project manager.

Proper version control for the test team includes the following steps:

1. Collect all prior physical (*e.g.*, disk-based) builds from the test team before distributing the new build. The prior versions should be staked together and archived until the project is complete. (When testing digital downloads, uninstall and delete or archive prior digital builds.)

2. Archive all paperwork. This includes not only any build notes you received from the development team, but also any completed test suites, screen shots, saved games, notes, video files, and any other material generated during the course of testing a build. It is sometimes important to retrace steps along the paper trail, whether to assist in isolating a new defect or determining in what version an old bug was re-introduced.

3. Verify the build number with the developer prior to distributing it.

4. In cases where builds are transmitted electronically, verify the byte count, file dates, and directory structure before building it. It is vital in situations where builds are sent via FTP, email, Dropbox (*www.dropbox.com*), or other digital means that the test team makes certain to test a version identical to the version the developers uploaded. Confirm the integrity of the transmitted build before distributing it to the testers.

5. Renumber all test suites and any other build-specific paperwork or electronic forms with the current version number.

6. Distribute the new build for smoke testing.

___

Configuration Preparation

Before the test team can work with the new build, some housekeeping is in order. The test equipment must be readied for a new round of testing. The test lead must communicate the appropriate hardware configuration to each tester for this build. Configurations typically change little over the course of game testing. To test a single-player-only console game, you need the game console, a controller, and a memory card or hard drive. That hardware configuration typically will not change for the life of the project. If, however, the new build is the first in which network play is enabled, or a new input device or PC video card has been supported, you will perhaps need to augment the hardware configuration to perform tests on that new code.

Perhaps the most important step in this preparation is to eliminate any trace of the prior build from the hardware. "Wiping" the old build of a disk-based game on a Nintendo Wii™ is simple, because the only recordable media for that system is an SD card or its small internal flash memory drive. All you have to do is remove and archive the saved game you created with the hold build. More careful test leads will ask their testers to go the extra step of reformatting the media, which completely erases it, to ensure that not a trace of the old build's data will carry forward during the testing of the new build.

Save your saves! Always archive your old player-created data, including game saves, options files, and custom characters, levels, or scenarios.

Not surprisingly, configuration preparation can be much more complicated for PC games. The cleanest possible testing configuration for a PC game is:

- A fresh installation of the latest version of the operating system, including any patches or security updates.

- The latest drivers for all components of the computer. This not only includes the obvious video card and sound card drivers, but also chipset drivers, motherboard drivers, Ethernet card drivers, WiFi firmware, and so on.

- The latest version of any "helper apps" or middleware the game requires in order to run. These can range from Microsoft's DirectX® multimedia libraries to third-party multiplayer matchmaking software.

The only other software installed on the computer should be the new build.

Chasing False Defects

We once walked into a QA lab that was testing a (then) very cutting-edge 3D PC game. Testing of the game had fallen behind, and we had been sent from the publisher to investigate. We arrived just as the testers were breaking for lunch, and were appalled to see the testers exit the game they were testing and fire up email, instant messenger clients, Web browsers, and file sharing programs—a host of applications that were installed on their test computers. Some even jumped into a game of *Unreal Tournament*. We asked the assistant test manager why he thought it was a good idea for the testers to run these extraneous programs on their testing hardware. "It simulates real-world conditions," he shrugged, annoyed by our question.

As you perhaps have already guessed, this lab's failure to wipe their test computers clean before each build led to a great deal of wasted time chasing false defects— symptoms testers thought were defects in the game, but which were in fact problems brought about by, for example, email or file sharing programs running in the background, taxing the system's resources and network bandwidth. This wasted tester time also meant a good amount of wasted programmer time, as the development team tried to figure out what in the game code might be causing such (false) defects.

The problem was solved by reformatting each test PC, freshly installing the operating system and latest drivers, and then using a drive image backup program to create a system restore file. From that point forward, testers merely had to reformat their hard drive and copy the system restore file over from a CD-ROM.

As will be discussed further in Chapter 12, "Ad Hoc Testing and Gameplay Testing," testing takes place in a "lab," and labs should be clean. So should test hardware. It's difficult to be too fastidious or paranoid when preparing test configurations. When you get a new build, reformat your PC rather than merely uninstall the new build.

You should be careful not to be complacent about deleting old builds in this new era of Internet browser and mobile games.

Browser games should be purged from each browser's cache and the browser should be restarted before you open the new game build. In the case of Flash® games, you can right-click on the old build and select "Global

Settings . . ." This will launch a separate browser process and will connect you to the Flash Settings Manager. Choosing the "Website Storage Settings panel" will launch a Flash applet. Click the "Delete all sites" button and close all of your browser processes. Now you can open the new build of your Flash game.

iOS™ games should be deleted both from the device and the iTunes® client on the computer the device is synched to. When prompted by iTunes, choose to delete the app entirely (this is the "Move to Recycle Bin" or "Move to Trash" button). Now, synch your device and make certain the old build has been removed both from iTunes and your device. Empty the Recycle Bin (or the Trash), relaunch iTunes, copy the new build, and synch your device again.

Android™ games, like iOS games, should be deleted entirely from the device and your computer. Always synch your device to double-check that you have scrubbed the old build off before you install the new build.

Whatever protocol is established, *config prep* is crucial prior to the distribution of a new build.

Smoke Testing

The next step after accepting a new build and preparing to test it is to certify that the build is worthwhile to submit to formal testing. This process is sometimes called *smoke testing*, because it's used to determine whether a build "smokes" (malfunctions) when run. At a minimum, it should consist of a "load & launch," that is, the lead or primary tester should launch the game, enter each module from the main menu, and spend a minute or two playing each module. If the game launches with no obvious performance problems and each module implemented so far loads with no obvious problems, it is safe to certify the build, log it, and duplicate it for distribution to the test team.

Now that the build is distributed, it's time to test for new bugs, right? Not just yet. Before testing can take a step forward, it must first take a step backward and verify that the bugs the development team claims to have fixed in this build are indeed fixed. This process is known as *regression testing*.

Regression Testing

Fix verification can be at once very satisfying and very frustrating. It gives the test team a good sense of accomplishment to see the defects they report disappear one by one. It can be very frustrating, however, when a fix of one defect creates another defect elsewhere in the game, as can often happen.

The test suite for regression testing is the list of bugs the development team claims to have fixed. This list, sometimes called a *knockdown list*, is ideally communicated through the bug database. When the programmer or artist fixes the defect, all they have to do is change the value of the Developer Status field to "Fixed." This allows the project manager to track the progress on a minute-to-minute basis. It also allows the lead tester to sort the regression set (by bug author or by level, for example). At a minimum, the knockdown list can take the form of a list of bug numbers sent from the development team to the lead tester.

Don't accept a build into test unless it is accompanied by a knockdown list. It is a waste of the test team's time to regress every open bug in the database every time a new build enters test.

Each tester will take the bugs they've been assigned and perform the steps in the bug write-up to verify that the defect is indeed fixed. The fixes for many defects are easily verified (typos, missing features, and so on). Some defects, such as hard-to-reproduce crashes, could *seem* fixed, but the lead tester might want to err on the side of caution before he closes the bug. By flagging the defect as *verify fix*, the bug can remain in the regression set (i.e., stay on the knockdown list) for the next build (or two), but out of the set of open bugs that the development team is still working on. Once the bug has been verified as fixed in two or three builds, the lead tester can then close the bug with more confidence. (For a more complete discussion of regression, see Chapter 14, "Regression Testing and Test Reuse.")

At the end of regression testing, the lead tester and project manager can get a very good sense of how the project is progressing. A high fix rate (number of bugs closed divided by the number of bugs claimed to have been fixed) means the developers are working efficiently. A low fix rate could be cause for concern. Are the programmers arbitrarily marking bugs as fixed if they think they've implemented new code that might address the defect, rather than troubleshooting the defect itself? Are the testers not writing clear bugs? Is there a version control problem? Are the test systems configured properly? While the lead tester and project manager mull over these questions, it's time for you to move on to the next step in the testing process: performing structured tests and reporting the results.

Testing "Around" a Bug

The old saying in carpentry is "measure twice, cut once." Good game testers thoroughly investigate a defect before they write it up, anticipating any questions the development team might have.

Before you begin to write a defect report, ask yourself some questions:

1. Is this the only location or level where the bug occurs?

2. Does the bug occur while using other characters or units?

3. Does the bug occur in other game modes (for example, multiplayer as well as single player, skirmish as well as campaign)?

4. Can I eliminate any steps along the path to reproducing the bug?

5. Does the bug occur across all platforms (for example, does it occur on both the Xbox 360 and PlayStation 3 builds)?

6. Is the bug machine-specific (for example, does it occur only on PCs with a certain hardware configuration)?

These are the types of questions you will be asked by the lead tester, project manager, or developer. Try to develop the habit of second-guessing such questions by performing some quick additional testing before you write the bug. Test to see whether the defect occurs in other areas. Test to determine whether the bug happens when you choose a different character. Test to check which other game modes contain the issue. This practice is known as testing "around" the bug.

Once you are satisfied that you have anticipated any questions that the development team might ask, and you have all your facts ready, you are finally ready to write the bug report.

ON WRITING BUGS WELL

Good bug writing is one of the most important skills a tester must learn. A defect can be fixed only if it is communicated clearly and effectively. One of the oldest jokes in software development goes something like this:

Q: How many programmers does it take to screw in a light bulb?

A: None—it's not dark where they're sitting.

Good bug report writing gets the development team to "see the light" of the bug. The developers are by no means the only people who will read your bug, however. Your audience could include:

- The lead tester or primary tester, who might wish to review the bug before she gives it an "open" status in the bug database.

- The project manager, who will read the bug and assign it to the appropriate member of the development team.

- Marketing and other business executives, who might be asked to weigh in on the possible commercial impact of fixing (or not fixing) the bug.

- Third parties, such as middleware developers, who could be asked to review a bug that is possibly related to a project they supply to the project team.

- Customer service representatives, who might be asked to devise work-arounds for the bug.

- Other testers, who will reproduce the steps if they are asked to verify a fix during regression testing.

Because you never know exactly who will be reading your bug report, you must always write in as clear, objective, and dispassionate a manner as possible. You can't assume that everyone reading your bug report will be as familiar with the game as you are. Testers spend more time in the game—exploring every hidden path, closely examining each asset—than almost anyone else on the entire project team. A well-written bug will give a reader who is not familiar with the game a good sense of the type and severity of the defect it describes.

Just the Facts, Ma'am

The truth is that defects stress out development teams, especially during "crunch time." Each new bug added to the database means more work still has to be done. An average-sized project can have hundreds or thousands of defects reported before it is completed. Developers can feel overwhelmed and might, in turn, get hostile if they feel their time is being wasted by frivolous or arbitrary bugs. That's why good bug writing is fact based and unbiased.

```
The guard's hat would look better if it was blue.
```

This is neither a defect nor a fact; it's an unsolicited and arbitrary opinion about design. There are forums for such opinions—discussions with the lead tester, team meetings, play testing feedback—but the bug database isn't one of them.

A common complaint in many games is that the artificial intelligence, or AI, is somehow lacking. (AI is a catch-all term that means any opponents or NPCs controlled by the game code.)

```
The AI is weak.
```

This could indeed be a fact, but it is written in such a vague and general way that it is likely to be considered an opinion. A much better way to convey the same information is to isolate and describe a specific example of AI behavior and write up that specific defect. By boiling issues down to specific facts, you can turn them into defects that have a good chance of being addressed.

Before you begin to write a bug report, you have to be certain that you have all your facts.

Brief Description

Larger databases could contain two description fields: Brief Description (or Summary) and Full Description (or Steps). The Brief Description field is used as a quick reference to identify the bug. This should not be a cute nickname, but a one-sentence description that allows team members to identify and discuss the defect without having to read the longer, full description each time. Think of the brief description as the headline of the defect report.

```
Crash to desktop.
```

This is not a complete sentence, nor is it specific enough to be a brief description. It could apply to one of dozens of defects in the database. The brief description must be brief enough to be read easily and quickly, but long enough to describe the bug.

```
The saving system is broken.
```

This is a complete sentence, but it is not specific enough. What did the tester experience? Did the game not save? Did a saved game not load? Does saving cause a crash?

```
Crash to desktop when choosing "Options" from Main Menu.
```

This is a complete sentence, and it is specific enough so that anyone reading it will have some idea of the location and severity of the defect.

```
Game crashed after I killed all the guards and dou-
bled back through the level to get all the pick-ups and
killed the first re-spawned guard.
```

This is a run-on sentence that contains far too much detail. A good way to boil it down might be

```
Game crashes after killing respawned guards.
```

The one-sentence program descriptions used by cable television guides and download stores can provide excellent examples of brief description writing—they boil an entire one-hour cop show or two-hour movie into one sentence.

Write the full description first, and then write the brief description. Spending some time polishing the full description will help you understand the most important details to include in the brief description.

Full Description

If the brief description is the headline of a bug report, the Full Description field provides the gory details. Rather than a prose discussion of the defect, the full description should be written as a series of brief instructions so that anyone can follow the steps and reproduce the bug. Like a cooking recipe—or computer code, for that matter—the steps should be written in second person imperative, as though you were telling someone what to do. The last step is a sentence (or two) describing the bad result.

```
1. Launch the game.

2. Watch the animated logos. Do not press ESC to skip
   through them.

--> Notice the bad strobing effect at the end of the
Developer logo.
```

The fewer steps, the better; and the fewer words, the better. Remember Brad Pitt's warning to Matt Damon in *Ocean's Eleven*: don't use seven steps when four will do. Time is a precious resource when developing a game. The less time it takes a programmer to read, reproduce, and understand the bug, the more time he has to fix it.

```
1. Launch game.

2. Choose multiplayer.

3. Choose skirmish.

4. Choose "Sorrowful Shoals" map.

5. Choose two players.

6. Start game.
```

These are very clear steps, but for the sake of brevity they can be boiled down to

```
1. Start a two player skirmish game on "Sorrowful
   Shoals."
```

Sometimes, however, you need several steps. The following bug describes a problem with a power-up called "mugging," which steals any other power-up from any other unit.

1. Create a game against one human player. Choose
   Serpent tribe.

2. Send a swordsman into a Thieves Guild to get the
   Mugging power-up.

3. Have your opponent create any unit and give that unit
   any power-up.

4. Have your Swordsman meet the other player's unit
   somewhere neutral on the map.

5. Activate the Mugging power-up.

6. Attack your opponent's unit.

--> Crash to desktop as Swordsman strikes.

This might seem like many steps, but it is the quickest way to reproduce the bug. Every step is important to isolate the behavior of the mugging code. Even small details, like meeting in a neutral place, are important, because meeting in occupied territory might bring allied units from one side or another into the fight, and the test might then be impossible to perform.

TIP   *Good bug writing is* precise *yet* concise.

Great Expectations

Oftentimes, the defect itself will not be obvious from the steps in the full description. Because the steps produce a result that deviates from player expectation, but does not produce a crash or other severe or obvious symptom, it is sometimes necessary to add two additional lines to your full description: Expected Result and Actual Result.

Expected Result describes the behavior that a normal player would reasonably expect from the game if the steps in the bug were followed. This expectation is based on the tester's knowledge of the design specification, the target audience, and precedents set (or broken) in other games, especially games in the same genre.

Actual Result describes the defective behavior. Here's an example.

1. Create a multiplayer game.

2. Click Game Settings.

3. Using your mouse, click any map on the map list. Remember the map you clicked on.

4. Press up or down directional keys on your keyboard.

5. Notice the highlight changes. Highlight any other map.

6. Click Back.

7. Click Start Game.

Expected Result: Game loads map you chose with the keyboard.

Actual Result: Game loads map you chose with the mouse.

Although the game loaded a map, it wasn't the map the tester chose with the keyboard (the last input device he used). That's a bug, albeit a subtle one. Years of precedent creates the expectation in the player's mind that the computer will execute a command based on the last input the player gave. Because the map-choosing interface failed to conform to player expectation and precedent, it could be confusing or annoying, so it should be written up as a bug.

Use the Expected/Actual Result steps sparingly. Most of the time, defects are obvious.

4. Choose "Next" to continue.

Expected Result: You continue.

Actual Result: Game locks up. You must reboot the console.

It is understood by all members of the project team that the game shouldn't crash. Don't waste time pointing out the obvious.

You should use expected/actual result statements sparingly in your bug reports, but you should use them. They can often make a difference when a developer wants to close a bug in the database by declaring it "by design," "working as intended," or "NAB" (Not a Bug).

Habits to Avoid

For the sake of clarity, effective communication, and harmony among members of the project team try to avoid two common bug writing pitfalls: humor and jargon.

Although humor is often welcome in high-stress situations, it is not welcome in the bug database. Ever. There are too many chances for misinterpretation and confusion. During crunch time, tempers are short, skins are thin, and nerves are frayed. The defect database could already be a point of contention. Don't make the problem worse with attempts at humor (even if you think your joke is hilarious). Finally, as the late William Safire warned, you should "avoid clichés like the plague."

It perhaps seems counterintuitive to want to avoid jargon in such a specialized form of technical writing as a bug report, but it is wise to do so. Although some jargon is unavoidable, and each project team quickly develops it own nomenclature specific to the project they're working on, testers should avoid using (or misusing) too many obscure technical terms or acronyms. Remember that your audience could range from programmers to financial or marketing executives, so use plain language as much as possible.

Summary

Although testing build after build might seem repetitive, each new build provides exciting new challenges with its own successes (fixed bugs and passed tests) and shortfalls (new bugs and failed tests). The purpose of going about the testing of each build in a structured manner is to reduce waste and to get the most out of the game team. Each time around, you get new build data that is used to re-plan test execution strategies and update or improve your test suites. From there, you prepare the test environment and perform a smoke test to ensure the build is functioning well enough to deploy to the entire test team. Once the test team is set loose, your top priority is typically regression testing to verify recent bug fixes. After that, you perform many other types of testing in order to find new bugs and to check that old ones have not re-emerged. New defects should be reported in a clear, concise, and professional manner after an appropriate amount of investigation. Once you complete this journey, you are rewarded with the opportunity to do it all over again.

Exercises

1. Briefly describe the difference between the Expected Result and the Actual Result in a bug write-up.

2. What's the purpose of regression testing?

3. Briefly describe the steps in preparing a test configuration.

4. What is a "knockdown list"?

5. Black box testing refers to examining the actual game code. True or False?

6. The Brief Description field of a defect report should include as much information as possible. True or False?

7. White box testing describes the testing of gameplay. True or False?

8. Version control should be applied only to the developers' code. True or False?

9. A "Verify Fix" status on a bug means it will remain on the knockdown list for at least one more test cycle. True or False?

10. A tester should write as many steps as possible when reporting a bug to ensure the bug can be reliably reproduced. True or False?

11. On a table next to a bed is a touch-tone landline telephone. Write step-by-step instructions for using that phone to dial the following local number: 555-1234. Assume the person reading the instructions has never seen or used a telephone before.

CHAPTER 7

TESTING BY THE NUMBERS

In This Chapter

- Testing progress
- Testing effectiveness
- Tester performance

P roduct metrics, such as the number of defects found per line of code, tell you how fit the game code is for release. Test metrics can tell you about the effectiveness and efficiency of your testing activities and results. A few pieces of basic test data can be combined in ways that reveal important information that you can use to keep testing on track, while getting the most out of your tests and testers.

TESTING PROGRESS

Collecting data is important to understanding where the test team is and where they are headed in terms of meeting the needs and expectations of the overall game project. Data and charts can be collected by the test lead or the individual testers. Take responsibility for knowing how well you're doing. For example, in order to estimate the duration of the test execution for any portion of the game project, estimate the total number of tests to be performed. This number is combined with data on how many tests can be completed per staff-day of effort, how much of a tester's calendar time is actually spent on testing activities, and how many tests you can expect to be redone.

Figure 7.1 provides a set of data for a test team starting to run tests against a new code release. The project manager worked with the test lead to use an estimate of 12 tests per day as the basis for projecting how long it would take to complete the testing for this release.

Date	Daily execution		Total execution	
	Planned	Actual	Planned	Actual
22-Dec	12	13	12	13
23-Dec	12	11	24	24
28-Dec	12	11	36	35
29-Dec	12	12	48	47
30-Dec	12	8	60	55
4-Jan	12	11	72	66
5-Jan	12	10	84	76
6-Jan	12	11	96	87
7-Jan	12	11	108	98
8-Jan	12	16	120	114
10-Jan	12	10	132	124
11-Jan	12	3	144	127
12-Jan	12	7	156	134

FIGURE 7.1 Planned and actual test execution progress data.

Thirteen days into the testing, the progress lagged what had been projected, as shown in Figure 7.2. It looks like progress started to slip on the fifth day, but the team was optimistic that they could catch up. By the tenth day they seemed to have managed to steer back toward the goal, but during the last three days the team lost ground again, despite the reassignment of some people on to and off of the team.

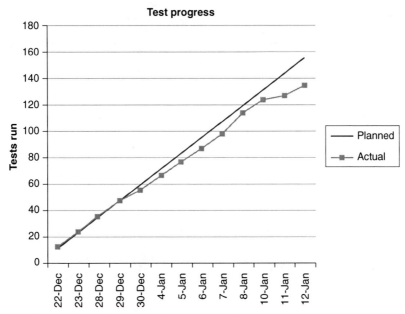

FIGURE 7.2 Planned and actual test execution progress graph.

To understand what is happening here, data was collected for each day that a tester was available to do testing, and the number of tests he or she completed each day. This information can be put into a chart, as shown in Figure 7.3. The totals show that an individual tester completes an average of about four tests a day.

Once you have the test effort data for each person and each day, you must compare the test effort people have contributed to the number of work days they were assigned to participate in system testing. Ideally, this ratio would come out to 1.00. The numbers you actually collect will give you a measurement of something you felt was true, but couldn't prove before: Most testers are unable to spend 100% of their time on testing. This being the case, don't plan on testers spending 100% of their time on a single task! Measurements will show you how much to expect from system testers, based on various levels of participation. Some testers will be dedicated to testing as their only assignment. Others perhaps perform a dual role, such as developer/tester or QA engineer/tester. Collect effort data for your team members that fall into each category, as shown in Figure 7.4.

Date	Tester					Tester days	Completed tests
	B	C	D	K	Z		
22-Dec	*				*	2	13
23-Dec	*				*	2	11
28-Dec	*				*	2	11
29-Dec	*				*	2	12
30-Dec	*				*	2	8
4-Jan	*		*		*	3	11
5-Jan	*		*		*	3	10
6-Jan	*		*		*	3	11
7-Jan	*		*		*	3	11
8-Jan		*	*	*	*	4	16
10-Jan	*	*	*			3	10
11-Jan	*	*	*			3	3
12-Jan			*			1	7
Totals						33	134
Tests/tester day							4.06

FIGURE 7.3 Test completion rate per tester per day.

Full-time testers

Week	1	2	3	4	5	6	7	Total
Tester days	15.5	21.5	35.5	31.5	36.5	22	23.5	186
Assigned days	44	50	51	53	50	41	41	330
Full-time tester availability								56%

Part-time testers

Week	1	2	3	4	5	6	7	Total
Tester days	0	0	0	18.5	18.5	6	15	58
Assigned days	0	0	0	49	54	53	46	202
Part-time tester availability								29%

Cumulative

Tester days	244
Assigned days	532
Availability	46%

FIGURE 7.4 Tester participation rate calculations.

These data lead to a number of important points. One is that, given tester "overhead" tasks such as training, meetings, preparing for demos, and so on, a full-time tester might be able to contribute only about 75% of his or her time at best, and 50%–60% on average, over the course of a long project. If you are counting on people with other responsibilities—for example, artists, developers, or QA—to help with testing, then expect only half as much participation as the full-time testers. Using the numbers in Figure 7.4, that would be about 30% of their total available time. You will need to make these measures for your own particular project.

Also, by combining the individual productivity numbers to find a team productivity number, you can see that this team performs only half as many tests as they could if they had 100% of their time to perform testing. This number can be combined with your effort estimate to give an accurate count of calendar work days remaining before testing will be finished. Using the number of 125 tests remaining, and a staff size of 11 testers, you would approximate 11 staff-days of testing remaining. Now that you know what the team's productivity is, however, you divide 11 by 46%, resulting in 24 calendar work days remaining, or nearly five "normal" work weeks. If you had committed to the original, optimistic number of 11 days, there would be much gnashing of teeth when the tests weren't actually completed until three weeks after they had been promised!

You need this kind of information to answer questions such as "How many people do you need to get testing done by Friday?" or "If I can get you two more testers, when can you be done?"

Burn into your mind that it's easier to stay on track by getting a little extra done day to day than by trying to make up a large amount in a panic situation; remember Rule #1: Don't Panic.

Going back to Figure 7.1, you can see that on 8-Jan the team was only six tests behind the goal. Completing one extra test on each of the previous six work days would have had the team on goal. If you can keep short-term commitments to stay on track, you will be able to keep the long-term commitment to deliver completed testing on schedule.

TESTING EFFECTIVENESS

Measure your Test Effectiveness (TE) by adding up defects and dividing by the number of tests completed. This measurement tells you not only how "good" the current release is compared to previous ones, it can also be used to predict how many defects will be found by the remaining tests for that release. For example, with 30 tests remaining and a TE of 0.06, testers should find approximately two more defects. This could be a sign to developers to delay a new code release until the two expected defects are identified, classified, and removed. An example table of TE measurements is shown in Figure 7.5.

Code release	Defects		Tests run		Defects/test	
	New	Total	Release	Total	Release	Total
Dev1	34	34	570	570	0.060	0.060
Dev2	47	81	1230	1800	0.038	0.045
Dev3	39	120	890	2690	0.044	0.045
Demo1	18	138	490	3180	0.037	0.043
Alpha1	6	144	220	3400	0.027	0.042

FIGURE 7.5 Test Effectiveness measurements.

You should measure TE for each release as well as for the overall project. Figure 7.6 shows a graphical view of this TE data.

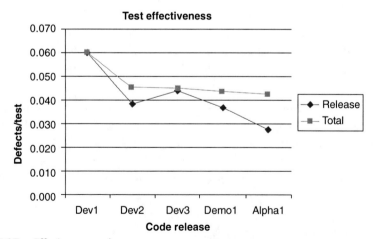

FIGURE 7.6 Test Effectiveness graph.

Notice how the cumulative TE reduced with each release and settled at .042. You can take this measurement one step further by using test completion and defect detection data for each tester in order to calculate individual TEs. Figure 7.7 shows a snapshot of tester TEs for the overall project. You can also calculate each tester's TE per release.

Tester	B	C	D	K	Z	Total
Tests run	151	71	79	100	169	570
Defects found	9	7	6	3	9	34
Defects/test	0.060	0.099	0.076	0.030	0.053	0.060

FIGURE 7.7 TE measured for individual testers.

Note that for this project, the effectiveness of each tester ranges from 0.030 to 0.099, with an average of 0.060. The effectiveness is perhaps as much a function of the particular tests each tester was asked to perform as it is a measure of the skill of each tester. Like the overall TE measurement, however, this number can be used to predict how many additional defects a particular tester could find when performing a known number of tests. For example, if tester C has 40 more tests to perform, expect her to find about four more defects.

In addition to measuring how many defects you detect (quantitative), it is important to understand the severity of defects introduced with each release (qualitative). Using a defect severity scale of 1 to 4, where 1 is the highest severity, detection of new severity 1 and 2 defects should be reduced to 0 prior to shipping the game. Severity 3 and 4 defect detection should be on a downward trend approaching 0. Figure 7.8 provides examples of severity data.

Release	Defects by severity				
	1	2	3	4	All
Dev1	7	13	13	1	34
Dev2	4	11	30	2	47
Dev3	2	3	34	0	39
Demo1	1	2	12	3	18
Alpha1	0	0	6	0	6

FIGURE 7.8 Defect severity trend data.

Figure 7.9 graphs the trend of the severity data listed in Figure 7.8. Take a moment to examine the graph. What do you see?

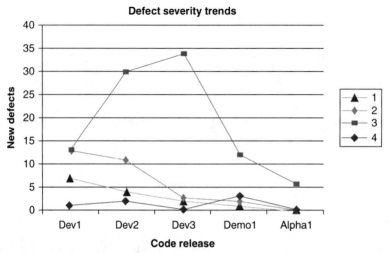

FIGURE 7.9 Defect severity trend graph.

Notice that the severity 3 defects dominate. They are also the only category to significantly increase after Dev1 testing, except for some extra 4s popping up in the Demo1 release. When you set a goal that does not allow any severity 2 defects to be in the shipping game, there will be a tendency to push any borderline severity 2 issues into the severity 3 category. Another explanation could be that the developers focus their efforts on the 1s and 2s so they leave the 3s alone early in the project, with the intention of dealing with them later. This approach bears itself out in Figures 7.8 and 7.9, where the severity 3 defects are brought way down for the Demo1 release and continue to drop in the Alpha1 release. Once you see "what" is happening, try to understand "why" it is happening that way.

TESTER PERFORMANCE

You can implement some other measurements to encourage testers to find defects and to give them a sense of pride in their skills. One of them is the "Star Chart." This chart is posted in the testing area and shows the accomplishments of each tester according to how many defects they find of each severity. Tester names are listed down one side of the chart and each defect is indicated by a stick-on star. The star's color indicates the defect's severity. For example, you can use blue for 1, red for 2, yellow for 3, and silver for 4. Points can also be assigned to each severity (for example, A = 10, B = 5, C = 3, D = 1), and a "Testing Star" can be declared at the end of the project based on who has the most points.

NOTE

In our experience, this chart has led to a sense of friendly competition among testers, increased their determination to find defects, promoted tester ownership of defects, and has caused testers to pay more attention to the severity assigned to the defects they find. This approach turns testing into a game for the testers to play while they're testing games.

Figure 7.10 shows what a Star Chart looks like prior to applying the testers' stars.

Star chart for xyzzy	
Testers	Stars (sev. 1 = blue, 2 = red, 3 = yellow, 4 = silver)
B	
C	
D	
K	
Z	

FIGURE 7.10 Empty Star Chart.

If you're worried about testers getting into battles over defects and not finishing their assigned tests quickly enough, you can create a composite measure of each tester's contribution to test execution and defects found. Add the total number of test defects found and calculate a percentage for each tester, based on how many they found divided by the project total.

Then do the same for tests run. You can add these two numbers for each tester. Whoever has the highest total is the "Best Tester" for the project. This might or might not turn out to be the same person who becomes the Testing Star. Here's how this works for testers B, C, D, K, and Z for the Dev1 release:

- Tester B executed 151 of the team's 570 Dev1 tests. This comes out to 26.5%. B has also found 9 of the 34 Dev1 defects, which is also 26.5%. B's composite rating is 53.

- Tester C ran 71 of the 570 tests, which is 12.5%. C found 7 out of the 34 total defects in Dev1, which is 20.5%. C's rating is 33.

- Tester D ran 79 tests, which is approximately 14% of the total. D also found 6 defects, which is about 17.5% of the total. D earns a rating of 31.5.

- Tester K ran 100 tests and found 3 defects. These represent 17.5% of the test total and about 9% of the defect total. K has a 26.5 rating.

- Tester Z ran 169 tests, which is about 29.5% of the 570 total. Z found 9 defects, which is 26.5% of that total. Z's total rating is 56.

- Tester Z has earned the title of "Best Tester."

When you have people on your team who keep winning these awards, take them to lunch and find out what they are doing so you can win some too!

Be careful to use this system for good and not for evil. Running more tests or claiming credit for new defects should not come at the expense of other people or the good of the overall project. You could add factors to give more weight to higher-severity defects in order to discourage testers from spending all their time chasing and reporting low-severity defects that won't contribute as much to the game as a few very important high-severity defects.

Use this system to encourage and exhibit positive test behaviors. Remind your team (and yourself!) that some time spent automating tests could have generous payback in terms of test execution. Likewise, spending a little time up front to effectively design your tests, before you run off to start banging on the game controller, will probably lead you to more defects. You will learn more about these strategies and techniques in the remaining chapters of this book.

Summary

This chapter introduced you to a number of metrics you can collect to track and improve testing results. Each metric from this chapter is listed below, together with the raw data you need to collect for each, mentioned in parentheses:

- Test Progress Chart (# of tests completed by team each day, # of tests required each day)

- Test Completed/Days of Effort (# of tests completed, # days of test effort for each tester)

- Test Participation (# of days of effort for each tester, # of days each tester assigned to test)

- Test Effectiveness (# of defects, # of tests for each release and/or tester)

- Defect Severity Profile (# of defects of each severity for each release)

- Star Chart (# of defects of each severity for each tester)

- Testing Star (# of defects of each severity for each tester, point value of each severity)

- Best Tester (# of tests per tester, # of total tests, # of defects per tester, # of total defects)

Testers or test leads can use these metrics to aid in planning, predicting, and performing game testing activities. Then you will be *testing by the numbers*.

Exercises

1. How does the data in Figure 7.3 explain what is happening on the graph in Figure 7.2?

2. How many testers do you need to add to the project represented in Figures 7.1 and 7.2 in order to bring the test execution back on plan in

the next 10 working days? The testers will begin work on the very next day that is plotted on the graph.

3. Tester C has the best TE as shown in Figure 7.7, but did not turn out to be the "Best Tester." Explain how this happened.

4. You are tester X working on the project represented in Figure 7.7. If you have run 130 tests, how many defects do you need to find in order to become the "Best Tester?"

5. Describe three positive and three negative aspects of measuring the participation and effectiveness of individual testers. Do not include any aspects already discussed in this chapter.

CHAPTER 8

COMBINATORIAL TESTING

In This Chapter

- Pairwise combinatorial testing
- Constructing tables
- Combinatorial templates
- Combinatorial test generation
- Combinatorial economics

L ike Goldilocks, testers and project managers are continually struggling with the issue of how much testing is too little, too much, or just right. Game quality has to be good enough for consumers, but testing can't go on forever if the game is going to hit its release date. Trying to test every possible combination of game events, configurations, functions, and options is neither practical nor economical under these circumstances. Taking shortcuts or skipping some testing, however, is risky business.

Pairwise combinatorial testing is a way to find defects and gain confidence in the game software, while keeping the test sets small relative to the amount of functionality they cover. "Pairwise" combination means that each value you use for testing needs to be combined at least once with each other value of the remaining parameters.

PARAMETERS

Parameters are the individual elements of the game that you want to include in your combinatorial tests. You can find test parameters by looking at various types of game elements, functions, and choices such as:

- Game events

- Game settings

- Gameplay options

- Hardware configurations

- Character attributes

- Customization choices

The test you create can be *homogenous*—designed to test combinations of parameters of the same type, or *heterogeneous*—designed to test more than one type of parameter in the same table.

For example, testing choices from a Game Options screen for their effect on gameplay is done with a homogenous combinatorial table. If you go through various menus to select different characters, equipment, and options to use for a particular mission, then that results in a heterogeneous table.

VALUES

Values are the individual choices that are possible for each parameter. Values could be entered as a number, entered as text, or chosen from a list. There are many choices for a gamer to make, but do they all need to be considered in your testing? That is, does every single value or choice have the same weight or probability of revealing a defect, or can you reduce the number of values you test without impacting your test's ability to reveal the defects in the game?

Defaults

Consider whether or not default values should be used in your tests. These are the settings and values that you get if you don't select anything special and just start playing the game as installed. You might also want to consider the first item in any list—say, a choice of hairstyle for your character—to be a kind of default value, because if you want to start playing as quickly as possible and bang on the Select key to get through all of the mandatory choices, these are the values you will be using.

If the combinatorial testing is the only testing that will be using these parameters, then the defaults should be included. They are the values that will be most often used, so you don't want to let bugs escape that will affect nearly everyone who plays the game.

On the other hand, if combinatorial testing is going to be a complement to other types of testing, then you can reduce your test burden by leaving the default values out of your tables. This strategy relies on the fact that the defaults will be used so often that you can expect them to show up in the other testing being done for the game. If you consider leaving these values out, get in touch with the other groups of people who are testing to make sure they *do* plan on using default values. If you have a test plan for your game, use it to document which sets of tests will incorporate default values and which will not.

Enumerations

Many choices in a game are made from a set of distinct values or options that do not have any particular numerical or sequential relationship to one another. Choosing which car to drive, or which baseball team to play, or which fighter to use are examples of this kind of choice.

Regardless of the number of unique choices (team, car, fighter, weapon, song, hairstyle, and so on), each one should be represented somewhere in your tests. It's easy to find bugs that happen independent of which particular choice is made. Those that do escape tend to happen for only a very few of the choices.

Ranges

Many of the game options and choices require the player to pick a number from a range or list. This could be done by directly entering a number or by scrolling through a list to make a selection. For each range of numbers, three particular values tend to have special defect-revealing properties: Zero, Minimum, and Maximum.

Anytime a zero (0) is presented as a possible choice or entry, it should be included in testing. This is partly due to the unique or ambiguous way that the value 0 might affect the game source code. Here is a partial list of possible unintended zero-induced effects:

- A loop could prematurely exit or could execute code in the body of the loop before checking for zero

- Confusion between starting loop counts at 0 or 1

- Confusion with arrays or lists starting at index 0 or 1

- 0 is often used to represent special meaning, such as to indicate an infinite timer or that an error has occurred

- 0 is the same value as the string termination (NULL) character in C

- 0 is the same value as the logical (Boolean) False value in C

Minimum values are also a good source of defects. They can be applied to numerical parameters or list choices. Look for the opportunity to use minimum values with parameters related to the following:

- Time

- Distance

- Speed

- Quantity

- Size

- Bet, sell, or purchase amount

For example, using a minimum time might not allow certain effects to be completed once they are started, or could make certain goals unachievable.

Maximum values can also cause undesirable side effects. They are especially important to use where they place an extra burden of time or skill for the tester to reach the maximum value. Both developers and testers will tend to pass over these values in favor of "easier" testing.

Use maximum values for the same parameter categories that you would test for minimum values. In addition to testing in-game elements, be sure to also include tests for the maximum number of players, maximum number of controllers connected, maximum number of saved files, and maximum storage—disk, cartridge, mobile device memory, and so on.

Boundaries

When a child (or even an adult) colors in a page of a coloring book, we judge how they do by how well they stay within the lines. Likewise, it is the responsibility of the game tester to check the game software around its boundaries. Game behavior that does not "stay within the lines" leads to defects.

Some of the boundaries to test might be physically rendered in the game space, such as the following:

- Town, realm, or city borders

- Goal lines, sidelines, foul lines, and end lines on a sports field or court

- Mission or race waypoints

- Start and finish lines

- Portal entrances and exits

Other boundaries are not physical. These can include:

- Mission, game, or match timers

- The speed that a character or vehicle can achieve

- The distance a projectile can travel

- The distance at which graphic elements become visible, transparent, or invisible

Dig deep into the rules of the game to identify hidden or implied boundaries.

For example, in football there are rules and activities tied in with the timing of the game. The timing of a football game is broken into four quarters of equal length, with a halftime pause in the game that occurs after the end of the second quarter. The game ends if one team has more points than another at the end of the fourth quarter. With two minutes left in each half, the referee stops the clock for the Two Minute Warning. To test a football game, two-minute quarters are a good boundary value to see if the second and fourth quarters of the game each start normally or with the special Two Minute Warning. A three-minute duration could also be interesting because it is the smallest duration that would have a period of play prior to the Two Minute Warning.

Another example is from the The CRIB™ feature in *ESPN NFL 2K5*, which awards players points for accomplishments during a single game, during the course of a season, and over the course of their career. Some of these accomplishments will not be rewarded if the game duration is less than five minutes and greater than eight minutes. This creates two additional quarter-length boundary values of interest.

CONSTRUCTING TABLES

To see how a combinatorial table is constructed, start with a simple table using parameters that have only two possible values. Games are full of these kinds of parameters, providing choices such as On or Off, Male or Female, Mario or Luigi, or Night or Day. This test combines character attributes for a Jedi character in a Star Wars™ game to test their effects on combat animations and damage calculations. The three test parameters are character Gender (Male or Female), whether the character uses a one-handed or two-handed Light Saber, and whether the character follows the Light side or the Dark side of the Force.

TUTORIAL

The table starts with the first two parameters arranged in the first two columns so that they cover all four possible combinations, as shown in Table 8.1.

TABLE 8.1 First Two Columns of Jedi Combat Test

Gender	Light Saber
Male	1-Handed
Male	2-Handed
Female	1-Handed
Female	2-Handed

To construct a full combinatorial table, repeat each of the Gender and Light Saber pairs, and then combine each with the two possible Force values. When the Light and Dark "Force" choices are added in this way, the size of the table doubles—determined by the number of rows—as shown in Table 8.2.

TABLE 8.2 Complete Three-Way Combinatorial Table for Jedi Combat Test

Gender	Light Saber	Force
Male	1-Handed	Light
Male	1-Handed	Dark
Male	2-Handed	Light
Male	2-Handed	Dark
Female	1-Handed	Light
Female	1-Handed	Dark
Female	2-Handed	Light
Female	2-Handed	Dark

For a pairwise combinatorial table, it's necessary to combine each value of every parameter with each value of every other parameter at least once somewhere in the table. A pair that is represented in the table is said to be "satisfied," while a pair not represented in the table is "unsatisfied." The following six pairings must be satisfied for the Jedi combat table:

1. Male Gender paired with each Light Saber choice (1-Handed, 2-Handed)

2. Female Gender paired with each Light Saber choice (1-Handed, 2-Handed)

3. Male Gender paired with each Force choice (Light, Dark)

4. Female Gender paired with each Force choice (Light, Dark)

5. One-Handed (1-Handed) Light Saber paired with each Force choice (Light, Dark)

6. Two-Handed (2-Handed) Light Saber paired with each Force choice (Light, Dark)

To make the pairwise table, rebuild from Table 8.1 by adding a column for the Force values. Next, enter the Light and Dark choices for the Male character, as shown in Table 8.3. This satisfies pairings 1 and 3—Male Gender with Light Saber choices and Male Gender with Force choices.

TABLE 8.3 Adding Force Choices for the Male Rows

Gender	Light Saber	Force
Male	1-Handed	**Light**
Male	2-Handed	**Dark**
Female	1-Handed	
Female	2-Handed	

Adding the "Dark" value to the first Female row will satisfy the criteria for pairing "1-Handed" Light Saber with each Force choice, as illustrated in Table 8.4.

TABLE 8.4 Adding the First Force Choice for the Female Character Tests

Gender	Light Saber	Force
Male	1-Handed	Light
Male	2-Handed	Dark
Female	**1-Handed**	**Dark**
Female	2-Handed	

Finally, fill in the Light value in the second Female row to produce Table 8.5 which completes the pairwise criteria for all parameters. This final entry takes care of the remaining pairings for Female Gender paired with each Light Saber choice, Female Gender paired with each Force choice, and Two-Handed (2-Handed) Light Saber paired with each Force choice.

This new table is only half the size of Table 8.2, which was developed to account for all possible three-way combinations, rather than concentrating on using parameter pairs. Including the Force parameter in these tests is "free" in terms of the resulting number of test cases. In many cases, pairwise combinatorial tables let you add complexity and coverage without increasing the number of tests you will need to run. This will not always be true; sometimes you will need a few more tests as you continue to add parameters to the table. The growth of the pairwise table, however, will be much slower than full combinatorial tables for the same set of parameters and their values.

TABLE 8.5 Completed Pairwise Combinatorial
Table for Three Jedi Combat Parameters

Gender	Light Saber	Force
Male	1-Handed	Light
Male	2-Handed	Dark
Female	1-Handed	Dark
Female	**2-Handed**	**Light**

In this simple example, the pairwise technique has cut the number of required tests in half compared by creating every mathematically possible combination of all of the parameters of interest. This technique and its benefits are not limited to tables with two-value parameters. Parameters with three or more choices can be efficiently combined with other parameters of any dimension. When it makes sense, incorporate more parameters to make your tables more efficient.

The number of choices (values) tested for a given parameter is referred to as its *dimension*. Tables are characterized by the dimensions of each parameter. They can be written in descending order, with a superscript to indicate the number of parameters of each dimension. In this way, the Jedi combat table completed in Table 8.5 is described as a 2^3 table. A table with one parameter of three values, two parameters of four values, and three parameters of two values is described as a $4^2 3^1 2^3$. Another way to describe the characteristics of the table is to list the parameter dimensions individually in descending order with a dash between each value. Using this notation, the Jedi combat table is a 2-2-2 table, and the second example mentioned above is described as 4-4-3-2-2-2. You can see how the second notation takes up a great deal of space when there are a significant number of parameters. Use whichever works best for you.

Create pairwise tables of any size for your game tests using the following short and simple process. These steps might not always produce the optimum (smallest possible) size table, but you will still achieve an efficient table.

1. Choose the parameter with the highest dimension.

2. Create the first column by listing each test value for the first parameter N times, where N is the dimension of the next-highest dimension parameter.

3. Start populating the next column by listing the test values for the next parameter.

4. For each remaining row in the table, enter the parameter value in the new column that provides the greatest number of new pairs with respect to all of the preceding parameters entered in the table. If no such value can be found, alter one of the values previously entered for this column and resume this step.

5. If there are unsatisfied pairs in the table, create new rows and fill in the values necessary to create one of the required pairs. If all pairs are satisfied, then go back to step 3.

6. Add more unsatisfied pairs using empty spots in the table to create the most new pairs. Go back to step 5.

7. Fill in empty cells with any one of the values for the corresponding column (parameter).

The next example is a little more complicated than the previous one. Use the preceding process to complete a pairwise combinatorial table for some of the *FIFA 11* Match parameters under the Game Settings menu in order to test their affect on gameplay and graphics. Figure 8.1 shows a relevant portion of the available Match settings.

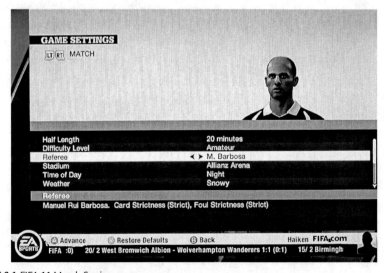

FIGURE 8.1 FIFA 11 Match Settings screen.

Half Length is the real-world amount of time it takes to complete each half of the match. Half Length times are selectable from 4–10 minutes, 15 minutes, or 20 minutes. This test design will use 4 and 10 as range boundaries and 20 because it is the maximum value for this parameter. Match Difficulty Level choices in the game range from Amateur to Legendary, so that these two extremes will be represented. Match Referees each have a different level of strictness with regard to calling fouls and issuing cards. We will test using referees that represent a Lenient, Average, or Strict approach toward fouls and cards. For example, you can use H. Pennyfeather as the "Lenient" referee, J. Rabault as the "Average" referee, and M. Barbosa as the "Strict" disciplinarian. Match Weather choices for this test will be Rainy, Snowy, or Dry. Pitch Wear (the amount of "messiness" shown on the most-used portions of the field) can be selected between None, Low, Medium, and High. For the purposes of this particular test design we will use None and High to serve as boundary values. Lastly, the two extreme Game Speed choices will be tested: Slow and Fast. As a result, you will create a $3^3 2^3$ table consisting of three parameters with three choices: Half Length, Weather, Referee, and three parameters with two choices: Difficulty Level, Pitch Wear, and Game Speed.

If you aren't familiar with the game or the detailed rules of soccer, that doesn't matter right now. You just need to be able to understand and follow the seven steps for constructing a pairwise combinatorial table.

Begin the process with steps 1 and 2 and list the Half Length values three times in the first column of the table. This is because Half Length is one of the parameters with the highest dimension (3). One of the parameters with the next highest dimension is Referee, which also has a dimension of three.

Next, apply step 3 and put each of the three Referee values in the first three rows of column 2. Table 8.6 shows what the matrix looks like at this point. A row number is included in the table so that each combination (test case) can be referenced easily.

TABLE 8.6 Starting the *FIFA 11* Match Settings Test Table

Row	Half Length	Referee
1	4 min	Lenient
2	10 min	Average

(Continued)

TABLE 8.6 Continued

Row	Half Length	Referee
3	20 min	Strict
4	4 min	
5	10 min	
6	20 min	
7	4 min	
8	10 min	
9	20 min	

Apply step 4 to continue filling in the next column. Starting with the fourth row, enter a Referee parameter that creates the most number of new pairs. Because this is only the second column, you can create only one new pair. The "Lenient" Referee has already been paired with the "4 min" Half Length, so you can put "Average" in row 4 to create a new pair. Likewise, "Strict" and "Lenient" should go in rows 5 and 6 to create new pairs with "10 min" and "20 min," respectively. Table 8.7 shows the resulting combinations at this point in the process.

TABLE 8.7 Adding the Second Set of Referee Values

Row	Half Length	Referee
1	4 min	Lenient
2	10 min	Average
3	20 min	Strict
4	4 min	Average
5	10 min	Strict
6	20 min	Lenient
7	4 min	
8	10 min	
9	20 min	

Continue with step 4 to complete the Referee column. At the seventh row, enter a Referee parameter that creates a new pair with the "4 min" Half Length value. "Lenient" (row 1) and "Average" (row 4) have already been paired, so "Strict" is the correct value for this row. By the same process,

"Lenient" goes in row 8 and "Average" in row 9. Table 8.8 shows the first two columns completed in this manner.

TABLE 8.8 Completing the Referee Column

Row	Half Length	Referee
1	4 min	Lenient
2	10 min	Average
3	20 min	Strict
4	4 min	Average
5	10 min	Strict
6	20 min	Lenient
7	4 min	Strict
8	10 min	Lenient
9	20 min	Average

Applying step 5, check that all of the pairs required for the first three columns are satisfied:

- Half Length = "4 min" is paired with "Lenient" (row 1), "Average" (row 4), and "Strict" (row 7).

- Half Length = "10 min" is paired with "Lenient" (row 8), "Average" (row 2), and "Strict" (row 5).

- Half Length = "20 min" is paired with "Lenient" (row 6), "Average" (row 9), and "Strict" (row 3).

Because all of the pairs required for the first two columns are represented in the table, step 5 sends us back to step 3 to continue the process with the Weather option and its three test values. Applying step 3, list the "Dry," "Rainy," and "Snowy" Weather values at the top of the third column, as shown in Table 8.9.

TABLE 8.9 Starting the Weather Column

Row	Half Length	Referee	Weather
1	4 min	Lenient	Dry
2	10 min	Average	Rainy

(Continued)

TABLE 8.9 Continued

Row	Half Length	Referee	Weather
3	20 min	Strict	Snowy
4	4 min	Average	
5	10 min	Strict	
6	20 min	Lenient	
7	4 min	Strict	
8	10 min	Lenient	
9	20 min	Average	

Proceed with step 4 to add the Weather value that creates the most pairs for row 4 ("4 min" and "Average"). "Dry" is already paired with "4 min" in row 1 and "Rainy" is already paired with "Average" in row 2, so "Snowy" is the correct entry for this row. In the same manner, "Dry" creates two new pairs in row 5, and "Rainy" creates two new pairs in row 6. Table 8.10 shows what the test table looks like at this point.

TABLE 8.10 Adding the Second Set of Weather Values

Row	Half Length	Referee	Weather
1	4 min	Lenient	Dry
2	10 min	Average	Rainy
3	20 min	Strict	Snowy
4	**4 min**	**Average**	**Snowy**
5	**10 min**	**Strict**	**Dry**
6	**20 min**	**Lenient**	**Rainy**
7	4 min	Strict	
8	10 min	Lenient	
9	20 min	Average	

Again, continue with step 4 to complete the Weather column. "Rainy" produces two new pairs in row 7, "Snowy" in row 8, and "Dry" in row 9. Table 8.11 shows the completed Weather column.

TABLE 8.11 Completing the Weather Column

Row	Half Length	Referee	Weather
1	4 min	Lenient	Dry
2	10 min	Average	Rainy
3	20 min	Strict	Snowy
4	4 min	Average	Snowy
5	10 min	Strict	Dry
6	20 min	Lenient	Rainy
7	**4 min**	**Strict**	**Rainy**
8	**10 min**	**Lenient**	**Snowy**
9	**20 min**	**Average**	**Dry**

It's time again to check that all the required pairs are satisfied. Because the first two columns have been previously verified, there's no need to check them again. Check the new Weather column against all of its predecessors, as follows:

- Half Length = "4 min" is paired with "Dry" (row 1), "Rainy" (row 7), and "Snowy" (row 4).

- Half Length = "10 min" is paired with "Dry" (row 5), "Rainy" (row 2), and "Snowy" (row 8).

- Half Length = "20 min" is paired with "Dry" (row 9), "Rainy" (row 6), and "Snowy" (row 3).

- Referee = "Lenient" is paired with "Dry" (row 1), "Rainy" (row 6), and "Snowy" (row 8).

- Referee = "Average" is paired with "Dry" (row 9), "Rainy" (row 2), and "Snowy" (row 4).

- Referee = "Strict" is paired with "Dry" (row 5), "Rainy" (row 7), and "Snowy" (row 3).

With all of the required pairs satisfied at this point, step 5 sends you back to step 3 to add the Difficulty Level ("Difficulty") parameter. Table 8.12 shows the two Difficulty test values added to the top of the fourth column.

TABLE 8.12 Starting the Difficulty Level Column

Row	Half Length	Referee	Weather	Difficulty
1	4 min	Lenient	Dry	Amateur
2	10 min	Average	Rainy	Legendary
3	20 min	Strict	Snowy	
4	4 min	Average	Snowy	
5	10 min	Strict	Dry	
6	20 min	Lenient	Rainy	
7	4 min	Strict	Rainy	
8	10 min	Lenient	Snowy	
9	20 min	Average	Dry	

Apply step 4 and add the Difficulty value in row 3 ("20 min," "Strict," and "Snowy") that creates the most pairs with column 4. Either "Amateur" or "Legendary" will create a new pair with all three of the other values in this row. For this exercise, choose "Amateur" for row 3. Continue from there and add the right values for rows 4 through 6. "Amateur" in row 4 would create only one new pair with "Average" so "Legendary" is the right value to put here, creating pairs with "4 min" and "Snowy." Rows 5 and 6 are populated with "Legendary" to create two new pairs in each of these rows as well—"Strict" and "Dry" in row 5 and "20 min" and "Rainy" in row 6. Table 8.13 shows the table with the newly satisfied pairs in BOLD in rows 3 through 6.

TABLE 8.13 Generating New Difficulty Pairs

Row	Half Length	Referee	Weather	Difficulty
1	4 min	Lenient	Dry	Amateur
2	10 min	Average	Rainy	Legendary
3	**20 min**	**Strict**	**Snowy**	**Amateur**
4	**4 min**	Average	**Snowy**	**Legendary**
5	10 min	**Strict**	**Dry**	**Legendary**
6	**20 min**	**Lenient**	Rainy	**Legendary**
7	4 min	Strict	Rainy	
8	10 min	Lenient	Snowy	
9	20 min	Average	Dry	

Now choose the right Difficulty values for the remaining rows. "Legendary" in row 7 does not create any new pairs, because "4 min" is already paired with "Legendary" in row 4, "Strict" is already paired with "Legendary" in row 5, and "Rainy" is already paired with "Legendary" in row 6. "Amateur" in row 7 does create a new pair with "Rainy," so it is the only correct choice. Rows 8 and 9 must also be populated with "Amateur" to create new pairs with "10 min" and "Average," respectively. Table 8.14 shows the completed Difficulty column.

TABLE 8.14 Completing the Difficulty Column

Row	Half Length	Referee	Weather	Difficulty
1	4 min	Lenient	Dry	Amateur
2	10 min	Average	Rainy	Legendary
3	20 min	Strict	Snowy	Amateur
4	4 min	Average	Snowy	Legendary
5	10 min	Strict	Dry	Legendary
6	20 min	Lenient	Rainy	Legendary
7	4 min	Strict	**Rainy**	**Amateur**
8	**10 min**	Lenient	Snowy	**Amateur**
9	20 min	**Average**	Dry	**Amateur**

Now check that all the required pairs for the Difficulty column are satisfied:

- Half Length = "4 min" is paired with "Amateur" (rows 1, 7) and "Legendary" (row 4).

- Half Length = "10 min" is paired with "Amateur" (row 8) and "Legendary" (rows 2, 5).

- Half Length = "20 min" is paired with "Amateur" (rows 3, 9) and "Legendary" (row 6).

- Referee = "Lenient" is paired with "Amateur" (rows 1, 8) and "Legendary" (row 6).

- Referee = "Average" is paired with "Amateur" (row 9) and "Legendary" (rows 2, 4).

- Referee = "Strict" is paired with "Amateur" (rows 3, 7) and "Legendary" (row 5).

- Weather = "Dry" is paired with "Amateur" (rows 1, 9) and "Legendary" (row 5).

- Weather = "Rainy" is paired with "Amateur" (row 7) and "Legendary" (rows 2, 6).

- Weather = "Snowy" is paired with "Amateur" (rows 3, 8) and "Legendary" (row 4).

So far, so good! Having satisfied all of the pairs required by the Difficulty column, go back again to step 3 to continue with the Pitch Wear option. Add the "None" and "High" Pitch Wear values to the top of the fifth column, as shown in Table 8.15.

TABLE 8.15 Starting the Pitch Wear Column

Row	Half Length	Referee	Weather	Difficulty	Pitch Wear
1	4 min	Lenient	Dry	Amateur	None
2	10 min	Average	Rainy	Legendary	High
3	20 min	Strict	Snowy	Amateur	
4	4 min	Average	Snowy	Legendary	
5	10 min	Strict	Dry	Legendary	
6	20 min	Lenient	Rainy	Legendary	
7	4 min	Strict	Rainy	Amateur	
8	10 min	Lenient	Snowy	Amateur	
9	20 min	Average	Dry	Amateur	

Step 4 requires the value in column 5 that creates the most for row 3. Only "High" creates a new pair with the four other values in this row ("20 min," "Strict," "Snowy," and "Amateur"). Repeat for row 4 and choose "None," which creates three new pairs ("Average," "Snowy," and "Legendary"), while "High" would provide only one new pair with "1 min." Populating rows 5 and 6 with "None" creates two new pairs in each of these rows, while "High" would add only one new pair in each case. Table 8.16 shows "High" chosen for Pitch Wear in row 3, and "None" for rows 4, 5, and 6.

TABLE 8.16 Adding to the Pitch Wear Column

Row	Half Length	Referee	Weather	Difficulty	Pitch Wear
1	4 min	Lenient	Dry	Amateur	None
2	10 min	Average	Rainy	Legendary	High
3	20 min	Strict	Snowy	Amateur	High
4	4 min	Average	Snowy	Legendary	None
5	10 min	Strict	Dry	Legendary	None
6	20 min	Lenient	Rainy	Legendary	None
7	4 min	Strict	Rainy	Amateur	
8	10 min	Lenient	Snowy	Amateur	
9	20 min	Average	Dry	Amateur	

A "High" value in the remaining rows produces a new pair for each: "4 min," "Lenient," and "Dry." Table 8.17 shows the completed Pitch Wear column.

TABLE 8.17 Completing the Pitch Wear Column

Row	Half Length	Referee	Weather	Difficulty	Pitch Wear
1	4 min	Lenient	Dry	Amateur	None
2	10 min	Average	Rainy	Legendary	High
3	20 min	Strict	Snowy	Amateur	High
4	4 min	Average	Snowy	Legendary	None
5	10 min	Strict	Dry	Legendary	None
6	20 min	Lenient	Rainy	Legendary	None
7	**4 min**	Strict	Rainy	Amateur	**High**
8	10 min	**Lenient**	Snowy	Amateur	**High**
9	20 min	Average	**Dry**	Amateur	**High**

It's time again to check that all the required pairs for the new column are satisfied:

- Half Length = "4 min" is paired with "None" (rows 1, 4) and "High" (row 7).

- Half Length = "10 min" is paired with "None" (row 5) and "High" (rows 2, 8).

- Half Length = "20 min" is paired with "None" (row 6) and "High" (rows 3, 9).

- Referee = "Lenient" is paired with "None" (rows 1, 6) and "High" (row 8).

- Referee = "Average" is paired with "None" (row 4) and "High" (rows 2, 9).

- Referee = "Strict" is paired with "None" (row 5) and "High" (rows 3, 7).

- Weather = "Dry" is paired with "None" (rows 1, 5) and "High" (row 9).

- Weather = "Rainy" is paired with "None" (row 6) and "High" (rows 2, 7).

- Weather = "Snowy" is paired with "None" (row 4) and "High" (rows 3, 8).

- Difficulty = "Amateur" is paired with "None" (row 1) and "High" (rows 3, 7, 8, 9).

- Difficulty = "Legendary" is paired with "None" (rows 4, 5, 6) and "High" (row 2).

This confirms that the pairs required for the Pitch Wear column are all satisfied. The process sends you back to step 3 to pair the Game Speed values in the final column. Add the "Slow" and "Fast" values to the top of this column, as shown in Table 8.18.

TABLE 8.18 Starting the Game Speed Column

Row	Half Length	Referee	Weather	Difficulty	Pitch Wear	Game Speed
1	4 min	Lenient	Dry	Amateur	None	Slow
2	10 min	Average	Rainy	Legendary	High	Fast
3	20 min	Strict	Snowy	Amateur	High	
4	4 min	Average	Snowy	Legendary	None	
5	10 min	Strict	Dry	Legendary	None	
6	20 min	Lenient	Rainy	Legendary	None	
7	4 min	Strict	Rainy	Amateur	High	
8	10 min	Lenient	Snowy	Amateur	High	
9	20 min	Average	Dry	Amateur	High	

As you proceed from here, something new happens. Neither of the Game Speed values added to row 3 creates four new pairs, so neither value can be selected. A "Slow" creates new pairs with "20 min," "Strict," "Snowy," and "High," while a "Fast" creates new pairs with "20 min," "Strict," "Snowy," and "Amateur." As you go through the table, you will find that no preferred value can be found for any of the remaining rows. Don't trust me on this (remember Rule #2?)—check for yourself! According to step 4, "If no such value can be found, alter one of the values previously entered for this column and resume this step." So, one of the Game Speed values in the first two rows should be changed. Table 8.19 shows the updated table with the second Game Speed value changed to "Slow."

TABLE 8.19 Restarting the Game Speed Column

Row	Half Length	Referee	Weather	Difficulty	Pitch Wear	Game Speed
1	4 min	Lenient	Dry	Amateur	None	Slow
2	10 min	Average	Rainy	Legendary	High	Slow
3	20 min	Strict	Snowy	Amateur	High	
4	4 min	Average	Snowy	Legendary	None	
5	10 min	Strict	Dry	Legendary	None	
6	20 min	Lenient	Rainy	Legendary	None	
7	4 min	Strict	Rainy	Amateur	High	
8	10 min	Lenient	Snowy	Amateur	High	
9	20 min	Average	Dry	Amateur	High	

Continue to step 4 from this point and see that there are now clear choices for the remaining rows. A "Fast" in row 3 provides new pairs with all of the first five columns, versus only four new pairs that would be provided by a "Slow." Another "Fast" in row 4 provides four new pairs versus three from using "Slow," and rows 5 and 6 get two new pairs from a "Fast" versus only one from a "No." Table 8.20 shows how the table looks with these values filled in.

TABLE 8.20 Adding to the Game Speed Column

Row	Half Length	Referee	Weather	Difficulty	Pitch Wear	Game Speed
1	4 min	Lenient	Dry	Amateur	None	Slow
2	10 min	Average	Rainy	Legendary	High	Slow

(Continued)

TABLE 8.20 Continued

Row	Half Length	Referee	Weather	Difficulty	Pitch Wear	Game Speed
3	**20 min**	**Strict**	**Snowy**	**Amateur**	**High**	**Fast**
4	**4 min**	**Average**	Snowy	**Legendary**	**None**	**Fast**
5	**10 min**	Strict	**Dry**	Legendary	None	**Fast**
6	20 min	**Lenient**	**Rainy**	Legendary	None	**Fast**
7	4 min	Strict	Rainy	Amateur	High	
8	10 min	Lenient	Snowy	Amateur	High	
9	20 min	Average	Dry	Amateur	High	

Complete the final three values for the table in the same manner. "Slow" is the only value that produces a new pair in each of these rows. The completed table is shown in Table 8.21.

TABLE 8.21 The Completed Match Settings Test Table

Row	Half Length	Referee	Weather	Difficulty	Pitch Wear	Game Speed
1	4 min	Lenient	Dry	Amateur	None	Slow
2	10 min	Average	Rainy	Legendary	High	Slow
3	20 min	Strict	Snowy	Amateur	High	Fast
4	4 min	Average	Snowy	Legendary	None	Fast
5	10 min	Strict	Dry	Legendary	None	Fast
6	20 min	Lenient	Rainy	Legendary	None	Fast
7	4 min	**Strict**	Rainy	Amateur	High	**Slow**
8	10 min	Lenient	**Snowy**	Amateur	High	**Slow**
9	**20 min**	Average	Dry	Amateur	High	**Slow**

Now, for perhaps the last time, check that all the required pairs for the Game Speed column are satisfied:

- Half Length = "4 min" is paired with "Slow" (rows 1, 7) and "Fast" (row 4).

- Half Length = "10 min" is paired with "Slow" (row 2) and "Fast" (rows 5, 8).

- Half Length = "20 min" is paired with "Slow" (row 9) and "Fast" (rows 3, 6).

- Referee = "Lenient" is paired with "Slow" (rows 1, 8) and "Fast" (row 6).

- Referee = "Average" is paired with "Slow" (rows 2, 9) and "Fast" (row 4).

- Referee = "Strict" is paired with "Slow" (row 7) and "Fast" (rows 3, 5).

- Weather = "Dry" is paired with "Slow" (rows 1, 9) and "Fast" (row 5).

- Weather = "Rainy" is paired with "Slow" (rows 2, 7) and "Fast" (row 6).

- Weather = "Snowy" is paired with "Slow" (row 8) and "Fast" (rows 3, 4).

- Difficulty = "Amateur" is paired with "Slow" (rows 1, 7, 8, 9) and "Fast" (row 3).

- Difficulty = "Legendary" is paired with "Slow" (row 2) and "Fast" (rows 4, 5, 6).

- Pitch Wear = "None" is paired with "Slow" (row 1) and "Fast" (rows 4, 5, 6).

- Pitch Wear = "High" is paired with "Slow" (rows 2, 7, 8, 9) and "Fast" (row 3).

Well done! By creating a pairwise combinatorial table, you developed nine tests that can test this set of parameters and values comprising 216 possible mathematical combinations (3*3*3*2*2*2). It was certainly worth the effort to create the table in order to save 207 test cases! Also note that for this table you didn't have to resort to steps 6 and 7. That won't be true in every case, so don't rule it out for the future.

Now you are ready to test the game using the combinations in the table and check for any irregularities or discrepancies with what you expect to happen. Create test tables as early as possible, for example, by using information provided in the design document long before any working code is produced. Check any available documentation to see if there is a clear definition of what should happen for each of your combinations. That will equip you to raise questions about the game that perhaps had not been considered. This is an easy way to prevent bugs and improve gameplay.

A second approach is to ask people involved with code or requirements "What happens if …" and read your combinations. You might be surprised by how many times you will get an answer like "I don't know" or "I'll have to check and get back with you." This is a much more economic alternative to finding surprises late in the project. It is also much more likely that your issues will be fixed, or at least considered, by the time the code is written.

Don't just check for immediate or near-term effects of your combinatorial tests. It's important to make sure that a menu selection is available or a button performs its function when pressed, but mid-term and far-term effects can lock up or spoil the game down the road. Some of the effects to consider are as follows:

- ☐ Does my game or session end properly?

- ☐ Do achievements get recorded properly?

- ☐ Can I progress to appropriate parts of the game or story?

- ☐ Did actions taken in the game get properly counted toward season/career accomplishments and records?

- ☐ Can I properly start and play a new session?

- ☐ Can I store and retrieve sessions or files?

Some unusual behaviors you might observe from running the *FIFA 11* Match Settings tests you completed in Table 8.21 are listed in the sidebar, "Issues with Goal Scoring"

Issues with Goal Scoring

In the first long game I tested, I noticed late into the game that when play resumed after scoring a goal, the time of the goal and the goal scorer was being reported incorrectly. The time was in the past and the same time and player's name was always being shown. Examining the game's Match Events screen showed that the goal which was being reported was the 30th goal that was scored by my team. Going through a few other test cases from the table confirmed that this happened consistently and occurred whether the 30th goal is scored in the first half or second half of the game.

A second issue appeared when I finished one match with a score of 107-0. The individual Player Ratings: Goals screen recorded a total of only 100 goals and the Match Events: Goals screen listed only the 100 most recent goals—goals scored in the first 4 minutes were not listed.

In the games I played with the 10-minute and 20-minute Half Length, I experienced some delays and stuttering on screen transitions during gameplay toward the end of the match. Perhaps this was due to the accumulation of all of the events that get logged during the game, a graphics memory management issue, or some other nefarious problem.

At some point in the sequence of games I was playing, I noticed that when starting a game with Weather = Rainy, the rain is initially visible in the "lobby" but stops coming down after a short period of time. There was also no rain coming down during the match. This is one of those cases where the tester needs to run further experiments to determine which combination or sequence of combinations triggers this phenomenon.

■ Figure 8.2 shows how a second-half goal scored in the 55th minute of the match is reported as occurring in the 23rd minute of the previous half.

FIGURE 8.2 Incorrect reporting of goal event.

COMBINATORIAL TEMPLATES

Some preconstructed tables are included in Appendix C and on the DVD you got with this book. You can use them by substituting the names and values of the parameters you want to test for the entries in the template. This will be a fast way to produce tables of fewer than 10 tests without having to develop them from scratch and then verify that all of the necessary pairs are covered. Wherever a "*" appears after a letter in the template, such as B*, that means you can substitute any of the test values for that parameter and the table will still be correct.

To see how this works, create a test table based on the Advanced Controls settings screen for *HALO Reach* (Figure 8.3). Start by determining how many parameters and values you want to test. Figure 8.3 shows nine Advanced Controls parameters and examples of their values. For this exercise, test the Look Inversion, Look Sensitivity, AutoLook Centering, Crouch Behavior, and Clench Protection settings in combination with one another. The Look Sensitivity parameter can be a value from 1 to 10 and the remaining parameters have Yes/No, Enabled/Disabled, or Toggle/Hold choices. Because Look Sensitivity ranges from 1 to 10, a good set of values to test would be the default, minimum, and maximum values, which are 3, 1, and 10, respectively. This test requires a combinatorial table of five parameters, where one parameter (Look Sensitivity) has three values and the remaining parameters have two test values. Scan through Appendix C and you'll find that Table C.18 corresponds to this configuration.

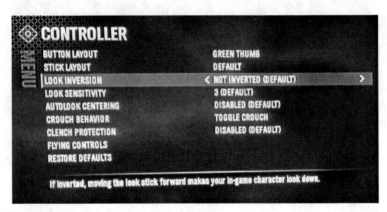

FIGURE 8.3 Advanced Controls parameters with their values.

For each parameter, assign one of the test values to the alphanumeric placeholders in the table template. Because Look Sensitivity is the only parameter with three values, it goes in the first column. The default value (3) will be assigned to A1, the minimum value (1) to A2, and the maximum (10) to A3. Replace each instance of A1, A2, and A3 in the table with their assigned values. The table at this point should look like Table 8.22.

TABLE 8.22 Look Sensitivity Values Placed into Table Template

Test	Look Sensitivity	Param B	Param C	Param D	Param E
1	3	B1	C1	D1	E1
2	1	B2	C2	D1	E1
3	10	B1	C2	D2	E1
4	3	B2	C2	D2	E2
5	1	B1	C1	D2	E2
6	10	B2	C1	D1	E2

Next, choose one of the two-value parameters, and substitute its name and values in the template's Param B column. Choose the Look Inversion parameter, assigning the default value (NO) to each instance of B1 in the table and the YES value to each B2. The table now looks like Table 8.23.

TABLE 8.23 Look Inversion Values Added to the Table

Test	Look Sensitivity	Look Inversion	Param C	Param D	Param E
1	3	NO	C1	D1	E1
2	1	YES	C2	D1	E1
3	10	NO	C2	D2	E1
4	3	YES	C2	D2	E2
5	1	NO	C1	D2	E2
6	10	YES	C1	D1	E2

Continue this process for the remaining columns using the default values for the first entry and the remaining value for the other choice. The complete design is shown in Table 8.24.

TABLE 8.24 Completed Controller Settings Table

Test	Look Sensitivity	Look Inversion	Autolook Centering	Crouch Behavior	Clench Protection
1	3	NO	NO	HOLD	DISABLED
2	1	YES	YES	HOLD	DISABLED
3	10	NO	YES	TOGGLE	DISABLED
4	3	YES	YES	TOGGLE	ENABLED
5	1	NO	NO	TOGGLE	ENABLED
6	10	YES	NO	HOLD	ENABLED

To use one of the template files included in the book's DVD start by selecting the right file based on your table dimensions. If all of your test parameters have only two values, then use the file *CombTemplates2Values.xls.* If one or more of your parameters has three values, use the file *CombTemplates3Values.xls.* If you have any parameters with four or more values, then you need to construct your table by hand or see the "Combinatorial Tools" section that follows.

Once you have identified the right template file to use, click the tab at the bottom of the worksheet that corresponds to the number of test parameters you are using. Then find the template on that sheet that matches your parameter configuration.

For the *HALO Reach* Controller Settings test, you would open the *CombTemplates3Values.xls* file and click the "5 params" tab at the bottom of the worksheet. Scroll down until you find the table labeled "1 parameter with 3 values, 4 parameters with 2 values." You will see that this table is identical in structure to the one in Appendix C that produced the test in Table 8.24. Cut this table out and paste it into your own test file. Finally, do a textual substitution for each of the test values to arrive at the same result.

COMBINATORIAL TEST GENERATION

At some point, you will find it difficult to construct and verify large parameter and value counts. Fortunately, James Bach has made a tool, available to the public at *www.satisfice.com/tools.shtml*, which handles this for you. It is also provided on the DVD that comes with this book. The Allpairs tool uses a tab-delimited text file as input and produces an output file that includes a pairwise combinatorial table as well as a report on how many times each pair was satisfied in the table.

TUTORIAL

To use Allpairs, start by creating a file that contains tab-delimited columns of parameter names with the test values in the following table. Here is an example based on match settings from the fighting game *Dead or Alive 3* (DOA3):

Difficulty	MatchPoint	LifeGauge	RoundTime
Normal	1	Smallest	NoLimit
Easy	2	Small	30
Hard	3	Normal	40
VeyHard	4	Large	50
	5	Largest	60
			99

Remember, this is not an attempt at a combinatorial table—the Allpairs tool will provide that. This is a description of the parameters you want to test: Difficulty level, Match Points needed to win a match, Life Gauge size displayed on the screen, and Round Time in seconds. Even though there are only four parameters, the fact that they have 4, 5, 5, and 6 values each to test would make this difficult to construct and validate by hand. That also means there are 600 (4*5*5*6) values if you try to test all 4-way combinations. You should expect a much smaller test set from a pairwise combinatorial test of these options—somewhere in the 30 to 40 range—based on the dimensions of the two largest parameters (6*5).

Now open a DOS (yes—DOS!) window and enter "**allpairs *input.txt > output.txt*"** where *input.txt* is the name of your tab-delimited parameter list file and *output.txt* is the name of the file where you want to store the generated combinatorial table. Make sure you are in the directory where the files are located, or provide the full path.

For this *DOA3* table, the command might be *allpairs doaparams.txt > doapairs.txt*. Here's what the test case portion of the output looks like:

TEST CASES

case	Difficulty	MatchPoint	LifeGauge	RoundTime	pairings
1	Normal	1	Smallest	NoLimit	6
2	Easy	2	Small	NoLimit	6
3	Hard	3	Normal	NoLimit	6
4	VeryHard	4	Large	NoLimit	6
5	Hard	1	Small	30	6
6	VeryHard	2	Smallest	30	6
7	Normal	3	Large	30	6

8	Easy	4	Normal	30	6
9	VeryHard	1	Normal	40	6
10	Hard	2	Large	40	6
11	Easy	3	Smallest	40	6
12	Normal	4	Small	40	6
13	Easy	1	Large	50	6
14	Normal	2	Normal	50	6
15	VeryHard	3	Small	50	6
16	Hard	4	Smallest	50	6
17	Normal	5	Largest	60	6
18	Easy	1	Largest	60	4
19	Hard	2	Largest	60	4
20	VeryHard	3	Largest	60	4
21	Easy	5	Smallest	99	5
22	Normal	4	Largest	99	4
23	Hard	5	Small	99	4
24	VeryHard	5	Normal	99	4
25	~Normal	5	Large	NoLimit	2
26	~Easy	5	Largest	30	2
27	~Hard	5	Largest	40	2
28	~VeryHard	5	Largest	50	2
29	~Hard	4	Smallest	60	2
30	~Hard	1	Large	99	2
31	~VeryHard	~1	Largest	NoLimit	1
32	~Normal	~1	Small	60	1
33	~Easy	~2	Normal	60	1
34	~Easy	~3	Large	60	1
35	~Normal	2	~Smallest	99	1
36	~Easy	3	~Small	99	1

Aren't you glad you didn't have to do that by hand! The "case" and "pairings" columns are added to the output by the Allpairs tool. "Case" is a sequential number uniquely identifying each test case. The "pairings" number indicates how many necessary parameter pairs are represented by the set of values in each row. For example, the "pairings" value in row 18 is 4. You can check for yourself that row 18 produces four new pairs: Easy-Largest, Easy-60, 1-Largest, and 1-60. The Largest-60 pair was satisfied earlier in the table at row 17, and the Easy-1 pair first appears in row 13.

Values that begin with the "~" symbol are wildcards. That is, any value of that parameter could be placed there without removing one of the necessary pairings to complete the table. The tool arbitrarily chooses, but you, the knowledgeable tester, can replace those with more common or notorious values, such as defaults or values that have caused defects in the past.

The output from Allpairs also produces a Pairing Details list, which is an exhaustive list of each necessary pair and all of the rows that include that pair. One of the pairings listed for the DOA3 table is

MatchPoint   Difficulty   1   Easy   2   13, 18,

which means that the pair Match Point = 1 and Difficulty = Easy occurs 2 times, in rows 13 and 18 of the table.

In the same list, the entry

RoundTime   LifeGauge   60   Largest   4   17, 18, 19, 20

traces the RoundTime = 60 and LifeGauge = Largest pair to rows 17–20 of the combinatorial table. This kind of information is especially useful if you want to limit your testing to all the instances of a particular pair. One reason for doing that would be to limit verification testing of a release that fixed a bug caused by one specific pair.

Another use for the Pairing Details information is to quickly narrow down the possible cause of a new defect by immediately testing the other entries in the table that had the same pairs as the test that just failed. For example, if the test in row 13 fails, search the Pairing Details list for other pairs that were included in row 13. Then run the tests on any rows listed in addition to row 13. Here are the pairs that are satisfied by row 13:

RoundTime	MatchPoint	50	1	1	13
RoundTime	LifeGauge	50	Large	1	13
RoundTime	Difficulty	50	Easy	1	13

MatchPoint	LifeGauge	1	Large	2	13, 30
MatchPoint	Difficulty	1	Easy	2	13, 18
LifeGauge	Difficulty	Large	Easy	2	13, 34

From this information, tests 18, 30, and 34 could be run next to help identify the pair that causes the defect. If none of those tests fail, then the cause is narrowed down to the first three pairs, which are only found in row 13: 50-1, 50-Large, or 50-Easy. If test 18 fails, then look for the 1-Easy pair to be the cause of the problem. Likewise, if test 30 fails then suspect the 1-Large combination. If test 34 fails you can suggest Large-Easy as the cause of the problem in your defect report.

The Allpairs output file is tab delimited so you can paste it right into Microsoft Excel or any other program supporting that format. The Allpairs tool files and the examples from this chapter, including the complete output file, are provided on the book's DVD.

COMBINATORIAL ECONOMICS

The examples used in this chapter have produced tables with significant efficiency, covering hundreds of potential combinations in no more than a few dozen tests. As it turns out, these are very modest examples. Some configurations can yield reductions of more than 100:1, 1000:1, and even beyond 1,000,000:1. It all depends on how many parameters you use and how many test values you specify for each parameter. Do you always want to do *less* testing, however?

Some game features are so important that they deserve more thorough testing than others. One way to use pairwise combinatorial tests for your game is to do full combinatorial testing for critical features, and pairwise for the rest. Suppose you identify 10% of your game features as "critical" and that each of these features has an average of 100 tests associated with it (approximately a 4 × 4 × 3 × 2 matrix). It is reasonable to expect that the remaining 90% of the features could be tested using pairwise combinatorial tables, and only cost 20 tests per feature. The cost of full combinatorial testing of all features is 100*N, where N is the total number of features to be tested. The cost of pairwise combinatorial testing 90% of those features is

$100 \ast 0.1 \ast N + 20 \ast 0.9 \ast N = 10 \ast N + 18 \ast N = 28 \ast N$. This provides a 72% savings by using pairwise for the noncritical 90%.

Another way to use combinatorial tests in your overall strategy is to create some tables to use as "sanity" tests. The number of tests you run early in the project will stay low, and then you can rely on other ways of doing "traditional" or "full" testing once the game can pass the sanity tests. Knowing which combinations work properly can also help you select which scenarios to feature in prerelease videos, walkthroughs, or public demos.

Summary

In each of these situations, the least expensive way for your team to find and remove the defects is to create pairwise combinatorial tables as early as possible in the game life cycle and to investigate the potential results of each test case. Once the design document or storyboards become available, create combinatorial tables based on the information available to you at the time and question the designers about the scenarios you generate.

If you know your testing budget in terms of staff, effort, or dollars early in the project, you have to make choices about how to distribute your resources to test the game the best you can. Pairwise combinatorial tests provide a good balance of breadth and depth of coverage, which allows you to test more areas of the game than if you concentrate resources on just a few areas.

Exercises

1. Explain the difference between a pairwise combinatorial table and a full combinatorial table.

2. Explain the difference between a parameter and a value.

3. Use the appropriate template to add the Offsides (On/Off) parameter from the Game Settings: Rules screen to the FIFA 11 Match Settings test in Table 8.21.

4. Because some of the issues found with the *FIFA 11* table are events that happen related to the Half Length, add three new rows to the Match Settings test table that pair the "15 min" Half Length with the other 5 parameters.

5. Use the Allpairs tool to create a combinatorial table for the *HALO Reach* Custom Game: Game Options: General Settings: Base Player Traits: Shields and Health when playing the Land Grab game type. The first parameter to test is "Damage Resistance" using the values Unchanged, 10% (minimum), 2000% (maximum), and Invulnerable. The second parameter is the "Shield Multiplier" with the values Unchanged, No Shields, Normal Shields, 1.5x Overshields, and 4x Overshields. For the third parameter—"Shield Recharge Rate"— incorporate the values Unchanged, 0% (No Recharge), 10% (Slower), and 200% (Faster). The values Unchanged, Disabled, and Enabled should be used in the test table for both the "Immune to Headshots" and "Immune to Assassination" parameters.

CHAPTER 9

TEST FLOW DIAGRAMS

In This Chapter

- Creating Test Flow Diagrams
- Defining the Data Dictionary
- Path strategies
- Producing test cases

Test Flow Diagrams (TFDs) are graphical models representing game behaviors from the player's perspective. Testing takes place by traveling through the diagram to exercise the game in both familiar and unexpected ways.

TFDs provide a formal approach to test design that promotes modularity and completeness. Testers can enjoy a high degree of TFD reuse if the same behaviors are consistent across multiple game titles or features. This benefit extends to sequels and ports to other platforms. The graphical nature of the TFD gives testers, developers, and producers the ability to easily review, analyze, and provide feedback on test designs.

TFD ELEMENTS

A TFD is created by assembling various drawing components called "elements." These elements are drawn, labeled, and interconnected according to certain rules. Following the rules will make it possible for your tests to be understood throughout your test organization and makes them easier to reuse in future game projects. The rules will become even more important if your team develops software tools to process or analyze the TFD contents.

Flows

Flows are drawn as a line connecting one game "state" to another, with an arrow indicating the direction of flow. Each Flow also has a unique identification number, one *Event* and one *Action*. A colon (":") separates the Event name from the flow ID number and a slash ("/") separates the Action from the Event. During testing, you *do* what is specified by the Event and then *check* for the behavior specified by both the Action and the Flow's destination State. An example flow and each of its components are shown in Figure 9.1.

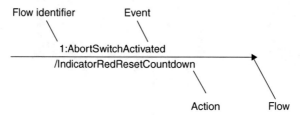

FIGURE 9.1 Flow components.

Events

Events are operations initiated by the user, peripherals, multiplayer networks, or internal game mechanisms. Think of an Event as something that is explicitly done during the game. Picking up an item, selecting a spell to cast, sending a chat message to another player and an expiring game timer are all examples of Events. The TFD does not have to represent all possible events for the portion of the game being tested. It is left up to each tester, who is now in the role of a test designer, to use his knowledge and judgment in selecting the right events that will achieve the purpose of a single TFD or a set of related TFDs. There are three factors that should be considered for including a new event:

1. Possible interactions with other Events

2. Unique or important behaviors associated with the Event

3. Unique or important game states that are a consequence of the Event

Only one Event can be specified on a flow, but multiple operations can be represented by a single event. An Event name can appear multiple times on a TFD when each instance carries the exact same meaning. Events could possibly cause a transition to a new game state.

Actions

An *Action* exhibits temporary or transitional behavior in response to an Event. It is something for the tester to check as a result of causing or performing an Event. Actions can be perceived through human senses and gaming platform facilities, including sounds, visual effects, game controller feedback, and information sent over a multiplayer game network. Actions do not persist over time. They can be perceived, detected, or measured when they occur but can no longer be perceived, detected, or measured some time later.

Only one Action can be specified on a Flow, but multiple operations can be represented by a single Action. An Action name can appear multiple times on a TFD when each instance carries the exact same meaning.

States

States represent persistent game behavior and are re-entrant. As long as you don't exit the State you will continue to observe the same behavior and each time you return to the State you should detect the exact same behavior.

A State is drawn as a "bubble" with a unique name inside. If the same behavior applies to more than one state on your diagram, consider whether they could be the same state. If so, remove the duplicates and reconnect the flows accordingly. Each state must have at least one Flow entering and one Flow exiting.

Primitives

Events, Actions, and States are also referred to as *Primitives*.

Primitive definitions provide details of the behavior represented on the TFD without cluttering the diagram. Primitive definitions form a "Data Dictionary" for the TFD. These definitions could be in text (e.g., English), a software language (e.g., C++), or an executable simulation or test language (e.g., TTCN). See the Data Dictionary section below for details and examples.

Terminators

These are not machines from the future programmed for war. Terminators are special boxes placed on the TFD that indicate where testing starts and where it ends. Exactly two Terminators should appear on each TFD. One is the IN box, which normally has a single Flow that goes to a State. The other is the OUT box, which has one or more Flows entering from one or more States.

TFD DESIGN ACTIVITIES

Creating a TFD is not just a matter of mechanically typing or drawing some information you already have in another form. It is a design activity which requires the tester to become a *designer*. A sound approach to getting your TFDs off and running is to go through three stages of activities: Preparation, Allocation, and Construction.

Preparation

Collect sources of game feature requirements.

Identify the requirements that fall within the scope of the planned testing, based on your individual project assignment or the game's Test Plan. This would include any storyboards, design documents, demo screens, or formal software requirements, as well as legacy titles that the new game is based on, such as a sequel or a spin-off.

Allocation

Estimate the number of TFDs required and map game elements to each.

Separate large sets of requirements into smaller chunks and try to cover related requirements in the same design. One way to approach this is to test various *abilities* provided in the game, such as picking up a weapon, firing a weapon, healing, and so forth. Plan on having one or more TFDs for each ability, depending on how many variations exist, such as distinct weapon types or different ways to regain health. Another approach is to map situations or scenarios to individual TFDs with a focus on specific *achievements*. These could be individual missions, quests, matches, or challenges, depending on the type of game you are testing. In this case, you are establishing that particular goals or outcomes are achievable according to which path you take in the game. TFD design based on achievements could be used either instead of or in addition to the abilities approach. Don't try to squeeze too much into a single design. It's easier to complete and manage a few simple TFDs than one that is complex.

Construction

Model game elements on their assigned TFDs using a "player's perspective."

A TFD should not be based on any actual software design structures within the game. The TFD is meant to represent the tester's interpretation of what she expects to happen as the game flows to and from the game States represented on the diagram. Creating a TFD is not as mechanical as constructing a Combinatorial Table. There is an element of art to it. TFDs for the same game feature could turn out quite differently depending on which tester developed them.

Begin the TFD with a blank sheet or a template. You can start on paper and then transfer your work to an electronic form or do the whole thing in one shot on your computer. The use of templates is discussed later in this chapter. Follow the steps below to begin constructing your TFD from scratch. An example appearing later in this chapter illustrates the application of these steps.

1. Open a file and give it a unique name that describes the scope of the TFD.

2. Draw a box near the top of the page and add the text "IN" inside of it.

3. Draw a circle and put the name of your first State inside of it.

4. Draw a Flow going from the IN box to your first State. Add the Event name "Enter" to the Flow. Note: Do not number any of the flows at this time. This will be done at the end to avoid recordkeeping and editing the numbers if you change the diagram during the rest of the design process.

Unlike the steps given for developing a pairwise combinatorial table in Chapter 8, "Combinatorial Testing," the middle steps for creating a Test Flow Diagram do not have to be followed in any particular order. Construct your diagram as your mind flows through the game scenario you are testing. The creation of the diagram should be iterative and dynamic as the diagram itself raises questions about possible events and their outcomes. Refer to the steps below when you get stuck or when you think you are done, to make sure you don't leave out any parts of the process.

1. From your first State, continue to add Flows and States. Flows can be connected back to the originating State in order to test required behavior that is transient (Action) or missing (ignored, resulting in no Action).

2. Record the traceability of each Flow to one or more requirements, options, settings, or functions. This could be as simple as ticking it off from a list or highlighting portions of the Game Design Document; or it can be done formally by documenting this information in a Requirements Traceability Matrix (RTMX).

3. For each Flow going from one State (A) to another State (B), check the requirements for possible ways to go from B to A, and add Flows as appropriate. If the requirements neither prohibit nor allow the possibility, review this with the game, feature, or level designer to determine if a requirement is missing (most likely), wrong, or ambiguous.

Once all requirements are traced to at least one Flow, check the diagram for alternative or additional ways to exercise each requirement. If a Flow seems appropriate, necessary, or obvious but can't be traced to any game documentation, determine if there might be a missing or ambiguous requirement. Otherwise, consider whether the Flow is outside of the defined scope of the TFD currently being constructed.

Go through these final steps in the order they appear here:

4. Add the OUT box.

5. Select which State or States should be connected to the OUT box. Your criteria should include choosing places in the test that are appropriate for stopping one test and starting the next one or selecting States that naturally occur at the end of the *ability* or *achievement* modeled by the TFD. For each of these States, provide a connecting flow to the OUT box with an "Exit" Event. There should be no more than one such flow coming from any State.

6. Update your IN and OUT box names to IN_xxx and OUT_xxx where xxx is a brief descriptive name for the TFD. This is done at the end in case your scope or focus has changed during the process of creating the TFD.

7. Number all of the flows.

A TFD EXAMPLE

In order to draw a TFD, you need a drawing application that can draw circles, lines with arrows, rounded or square rectangles, and the ability to attach numbers and text to each element. Microsoft PowerPoint® is an adequate and quite accessible tool that will do the job, or you might prefer the richer features in Microsoft Visio® or eazydraw® for Macintosh computers.

Your first TFD example will be based on the ability to pick up a weapon and its ammo while the game properly keeps track of your ammo count and performs the correct audible and visual effects. This is an ability required in first-person shooters, role playing games, action/adventure games, arcade games, and even some racing games. It might seem like a trivial thing to test, but the first four patches for *Unreal Tournament 2004* fixed five ammo-related defects and 14 other weapon-related bugs that were in the original release. This continued to be an area that needed tweaking in *Unreal Tournament 3*, with 13 weapon-related fixes in their first two patches.

NOTE *Use your favorite drawing tool to create your own diagram files as you follow the examples in this chapter. Do your own layout and editing and then compare what you designed with the example diagrams each step along the way.*

All TFDs start with an IN box, followed by a flow to the first state of the game that you want to observe or that you need to reach in order to begin testing. Don't begin every test with the startup screen unless that's what you are trying to test with the TFD. Jump right to the point in the game where you want to start doing things (Events) with the game that you want the tester to check (Actions, States).

In this TFD, the first State will represent the situation where the player has no weapon and no ammo. Draw a flow to connect the IN box to the NoGunNoAmmo state. Per the process described earlier in this chapter, provide the Event name "Enter" on the flow but don't provide an ID number yet. Figure 9.2 shows how the TFD looks at this point.

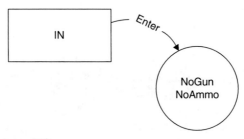

FIGURE 9.2 Starting the Ammo TFD.

The next step is to model what happens when the player does something in this situation. One likely response is to find a gun and pick it up. Having a gun creates observable differences from not having a gun. A gun appears in your inventory, your character is shown holding the gun, and a crosshair now appears at the center of the screen. These are reasons to create a separate state for this situation. Keep the naming simple and call the new state "HaveGun." Also, in the process of getting the gun, the game could produce some temporary effects like playing the sound of a weapon being picked up and identifying the weapon on the display. The temporary effects are represented by an Action on the flow. Name the flow's Event "GetGun" and name the Action "GunEffects." The TFD with the gun flow and new state is shown in Figure 9.3.

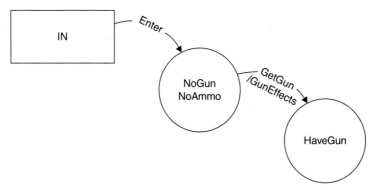

FIGURE 9.3 TFD after picking up weapon.

Because it's possible that the player could find and pick up ammo before getting the weapon, add another flow from NoGunNoAmmo to get ammo and check for the ammo sound and visual effects. A new destination state should also be added. Call it "HaveAmmo" to be consistent with the "HaveGun" state name format. Your TFD should look like Figure 9.4 at this point.

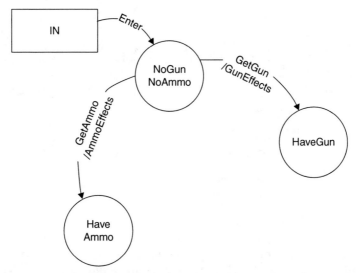

FIGURE 9.4 TFD with HaveGun and HaveAmmo states.

Now that there are a few states on the diagram, check if there are any flows you can add that go back from each state to a previous one. You got to the HaveGun state by picking up a weapon. It could also be possible to go back to the NoGunNoAmmo state by dropping the weapon. Likewise, there should be a flow from HaveAmmo going back to NoGunNoAmmo when the player somehow drops his ammo. If there are multiple ways to do this, each should appear on your TFD. One way might be to remove the ammo from your inventory and another might be to perform a reload function. For this example, just add the generic DropAmmo event and its companion DropSound action. In order to illustrate how actions might be reused within a TFD, the diagram will reflect that the same sound is played for dropping either a weapon or ammo. That means the DropGun event will also cause the DropSound action. The return flows from HaveGun and HaveAmmo are shown in Figure 9.5.

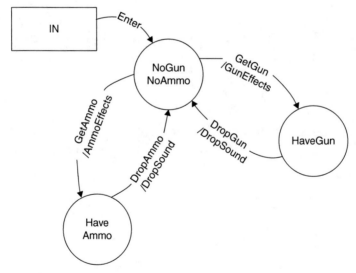

FIGURE 9.5 Return flows added from HaveGun and HaveAmmo.

Now that the test represents gun-only and ammo-only states, tie the two concepts together by grabbing ammo once you have the gun. Call the resulting state "HaveGunHaveAmmo." You should recognize that picking up the gun once you have the ammo will also take you to this very same state. Figure 9.6 shows the new flows and the HaveGunHaveAmmo state added to the TFD.

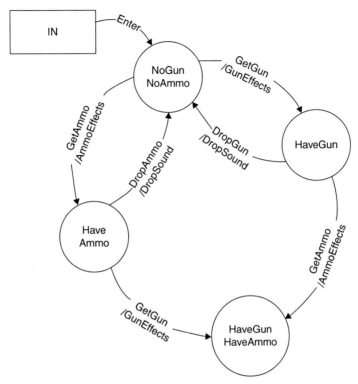

FIGURE 9.6 Flows added to get both gun and ammo.

You perhaps have noticed that when new states are added it's good to leave some room on the diagram for flows or states that you might decide to add when you get further into the design process. Use up some of that empty space now by doing the same thing for HaveGunHaveAmmo that you did with the HaveAmmo and HaveGun states: create return flows to represent what happens when the gun or the ammo is dropped. One question that arises is whether the ammo stays in your inventory or is lost when the gun is dropped. This test is based on the ammo automatically loading when you have the matching weapon, so the DropGun event will take you all the way from HaveGunHaveAmmo to NoGunNoAmmo. Be careful not to get caught up in the symmetry that sometimes arises from the diagram. Flows coming out of states don't always return to the previous state. The TFD with these additional flows is shown in Figure 9.7.

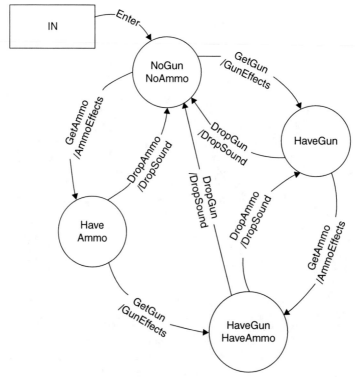

FIGURE 9.7 Return flows added from HaveGunHaveAmmo.

At this point, evaluate whether there's anything else that could be added that remains consistent with the purpose of this test. That is, are there any ways to manipulate the ammo or the gun that would require new flows and/or states on the TFD? Start from the furthest downstream state and work your way up. If you have the gun and ammo, is there any other way to end up with the gun and no ammo besides dropping the ammo? Well, shooting the gun uses ammo, so you could keep shooting until all of the ammo is used up and then end up back at HaveGun. Because both of the states involved in this transition are already on the diagram, you need to add a new flow only from HaveGunHaveAmmo to HaveGun. Likewise, besides picking up an empty gun, you might get lucky and get one with some ammo in it. This creates a new flow from NoGunNoAmmo to HaveGunHaveAmmo. Figure 9.8 shows the diagram with these new interesting flows added.

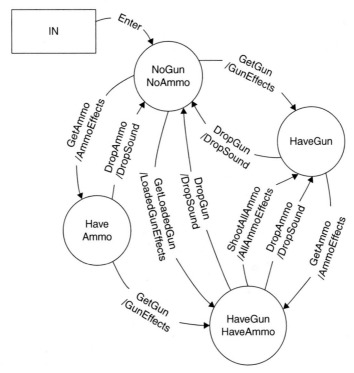

FIGURE 9.8 Loaded gun and shooting flows added.

Note that some of the existing flows were moved around slightly to make room for the new flows and their text. ShootAllAmmo will cause sounds, graphic effects, and damage to another player or the environment. Doing GetLoadedGun will cause effects similar to the combined effects of separately picking up an unloaded gun and its ammo. The actions for these new events were named AllAmmoEffects and LoadedGunEffects to reflect the fact that these multiple effects are supposed to happen and need to be checked by the tester. The ShootAllAmmo event illustrates that your test events do not have to be atomic. You do not need a separate event and flow for firing each individual round of ammo, unless that is exactly what your test is focusing on.

Do the same for HaveGun and HaveAmmo that you just did for HaveGunHaveAmmo. Question whether there are other things that could happen in those states to cause a transition or a new kind of action. You should recognize that you can attempt to fire the weapon at any time, whether or not you have ammo, so a flow should come out from HaveGun to represent the game behavior when you try to shoot with no ammo. Where does this flow go to? It ends up right back at HaveGun. This is drawn as a loop as shown in Figure 9.9.

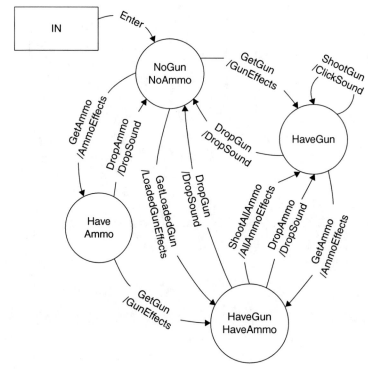

FIGURE 9.9 Flow added to shoot gun with no ammo.

At this point, only two things remain to do according to the procedures given earlier in this chapter: add the OUT box and number the flows. Keep in mind that the numbering is totally arbitrary. The only requirement is that each flow has a unique number.

Another thing that has been done is to name the IN and OUT boxes to identify this specific TFD which might be part of a collection of multiple TFDs created for various features of a game. This also makes it possible to uniquely specify the test setup and tear-down procedures in the Data Dictionary definition for these boxes. This is described in further detail later in this chapter.

Once you complete your diagram, be sure to save your file and give it an appropriate descriptive name. Figure 9.10 shows the completed Ammo TFD.

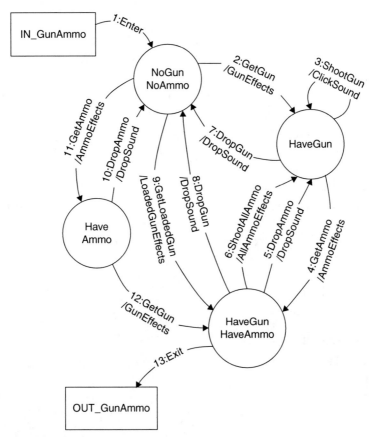

FIGURE 9.10 The completed Ammo TFD.

DATA DICTIONARY

The Data Dictionary provides detailed descriptions for each of the uniquely named primitive elements in your TFD collection. This also implies that any primitive name you reuse within a TFD and across multiple TFDs will carry the same meaning during testing. Think of the primitive names on the TFD as a hyperlink to pages that contain their definitions.

When you mentally "click" on one of those names, you get the same definition, regardless of which instance of the name you click on.

Data Dictionary Application

If you are using SmartDraw to create and maintain your TFDs, you can do this literally by highlighting the text for an event, action, or state and selecting "Insert Hyperlink" from the "Tools" pulldown menu. Then manually browse for a text or html file that contains the description of the primitive. If you use html files for the description, then you can also export your diagram to make your test accessible as a Web page. Do this by selecting "Publish to the Web" from the "File" menu.

It is up to you to decide how formal your definitions should be. In small teams intimate with the product, the TFD by itself might be sufficient if you can trust the person running the test (Rule #2…) to remember and consistently apply all of the details of each primitive. For large teams, especially when new people are moving in and out of the test team during the course of the project, the Data Dictionary will provide more consistent and thorough checking, as well as better adherence to the intent of the test. You will perhaps also want to keep TFD use informal in early development stages until the development team better understands how they really want the game to behave. Once the game stabilizes, capture that information in the Data Dictionary.

Data Dictionary Reuse

The Data Dictionary can also be an important tool for reusing your TFDs for different games or game elements. For example, the Ammo TFD in Figure 9.10 refers abstractly to "Gun" and "Ammo." Most games involving weapons provide multiple types of weapons and ammo that is specific for each. You could cover this by making copies of the TFD for each of the different weapon types, changing the event, action, and state names to match. An alternative is to keep a generic TFD and then apply different Data Dictionaries to interpret the TFD specifically for each weapon and ammo type.

A good strategy for *Unreal Tournament* or any other first-person shooter game would be to use a single TFD but have different data dictionaries for the various weapon/ammo pairs such as Flak Cannon/Flak Shells, Rocket Launcher/Rocket Pack, Shock Rifle/Shock Core, and so on. Each Data Dictionary could elaborate on the different audio, visual, and damage effects associated with each pair.

TUTORIAL

Data Dictionary Example

Build the Data Dictionary by defining each of the elements in the diagram. The "do" items (events) are written normally. The "check" items (actions and states) should be written in list form with a leading dash or bullet to visually separate them from the "do" items. You can also use an empty box character ☐ that can be checked off as the test is run. This is useful for providing a physical record of what the tester observed.

Some of the Ammo TFD data dictionary items for Figure 9.10 are defined below for the Bio-Rifle weapon, arranged in alphabetical order for easy searching. Individual definition files are also provided on the book's DVD.

AmmoEffects

    ☐ *Check that the Bio-Rifle ammo sound is made*

    ☐ *Check that the game temporarily displays "You picked up some Bio-Rifle ammo" in white text above the gun icons at the bottom of the screen*

    ☐ *Check that the temporary text on the display fades out slowly*

DropGun

Hit the "\" key to drop your selected weapon.

DropSound

Check that the item drop sound is made.

Enter

Select a match and click the FIRE button to start the match.

Exit

Hit the ESC key and exit the match.

GetAmmo

Find a Bio-Rifle ammo pack on the floor in the arena and walk over it.

GetGun

Find an unloaded Bio-Rifle hovering above the floor of the arena and walk into it.

GetLoadedGun

Find a Bio-Rifle loaded with ammo hovering above the floor of the arena and walk into it.

GunEffects

☐ *Check that the Bio-Rifle sound is made*

☐ *Check that the game temporarily displays "You got the Bio-Rifle" in white text above the gun icons at the bottom of the screen*

☐ *Check that the game simultaneously displays "Bio-Rifle" temporarily in blue text above the "You got the Bio-Rifle" message*

☐ *Check that all temporary text on the display fades out slowly*

HaveAmmo

☐ *Check that the Bio-Rifle icon is empty in the graphical weapon inventory at the bottom of the screen*

☐ *Check that the Bio-Rifle barrel is not rendered in front of your character*

☐ *Check that you cannot select the Bio-Rifle weapon using the mouse wheel*

☐ *Check that the aiming reticle in the center of the screen has not changed*

HaveGun

☐ *Check that the Bio-Rifle icon is present in the graphical weapon inventory at the bottom of the screen*

☐ *Check that the Bio-Rifle barrel is rendered in front of your character*

☐ *Check that you can select the Bio-Rifle weapon using the mouse wheel*

☐ *Check that the Bio-Rifle aiming reticle appears as a small blue broken triangle in the center of the screen*

☐ *Check that the ammunition count in the right hand corner of the screen is 0*

HaveGunHaveAmmo

☐ *Check that the Bio-Rifle icon is present in the graphical weapon inventory at the bottom of the screen*

☐ *Check that the Bio-Rifle barrel is rendered in front of your character*

☐ *Check that you can select the Bio-Rifle weapon using the mouse wheel*

☐ *Check that the Bio-Rifle aiming reticle appears as a small blue broken triangle in the center of the screen*

☐ *Check that the ammunition count in the right hand corner of the screen is 40*

IN_GunAmmo

Launch Unreal Tournament on the test PC

LoadedGunEffects

☐ *Check that the Bio-Rifle sound is made*

☐ *Check that the game temporarily displays "You got the Bio-Rifle" in white text above the gun icons at the bottom of the screen*

☐ *Check that the game simultaneously displays "Bio-Rifle" temporarily in blue text above the "You got the Bio-Rifle" message*

☐ *Check that all temporary text on the display fades out slowly*

NoGunNoAmmo

☐ *Check that the Bio-Rifle icon is empty in the graphical weapon inventory at the bottom of the screen*

☐ *Check that the Bio-Rifle barrel is not rendered in front of your character*

☐ *Check that you cannot select the Bio-Rifle weapon using the mouse wheel*

OUT_GunAmmo

At the main menu, click on "EXIT" to exit the game.

You can even include screen shots, art from design documents, or art from storyboards to provide a visual reference for the tester. This works well with the hyperlink and Web publishing approach. The reference graphics can be updated to reflect changes and maturing of the screen layout and art as the game gets closer to completion. For testing the Bio-Rifle, the AmmoEffects definition could include a screen shot like the one in Figure 9.11 below, which shows how the "picked up" confirmation text is rendered on the screen.

FIGURE 9.11 *Unreal Tournament 2004 Bio-Rifle AmmoEfffects.*

Likewise, Figure 9.12 illustrates a useful reference for showing the Bio-Rifle GunEffects action by capturing the on-screen indications that the Bio-Rifle has been picked up and is now the player's active weapon.

FIGURE 9.12 *Unreal Tournament 2004* Bio-Rifle GunEffects.

TFD PATHS

A test path is a series of Flows, specified by the flow numbers in the sequence in which they are to be traversed. Paths begin at the IN state and end at the OUT state. A set of paths provides behavior scenarios appropriate for prototyping, simulation, or testing.

A path defines an individual test case which can be "executed" to explore the game's behavior. Path execution follows the Events, Actions, and States on the TFD. A textual script can be constructed by cutting and pasting primitives in the order they occur along the path. Testers then follow the script to execute each test, referring to the Data Dictionary for details of each primitive. Automated scripts are created in the same manner, except lines of code are being pasted together rather than textual instructions for a human tester.

Many paths are possible for a single TFD. Tests can be executed according to single strategy for the duration of the project or path sets can vary according to the maturity of the game code as it progresses through different milestones. The TFD remains constant as long as the correct game requirements and behaviors do not change. Some useful strategies for selecting test paths are described below.

Minimum Path Generation

This strategy is designed to produce the smallest number of paths that will result in covering all of the flows in the diagram. In this context, "covering" means that a flow is used at least once somewhere in the test.

The benefits of using a Minimum path set are that you have a low test count and the knowledge that you exercised all parts of the diagram at least once. The drawbacks are that you tend to get long paths, which might keep you from testing some parts of the diagram until later in the project, when something goes wrong early in the test path.

Here's how to come up with a minimum path for the TFD in Figure 9.10. Start at the IN and take flow 1 to NoGunNoAmmo. Then go to HaveGun via flow 2. Since flow 3 loops back to HaveGun, take that next and then exit HaveGun via flow 4. The minimum path so far is 1, 2, 3, 4.

Now from HaveGunHaveAmmo, go back to HaveGun via flow 5. Since flow 6 also goes from HaveGunHaveAmmo to HaveGun, take flow 4 again and this time use flow 6 to return to HaveGun. At this stage, the Minimum path is 1, 2, 3, 4, 5, 4, 6, but there are still more flows to cover.

Take flow 7 out from HaveGun to go back to NoGunNoAmmo. From here you can take flow 9 to HaveGunHaveAmmo and return back using flow 8. Now the path is 1, 2, 3, 4, 5, 4, 6, 7, 9, 8. All that remains now is to use the flows on the left side of the TFD.

You are at NoGunNoAmmo again so take flow 11 to HaveAmmo and then return to NoGunNoAmmo via flow 10. Only flow 12 and 13 are left now, so take 11 back to HaveAmmo where you can take 12 to HaveGun-HaveAmmo and finally exit via flow 13 to the OUT box. The completed minimum path is 1, 2, 3, 4, 5, 4, 6, 7, 9, 8, 11, 10, 11, 12, 13. All 13 flows on the TFD are covered in 15 test steps.

There is usually more than one "correct" minimum path for any given TFD. For example, 1, 11, 10, 11, 12, 8, 9, 5, 7, 2, 3, 4, 6, 4, 13 is also a minimum path for the TFD in Figure 9.10. Diagrams that have more than one flow going to the OUT box will require more than one path. Even if you don't come up with the shortest path(s) mathematically possible, the purpose is to cover all of the flows in the least number of paths, which is one for the Ammo TFD.

Baseline Path Method

Baseline path generation begins by establishing as direct a path as possible from the IN Terminator to the OUT Terminator, which travels through as many states without repeating or looping back. This is designated as the Baseline path. Additional paths are derived from the Baseline by varying where possible, returning to the baseline path and following it to reach the OUT Terminator. The process continues until all Flows in the diagram are used at least once.

Baseline paths are more comprehensive than Minimum paths, but still more economical than trying to cover every possible path through the diagram. They also introduce small changes from one path to another, so a game defect can be traced back to the operations that were different among the paths that passed and the one(s) that failed. One drawback of Baseline paths is the extra effort to generate and execute the paths versus using the Minimum path approach.

Still using the TFD in Figure 9.10, create a baseline path starting at the IN box and then traveling across the most number of states you can in order to get to the OUT box. Once you get to the NoGunNoAmmo state from flow 1, the farthest distance to the OUT box is either through HaveGun and HaveGunHaveAmmo or through HaveAmmo and HaveGunHaveAmmo. Take the HaveGun route by taking flow 2, followed by flow 4 and exiting through flow 13. This results in the baseline path of 1, 2, 4, 13.

The next thing to do is to branch wherever possible from the first flow on the baseline. These branches are called "derived" paths from flow 1. Flow 2 is already used in the baseline, so take flow 9 to HaveGunHaveAmmo. From there flow 8 puts you back on the baseline path. Follow the rest of the baseline along flows 2, 4, and 13. The first derived path from flow 1 is 1, 9, 8, 2, 4, 13.

Continue to check for other possible branches after flow 1. Flow 11 comes out from NoGunNoAmmo and has not been used yet so follow it to HaveAmmo. Then use flow 10 to return to the baseline. Finish this path by following the remainder of the baseline to the OUT box. This second path derived from flow 1 is 1, 11, 10, 2, 4, 13.

At this point there are no more new flows to cover from NoGun NoAmmo, so move along the next flow on the baseline which is flow 2. Stop here and look for unused flows to follow. You need to create a path using flow 3. Because it comes right back to the HaveGun state, continue along the remainder of the baseline to get to the path 1, 2, 3, 4, 13. The only other flow coming out of HaveGun is flow 7, which puts you right back on the baseline at flow 2. The final path derived from flow 2 is 1, 2, 7, 2, 4, 13.

Now on to flow 4! Flow 4 takes you to HaveGunHaveAmmo, which has three flows coming out from it that aren't on the baseline: 5, 6, and 8. We already used flow 8 in an earlier path, so there is no obligation to use it here. Flows 5 and 6 get incorporated into our baseline the same way because they both go back to the HaveGun state. The derived path using flow 5 is 1, 2, 4, 5, 4, 13 and the derived path from flow 6 is 1, 2, 4, 6, 4, 13.

It might seem as though you are done now because the next flow along the baseline goes to the OUT box, and you have derived paths from each other flow along the baseline. Upon further inspection, however, there is still a flow on the diagram that is not included in any of your paths: flow 12 coming from the HaveAmmo state. It's not connected to a state that's along the baseline so it's easy to lose track of it, but don't fall into that trap. Pick up this flow by taking flows 1 and 11 to HaveAmmo and then use flow 12. You're now at HaveGunHaveAmmo and you must get back to the baseline to complete this path. Take flow 8, which is the shortest route and puts you back at NoGunNoAmmo. Finish the path by following the rest of the baseline. This final path is 1, 11, 12, 8, 2, 4, 13.

As you can see, the baseline technique produces many more paths and results in much more testing time than a minimum path. The final baseline and derived paths for our Ammo TFD are as follows:

Baseline:

1, 2, 4, 13

Derived from flow 1:

1, 9, 8, 2, 4, 13

1, 11, 10, 2, 4, 13

Derived from flow 2:

1, 2, 3, 4, 13

1, 2, 7, 2, 4, 13

Derived from flow 4:

1, 2, 4, 5, 4, 13

1, 2, 4, 6, 4, 13

Derived from flow 11:

1, 11, 12, 8, 2, 4, 13

Expert Constructed Paths

Expert Constructed paths are simply paths that a test or feature "expert" traces based on the expert's knowledge of how the feature is likely to fail or where she needs to establish confidence in a particular set of behaviors. They can be used by themselves or in combination with the Minimum or Baseline strategies. Expert Constructed paths do not have to cover all of the flows in the diagram, nor do they have to be any minimum or maximum length. The only constraint is that, like all other paths, they start at the IN and end at the OUT.

Expert paths can be effective at finding problems when there is organizational memory of what has failed in the past or what new game functions are the most sensitive. These paths could possibly have not shown up at all in a path list generated by the Minimum or Baseline criteria. The drawbacks of relying on this approach are the risks associated with not covering every flow and the possibility of tester bias producing paths that do not perform "unanticipated" sequences of Events.

Some Expert Constructed path strategies include:

- Repeat a certain flow or sequence of flows in combination with other path variations

- Create paths that emphasize unusual or infrequent events

- Create paths that emphasize critical or complex states

- Create extremely long paths, repeating flows if necessary

- Model paths after the most common ways the feature will be used

For example, the "emphasize critical or complex states" strategy can be used for the Ammo TFD in Figure 9.10. In this case, the HaveGun state will be emphasized. This means that each path will pass through HaveGun at least once. It is also a goal to cover all of the flows with this path set. To keep the paths short, head for the Exit flow once the HaveGun state has been used.

One path that works is to go to HaveGun, try to shoot, and then leave. This path would be 1, 2, 3, 4, 13. Another would incorporate the DropGun event in flow 7. The shortest way out from there is via flow 9 followed by 13, resulting in the path 1, 2, 7, 9, 13. You also need to include the two flows going into HaveGun from HaveGunHaveAmmo. This produces the paths 1, 2, 4, 5, 4, 13 and 1, 2, 4, 6, 4, 13. Finish covering all of the flows leaving HaveGunHaveAmmo by using flow 8 in the path 1, 2, 4, 8, 9, 13.

All that remains are some slightly longer paths that cover the left side of the TFD. Flows 1, 11, 12 get you to HaveGunHaveAmmo. The quickest way from there to HaveGun is either with flow 5 or 6. Choose flow 5, which results in the path 1, 11, 12, 5, 4, 13. You can eliminate or keep the earlier path that was made for the sole purpose of covering flow 5 (1, 2, 4, 5, 4, 13). It is no longer essential since is has now also been covered by the path you needed for flow 12.

The last flow to cover is flow 10. Go to HaveAmmo, take flow 10, go back through HaveGun and go out via flow 2. This gives you your final path of 1, 11, 10, 2, 4, 13. The list all of the paths that were just constructed for this set are as follows:

Expert path set:

1, 2, 3, 4, 13

1, 2, 7, 9, 13

1, 2, 4, 6, 4, 13

1, 2, 4, 8, 9, 13

1, 11, 12, 5, 4, 13

1, 11, 10, 2, 4, 13

Originally constructed but later eliminated:

1, 2, 4, 5, 4, 13

Combining Path Strategies

Testing uses time and resources that get more critical as the game project wears on. Here is one way to utilize multiple strategies that might make the best use of these resources for different stages of the project:

1. Use Expert Constructed Paths early, even when the game is not yet code complete and everything might not be working. Limit yourself to paths that only include the parts that the developers are most interested in or paths that target the only parts of the game that are available for testing.

2. Use Baseline Paths to establish some confidence in the feature(s) being tested. This can begin once the subject of the TFD is feature complete. You might even want to begin by seeing if the game can pass the baseline path before trying to use the other paths in the set. Anything that fails during this testing can be narrowed down to a few test steps that vary between the failed path(s) and the successful ones.

3. Once the Baseline Paths all pass, use the Minimum Paths on an ongoing basis to keep an eye on your feature to see that it hasn't broken.

4. As any kind of delivery point nears, such as going to an investor demo, a trade show, or getting ready to go gold, revert back to Baseline and/or Expert Paths.

This puts a greater burden on the construction of the test paths, but over the course of a long project it could be the most efficient use of the testers' and developers' time.

PRODUCING TEST CASES FROM PATHS

Here's how to produce a test case from a single TFD path. The subject of this example will again be the Ammo TFD in Figure 9.10. The test case will test getting ammo, then getting the gun, and then exiting. This is path 1, 11, 12, 13. To describe this test case, use the Data Dictionary definitions provided earlier in this chapter for the *Unreal Tournament* Bio-Rifle weapon.

TUTORIAL

Start constructing the test case with the Data Dictionary text for the IN box followed by the text for flow 1 which is the Enter flow:

Launch Unreal Tournament on the test PC.

Select a match and click the FIRE button to start the match.

Now add the text from the Data Dictionary for the NoGunNoAmmo state:

- ☐ *Check that the Bio-Rifle icon is empty in the graphical weapon inventory at the bottom of the screen*

- ☐ *Check that the Bio-Rifle barrel is not rendered in front of your character*

- ☐ *Check that you cannot select the Bio-Rifle weapon using the mouse wheel*

Now take flow 11 to get the Bio-Rifle ammo. Use the Data Dictionary entries for both the GetAmmo event and the AmmoEffects action:

Find a Bio-Rifle ammo pack on the floor in the arena and walk over it.

- ☐ *Check that the Bio-Rifle ammo sound is made*

Flow 11 goes to the HaveAmmo state so paste the HaveAmmo Data Dictionary text into the test case right after the text for flow 11:

- ☐ *Check that the Bio-Rifle icon is empty in the graphical weapon inventory at the bottom of the screen*

- ☐ *Check that the Bio-Rifle barrel is not rendered in front of your character*

- ☐ *Check that you cannot select the Bio-Rifle weapon using the mouse wheel*

- ☐ *Check that the aiming reticle in the center of the screen has not changed*

Next, add the text for the GetGun event and GunEffects action along flow 12:

Find an unloaded Bio-Rifle hovering above the floor of the arena and walk into it.

- ☐ *Check that the Bio-Rifle sound is made*

- ☐ *Check that the game temporarily displays "You got the Bio-Rifle" in white text above the gun icons at the bottom of the screen*

- ☐ *Check that the game simultaneously displays "Bio-Rifle" temporarily in blue text above the "You got the Bio-Rifle" message*

- ☐ *Check that all temporary text on the display fades out slowly*

Then paste the definition of the HaveGunHaveAmmo state:

- ☐ *Check that the Bio-Rifle icon is present in the graphical weapon inventory at the bottom of the screen*

- ☐ *Check that the Bio-Rifle barrel is rendered in front of your character*

- ☐ *Check that you can select the Bio-Rifle weapon using the mouse wheel*

- ☐ *Check that the Bio-Rifle aiming reticle appears as a small blue broken triangle in the center of the screen*

- ☐ *Check that the ammunition count in the right hand corner of the screen is 40*

Flow 13 is the last flow on the path. It is the Exit flow which goes to OUT_GunAmmo. Complete the test case by adding the text for these two elements:

Hit the ESC key and exit the match.

At the main menu, click on "EXIT" to exit the game.

That's it! Here's how all of the steps look when they're put together:

Launch Unreal Tournament on the test PC.

Select a match and click the FIRE button to start the match.

- ☐ *Check that the Bio-Rifle icon is empty in the graphical weapon inventory at the bottom of the screen*

- ☐ *Check that the Bio-Rifle barrel is not rendered in front of your character*

- ☐ *Check that you cannot select the Bio-Rifle weapon using the mouse wheel*

Find a Bio-Rifle ammo pack on the floor in the arena and walk over it.

- ☐ *Check that the Bio-Rifle ammo sound is made*

- ☐ *Check that the Bio-Rifle icon is empty in the graphical weapon inventory at the bottom of the screen*

- ☐ *Check that the Bio-Rifle barrel is not rendered in front of your character*

□ *Check that you cannot select the Bio-Rifle weapon using the mouse wheel*

□ *Check that the aiming reticle in the center of the screen has not changed*

Find an unloaded Bio-Rifle hovering above the floor of the arena and walk into it.

□ *Check that the Bio-Rifle sound is made*

□ *Check that the game temporarily displays "You got the Bio-Rifle" in white text above the gun icons at the bottom of the screen*

□ *Check that the game simultaneously displays "Bio-Rifle" temporarily in blue text above the "You got the Bio-Rifle" message*

□ *Check that all temporary text on the display fades out slowly*

□ *Check that the Bio-Rifle icon is present in the graphical weapon inventory at the bottom of the screen*

□ *Check that the Bio-Rifle barrel is rendered in front of your character*

□ *Check that you can select the Bio-Rifle weapon using the mouse wheel*

□ *Check that the Bio-Rifle aiming reticle appears as a small blue broken triangle in the center of the screen*

□ *Check that the ammunition count in the right hand corner of the screen is 40*

Hit the ESC key and exit the match.

At the main menu, click on "EXIT" to exit the game.

You can see how indenting the action and state definitions makes it easy to distinguish tester operations from things you want the tester to check for. When something goes wrong during this test you will be able to document the steps that led up to the problem and determine what specifically was different from what you expected.

There are two techniques you can use to reuse this test case for another type of weapon. One is to copy the Bio-Rifle version and substitute the name of another weapon and its ammo type for "Bio-Rifle" and "Bio-Rifle ammo." This only works if all of the other details in the events, flows, and states are the same except for the gun and ammo names. In this case, Bio-Rifle specific details were put into some of the definitions in order to give a precise description of what the tester should check.

GunEffects contains the following check, which references text color that varies by weapon. It is blue for the Bio-Rifle but different for other weapons, such as red for the Rocket Launcher and white for the Minigun.

☐ *Check that the game simultaneously displays "Bio-Rifle" temporarily in blue text above the "You got the Bio-Rifle" message*

Likewise, the HaveGunHaveAmmo state describes a specific color and shape for the Bio-Rifle aiming reticle as well as an ammunition count. Both vary by weapon type.

☐ *Check that the Bio-Rifle aiming reticle appears as a small blue broken triangle in the center of the screen*

☐ *Check that the ammunition count in the right hand corner of the screen is 40*

This leaves you with the option to copy the Bio-Rifle Data Dictionary files into a separate directory for the new weapon. These files should then be edited to reflect the details for the new weapon type you want to test. Use those files to construct your test cases for the new weapon in the same way you did for the Bio-Rifle.

Remember that using text in the Data Dictionary is not your only option. You can also use screen shots or automated code. When executable code for each TFD element along a test path is pasted together you should end up with an executable test case. Use the IN definition to provide introductory code elements, such as including header files, declaring data types, and providing main routine opening braces. Use the OUT definition to perform cleanup actions such as freeing up memory, erasing temporary files, and providing closing braces.

Storing Data Dictionary information in separate files is not your only option. You could keep them in a database and use a query to assemble the "records" for each TFD element into a report. The report could then be used for manual execution of the game test.

TFD TEMPLATES

Appendix D provides eight TFD templates you can apply to various situations for a wide variety of games. You can recreate the diagrams in your own favorite drawing tool or use the files provided on the book's DVD in SmartDraw (.sdf) and Windows Metafile (.wmf) format. In the drawing files, suggested baseline paths are indicated by blue flows.

Flows in the template files are not numbered. There will be times when you will need to edit or otherwise customize the TFD to match the specific behaviors for your game. If you need an action and none is there, put in what you need. If there's an action on the TFD but you don't have one in your game, take the action out. Change the names of events, actions, or states to suit your game. Also feel free to add any states you want to test that aren't already provided. Once you've done all that, *then* add the flow numbers and define your paths.

TO TFD OR NOT TO TFD?

Table 9.1 provides some guidelines for making a choice between using a Combinatorial Table or TFD for your test. If a feature or scenario has attributes that fall into both categories, consider doing separate designs of each type. Also, for anything critical to the success of your game, create tests using both methods when possible.

TABLE 9.1 Test Design Methodology Selection

Attribute/Dependency	Combinatorial	Test Flow Diagram
Game Settings	X	
Game Options	X	
Hardware Configurations	X	
Game State Transitions		X
Repeatable Functions		X
Concurrent States	X	
Operational Flow		X
Parallel Choices	X	X
Story Paths or Routes		X

Summary

Test Flow Diagrams are used to create models of how the game should work from the player's perspective. By exploring this model the tester can create unanticipated connections and discover unexpected game states. TFDs also incorporate invalid and repetitive inputs to test the game's behavior. TFD tests will demonstrate if expected behavior occurs and unexpected behavior doesn't. Complex features can be represented by complex TFDs, but a series of smaller TFDs is preferred. Good TFDs are the result of insight, experience, and creativity.

Exercises

1. Describe how you would apply the Ammo TFD in Figure 9.10 to an archer in an online role playing game. Include any modifications you would make to the TFD structure as well as to individual states, events, or actions.

2. Update the diagram in Figure 9.10 to account for what happens when the player picks up ammo that doesn't match the type of gun he has.

3. Create a set of Baseline and Minimum paths for the updated TFD you created in Exercise 2. Create Data Dictionary entries and write out the test case for your Minimum path. Reuse the Data Dictionary entries already provided in this chapter and create any new Data Dictionary entries you need.

4. Construct a TFD for a mobile game that is suspended when the user receives a call or opens the phone's s cover. Try to keep the number of states low. The game should be resumed once the call ends or the cover is lifted. HINT: only one criterion must be satisfied to suspend the game, but both criteria to resume the game must be met before it actually resumes.

CHAPTER 10

CLEANROOM TESTING

In This Chapter

- Usage probabilities
- Cleanroom test generation
- Inverted usage

C leanroom testing is a technique extracted from a software development practice known as Cleanroom Software Engineering. The original purpose of Cleanroom testing was to exercise software in order to make mean time to failure (MTTF) measurements over the course of the project. In this chapter, Cleanroom testing is applied to the problem of why customers find problems in games that have been through thousands of hours of testing before being released. If one measure of a game's success is that the users (players) will not find any bugs, then the game team's test strategy should include a way to detect and remove the defects that are most likely to be found by users.

So how do users find defects that testers missed? Users find defects in software by using it the way users use it. That's a little bit of a tongue twister, but it points to a testing approach that exercises the game according to the way the players are going to use it. That's what Cleanroom test development does; it produces tests that play the game the way players will play it.

USAGE PROBABILITIES

Usage probabilities, also referred to as usage frequencies, tell testers how often game functions should be used in order to realistically mimic the way customers will use the game. They can be based on actual data you might have from studies of game players or based on your own expectations about how the game will be played. Also take into account the possible evolution of a user's play during the life of the game. A player's patterns would be different just after running the tutorial than they would be by the time the player reaches the boss on the final level. Initially, the player would utilize fundamental operations and have few, if any, special items unlocked. Clicking dashboard icons would occur more frequently than key commands and user-defined macros. Matches or races might take longer at the end of the game due to the higher difficulty and closer matching of the player's skill to the in-game opponent(s). Usage information can be defined and utilized in three different ways:

- Mode-based usage

- Player-type usage

- Real-life usage

Mode-Based Usage

Game usage can change based on which mode the player is using, such as single player, campaign, multiplayer, or on-line.

Single-player mode could involve one or only a few confrontations or missions. The action usually starts right away so the player is less likely to perform "build-up" operations such as building advanced units and spending money or points on expensive skill-boosting items. Some features might not be available at all to the single player, such as certain characters, weapons, or vehicles. The single player's character might also have limited race, clan, and mission options.

Campaigns tend to start the player with basic equipment and opponents and then introduce more and more complex elements as the campaign progresses. For sports games, Franchise or Season modes provide unique options and experiences that aren't available when playing a single game, such as draft picks, training camp, trading players, and negotiating salaries. RPG games will provide more powerful spells, armor, weapons, and opponents as your characters level up. Racing games can provide more powerful vehicles, add-ons, and powerups, as well as more challenging tracks.

Multiplayer gaming can take place on the same machine, usually for 2–4 players, across two interconnected consoles, or over the Internet for more massive multiplayer experiences. Headset accessories are used for team confrontations, but aren't something you're likely to use by yourself unless the game has voice commands. Text chatting also is used in multiplayer PC games, giving the text keyboard a workout. Game controls can also be assigned to *smack talk* phrases and gestures, which you will also use to taunt your inferior opponents. The time spent on a multiplayer session can be much greater than that which a single player will spend, sometimes extending into the wee hours of the morning. This also brings up the fact that multiplayer games might involve players from different time zones and geographical regions, bringing together a variety of game clocks and language settings.

Player Type Usage

Another factor that influences game usage is the classification of four multi-user player categories described by Richard A. Bartle in "Hearts, Clubs, Diamonds, Spades: Players Who Suit MUDs" [BARTLE 96]. He describes players by their tendencies to emphasize either Achievement, Exploration, Socializing, or Killing when they participate in multiplayer games.

The Achiever wants to complete game goals, missions, and quests. He will gain satisfaction in advancing his character's level, point, and money totals in the most efficient way possible. Achievers often replay the game at a higher level of difficulty or under difficult circumstances such as using a last-place team or going into combat armed only with a knife. They will also be interested in reaching bonus goals and completing bonus missions.

Explorers are interested in finding out what the game has to offer. They will travel around to find obscure places and the edges of the map; unmapped territory will draw their attention. The Explorer will look around and appreciate the art and special beauty in the game such as a particularly nice moonrise or light shining through a stained glass cathedral window. She is also likely to attempt interesting features, animations, combos, and physics effects. Expect the Explorer to try to open every door and check the inventory at all of the stores. The Explorer wants to figure out how things work. Think of the phrase "I wonder what would happen if…?"

The goal of the Socializer is to use the game as a means to role play and get to know other players. Chat and messaging facilities are important to him, as well as joining social groups within the game such as clans, guilds, and so on. He will perhaps host meetings or tournaments, or bring many players together in one place for announcements, trading, or even an occasional wedding. Socializers will use special game features once they find out about them from other players.

Killers enjoy getting the best of other players. They engage in player versus player and real versus realm battles. Killers know where the taunt keys are and how to customize and activate an end zone celebration. Headsets, chats, and private messages are also tools that the Killer uses to bait and humiliate his opponents.

Finally, here are some other gamer "subtypes" to consider when you go to test your game the same way players play the game:

- *Casual gamer:* Sticks mostly to functions described in the tutorial, user manual, and on-screen user interface.

- *Hard-core gamer:* Uses function keys, macros, turbo buttons, and special input devices such as joysticks and steering wheels. Checks the Internet for tricks and tips. Might also have game hardware juiced up to run the highest graphics resolution and frame rate. MMORPGs and RTSs such as Blizzard's *World of Warcraft* and *Starcraft 2* are frequent hunting grounds for this gamer type, some of whom operate multiple characters and computers at the same time.

- *Button Masher:* Values speed and repetition over caution and defense. Wears out the A button on the controller to run faster, jump higher, or strike first. Will run out of ammo. Stylus-operated games on Nintendo DS devices and touch-enabled smartphones have bred the Button Masher's cousin: the *Screen Scratcher*. *Scribblenauts*™ is a great game for this gamer type.

- *Customizer:* Uses all of the game's customization features and plays the game with custom elements. Will also incorporate unlocked items, decals, jerseys, teams, and so on. You can find these capabilities in many sports titles, such as Electronics Arts' *Madden* and *FIFA* series.

- *Exploiter:* Always looking for a shortcut. Will use cheat codes, look for cracks in zone walls, and pick off opponents from a secret or unreachable spot. Creates bots to craft items, earn points, and level up. Uses infinite card combos against AI and human collectable card game (CCG) opponents.

Real-Life Usage

Some games have built-in mechanisms for capturing your in-game actions. This data might be available to you within the game, published on your game profile for other players to see, or even sent as raw data back to the game publisher for analysis or debugging. Capturing data from real-world gaming "friends" or in-game nonplayer characters (NPCs), such as coaches, goblins, war bunnies, etc., can be used to let you practice against their style of play so you can crush them the next time you battle for real.

The EA Madden team has blogged about how they use data collected from players to validate that their GameFlow feature, which recommends the next play to call in order to maintain continuity and suggests good plays based on the current situation, has a positive impact on play calling. They also collected data to understand why players would accidentally go into the "Hot Route" state during play calling [CUMMINGS 10].

Some of the stats collected by the Madden team include:

- 95% of games played had GameFlow as the default style of play calling

- 80% of offensive plays were chosen via GameFlow

- 86% of defensive plays were chosen via GameFlow

- More than 50% of players who activated the Hot Route feature never called a Hot Route

Presumably based on its measured success in *Madden NFL 10*, the GameFlow feature made its way into the mobile edition of *Madden NFL 11*. The player can turn it on or off any time from the control shown in the lower right hand corner of Figure 10.1.

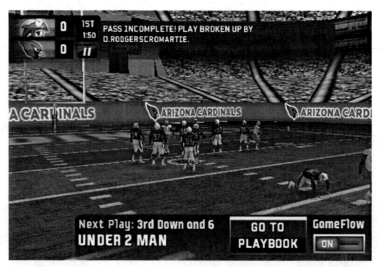

FIGURE 10.1 GameFlow mode activated in *Madden NFL 11* for iPhone/iPod Touch.

The Hot Route feature is also available in the mobile app. Setting up a Hot Route starts by clicking on the "playbook" icon in the bottom right of the screen which appears once the players have come out of the huddle and taken their positions. Prior to the ball being snapped, the user can modify the path any of their players will follow once the ball has been snapped (as shown in Figure 10.2).

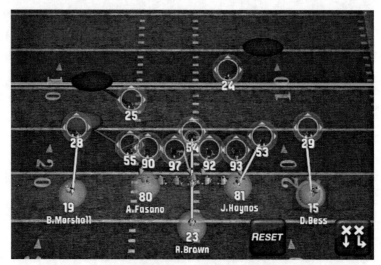

FIGURE 10.2 Hot Route mode activated in *Madden NFL 11* for iPhone/iPod Touch.

Armed with this kind of information—whether aggregated by the game company or from individual gamers' results, testers can exercise games according to different player styles and the expected frequency of use of various game actions, choices, and options. It is important to account for these tendencies because testing based entirely on balanced use of the game features would not reveal defects, such as a memory overflow caused by tapping the A button repeatedly on every play over the course of a maximum length game.

CLEANROOM TEST GENERATION

It's possible to generate Cleanroom tests using any of the methods covered in this book. You can also create your own Cleanroom tests on the fly. A usage probability must be assigned to each step in the test. This can be done in writing or you can keep track in your head. Use the usage probability to select test steps, values, or branches, and put them in sequence to produce tests that reflect your usages. For example, if you expect a simulation game player to develop residential property 50% of the time, commercial property 30% of the time, and industrial property 20% of the time, then your Cleanroom tests will reflect those same frequencies.

Cleanroom Combinatorial Tables

Cleanroom combinatorial tables will not necessarily be "pairwise" combinatorial tables (see Chapter 8, "Combinatorial Testing"). The number of tests to be created is determined by the test designer, and the values for each test will be chosen on the basis of their frequency of use rather than whether or not they satisfy one or more necessary value pairs.

To produce Cleanroom combinatorial tables, assign usage probabilities to the test values of each parameter. The probabilities of the set of values associated with a single parameter must add up to 100%.

To illustrate how this is done, revisit the parameter and value choices for the *HALO Reach* Advanced Controls table that you completed in Chapter 8, Table 8.24. The test values for each parameter are listed below with the default values identified.

- *Look Sensitivity*: 1, 3 (default), 10

- *Look Inversion*: Inverted, Not Inverted (default)

- *Autolook Centering*: Enabled, Disabled (default)
- *Crouch Behavior*: Hold to Crouch (default), Toggle
- *Clench Protection*: Enabled, Disabled (default)

Next, usage percentages need to be determined for each of the table's parameters. If you are considering testing against more than one player profile, you can make a separate usage table for each parameter with a column of usage percentages for each of the profiles you intend to test. Tables 10.1 through 10.5 show multiple profile usages for each of the five *HALO Reach* Advanced Controls parameters that you will incorporate into your Cleanroom combinatorial table.

NOTE

This chapter presents a variety of usage numbers in order to illustrate differences among user types, based on personal experience. If you have data gathered through scientific means, then that is what you should be using. If these numbers don't make sense to you, then please consider them "for educational purposes only" as you continue through the examples in this chapter.

Beginning with Table 10.1, distinct usage percentages for the Look Sensitivity parameter are provided to reflect the expected tendencies for each of the depicted player types.

TABLE 10.1 Look Sensitivity Values with Usage Percentages

Look Sensitivity	Casual	Achiever	Explorer	Multiplayer
1	10	0	10	5
3	85	75	70	75
10	5	25	20	20
Total	100	100	100	100

Table 10.2 provides a different set of usage values for the Inverted and Not Inverted options available for the Look Inversion parameter.

TABLE 10.2 Look Inversion Values with Usage Percentages

Look Inversion	Casual	Achiever	Explorer	Multiplayer
Inverted	10	40	30	50
Not Inverted	90	60	70	50
Total	100	100	100	100

Table 10.3 introduces a situation where the Disabled value for Autolook Centering has a 100% weighting. As a consequence, it will be tested using this same value throughout the entire set of cleanroom tests generated for the Achiever player type.

TABLE 10.3 Autolook Centering Values with Usage Percentages

Autolook Centering	Casual	Achiever	Explorer	Multiplayer
Enabled	30	0	20	10
Disabled	70	100	80	90
Total	100	100	100	100

Table 10.4 provides Crouch Behavior usage values that are mostly biased towards the Hold value, except for the Explorer, who is given an equal probability of selecting either the Hold or Toggle option.

TABLE 10.4 Crouch Behavior Values with Usage Percentages

Crouch Behavior	Casual	Achiever	Explorer	Multiplayer
Hold	80	75	50	90
Toggle	20	25	50	10
Total	100	100	100	100

Table 10.5 contains the final set of probabilities that are needed to proceed with Cleanroom test generation.

TABLE 10.5 Clench Protection Values with Usage Percentages

Clench Protection	Casual	Achiever	Explorer	Multiplayer
Enabled	25	60	50	90
Disabled	75	40	50	10
Total	100	100	100	100

Use Tables 10.1 through 10.5 as you work through the tutorial below to complete your first Cleanroom Combinatorial Table.

TUTORIAL

Cleanroom Combinatorial Example

A Cleanroom combinatorial table can be constructed for any of the player usage profiles you define. For this example, you will create one such table for the "Casual" player. To decide which value to choose for each parameter, you need a random number source. You could think of a number in your head, write a program to generate a list of numbers, or roll electronic dice on your smartphone. Microsoft Excel® can generate random numbers for you with the RAND ( ) function or the RANDBETWEEN ( ) function if you install the Analysis ToolPak add-in. You can also download free mobile apps to do the job for you, such as iGenerateRandomNumbers™ which provides random numbers one-at-a-time or Randoms™ which can give you up to 100 random numbers at a time. There is no wrong way as long as the number range is from 1–100, and selection is not biased toward any portion of the range.

Start building the table with an empty template that has column headings for each of the parameters. Decide how many tests you want and leave room for them in the table. A Cleanroom combinatorial table "shell" for the *HALO* Advanced Controls is shown in Table 10.6. It has room for six tests.

TABLE 10.6 *HALO Reach* Advanced Controls Cleanroom Combinatorial Table Shell

Test	Look Sensitivity	Look Inversion	Autolook Centering	Crouch Behavior	Clench Protection
1					
2					
3					
4					
5					
6					

Because there are five parameters, get five random numbers in the range of 1–100. These will be used one at a time to determine the values for each parameter in the first test. Construct the first test from the five numbers 30, 89, 13, 77, and 25.

Referring back to Table 10.1, the Casual player is expected to set the Look Sensitivity to "1" 10% of the time, to "3" 85% of the time, and to "10" 5% of the time. Assigning successive number ranges to each choice results in a mapping of 1–10 for Look Sensitivity = 1, 11–95 for Look Sensitivity = 3, and 96–100 for Look Sensitivity = 10. The first random number, 30, falls into the 11–95 range, so enter "3" in the first column of the test table.

Likewise, Table 10.2 provides a range of 1–10 for Look Inversion = Inverted and 11–100 for Look Inversion = Not Inverted. The second random number is 89, which is within the 11–100 range. Enter "Not Inverted" in the Look Inversion column for Test 1.

In Table 10.3, the Autolook Centering usage ranges for the Casual player are 1–30 for Enabled and 71–100 for Disabled. The third random number is 13, so enter "Enabled" in Test 1's Autolook Centering column.

Table 10.4 defines an 80% usage for Crouch Behavior = Hold and a 20% usage for Toggle. The fourth random number is 77, which is within the 1–25 range for the Yes setting. Enter "Hold" in the Crouch Behavior column for Test 1.

Last, Table 10.5 defines the Clench Protection Casual player usage as 25% for Enabled and 75% for Disabled. The last random number is 25, which is within the 1–25 range for the Enabled setting. Complete the definition of Test 1 by putting "Enabled" in the Clench Protection column for Test 1.

Table 10.7 shows the first test constructed from the random numbers 30, 89, 13, 77, and 25.

TABLE 10.7 The First Advanced Controls Cleanroom Combinatorial Test

Test	Look Sensitivity	Look Inversion	Autolook Centering	Crouch Behavior	Clench Protection
1	3	Not Inverted	Enabled	Hold	Enabled

A new set of five random numbers is required to produce the second test case. Use 79, 82, 57, 27, and 8.

The first number is 79, which is within the 11–95 range for Look Sensitivity = 3. Put a "3" again in the first column for Test 2. The second usage number is 82. It falls within the 11–100 range for Look Inversion = Not Inverted, so put "Not Inverted" that column for Test 2. Your third random number is 57. This number is in the 31–100 range for Autolook Centering, so enter "Disabled" into that column for Test 2. The fourth usage number is 27. This is within the 1–80 range for Crouch Behavior = Hold. Add "Hold" to the fourth column of values for Test 2. The last random number is 8. This usage value corresponds to the Enabled value range of 1–25 for the Clench Protection parameter. Complete Test 2 by entering "Enabled" in the last column. Table 10.8 shows the first two completed rows for this Cleanroom combinatorial table.

TABLE 10.8 Two Advanced Controls Cleanroom Combinatorial Tests

Test	Look Sensitivity	Look Inversion	Autolook Centering	Crouch Behavior	Clench Protection
1	3	Not Inverted	Enabled	Hold	Enabled
2	3	Not Inverted	Disabled	Hold	Enabled

The third test in this table is constructed from the random number sequence 32, 6, 11, 64, and 66. Once again, the first value corresponds to the default Look Sensitivity value of "3." The second usage number is 6, which results in the first "Inverted" entry for the Look Inversion parameter by virtue of being inside the 1–10 range for that value. The third random number for Test 3 is 11, which gives you an Enabled value for the Autolook Centering parameter. The number to use for determining the Crouch Behavior test value is 64, which maps to the 1–80 range for the Hold choice. The fifth number provides another "first"—a "Disabled" value for Clench Protection, because it falls within the 26–100 range. Table 10.9 shows the first three tests entered in the table.

TABLE 10.9 Three Advanced Controls Cleanroom Combinatorial Tests

Test	Look Sensitivity	Look Inversion	Autolook Centering	Crouch Behavior	Clench Protection
1	3	Not Inverted	Enabled	Hold	Enabled
2	3	Not Inverted	Disabled	Hold	Enabled
3	3	Inverted	Enabled	Hold	Disabled

Continue by using the random numbers 86, 64, 22, 95, and 50 for Test 4. The 86 is within the 11–95 range for Look Sensitivity =3, so put a "3" again in column one. A 64 is next in the usage number list. It maps to the Not Inverted range for Look Inversion. The next number, 22, corresponds to "Enabled" for Autolook Centering. The 95 provides the first Toggle value for Crouch Behavior in this set of tests. The Clench Protection number is 50, which puts another Disabled value in that column. Table 10.10 shows the table with four of the six tests defined.

TABLE 10.10 Four Advanced Controls Cleanroom Combinatorial Tests

Test	Look Sensitivity	Look Inversion	Autolook Centering	Crouch Behavior	Clench Protection
1	3	Not Inverted	Enabled	Hold	Enabled
2	3	Not Inverted	Disabled	Hold	Enabled
3	3	Inverted	Enabled	Hold	Disabled
4	3	Not Inverted	Enabled	Toggle	Disabled

Your fifth set of random numbers is 33, 21, 76, 63, and 85. The 33 puts a "3" in the Look Sensitivity column. The 21 is in the Not Inverted range for Look Inversion. An 85 is within the Not Inverted range for Invert Flight Control. The 63 corresponds to a Hold value for Crouch Behavior and the 85 causes another "Disabled" to be put in the last column for the Clench Protection parameter. Table 10.11 shows the Cleanroom combinatorial table with five tests defined. Only one more to go now!

TABLE 10.11 Five Advanced Controls Cleanroom Combinatorial Tests

Test	Look Sensitivity	Look Inversion	Autolook Centering	Crouch Behavior	Clench Protection
1	3	Not Inverted	Enabled	Hold	Enabled
2	3	Not Inverted	Disabled	Hold	Enabled
3	3	Inverted	Enabled	Hold	Disabled
4	3	Not Inverted	Enabled	Toggle	Disabled
5	3	Not Inverted	Disabled	Hold	Disabled

One more number set is needed to complete the table. Use 96, 36, 18, 48, and 12. The first usage number of 96 is high enough to be in the 96–100 range for the "10" Look Sensitivity value. This marks the first time that value appears in the table. Moving through the rest of the numbers, the 36 puts a No in the Invert Thumbstick column, 18 corresponds to Controller Vibration = Yes, 48 is in the range for Invert Flight Control = No, and 12 completes the final test row with a Yes for Auto-Center. Table 10.12 shows all six Cleanroom combinatorial test cases.

TABLE 10.12 Completed Advanced Controls Cleanroom Combinatorial Table

Test	Look Sensitivity	Look Inversion	Autolook Centering	Crouch Behavior	Clench Protection
1	3	Not Inverted	Enabled	Hold	Enabled
2	3	Not Inverted	Disabled	Hold	Enabled
3	3	Inverted	Enabled	Hold	Disabled
4	3	Not Inverted	Enabled	Toggle	Disabled
5	3	Not Inverted	Disabled	Hold	Disabled
6	10	Not Inverted	Enabled	Hold	Disabled

Your keen testing eye should have noticed that Look Sensitivity = 1 was never generated for this set of tests. That is a function of its relatively low probability (10%), the low number of test cases that you produced, and the particular random number set that was the basis for selecting the values for table. In fact, if you stopped generating tests after five test cases instead of six, the default value of "3" would have been the only value for Look Sensitivity that appeared in the table. This should not be considered a problem for a table of this size. If a value has a 5% or higher usage probability and you don't see it at all in a test set of 100 or more tests, then you can suspect that something is wrong with either your value selection process or your random number generation.

Also notice that some values appear more frequently or less frequently than their usage probability would suggest. Autolook Centering = Enabled has only a 30% usage for the Casual profile, but it appears in 67% (4/6) of the tests generated. This is mainly due to the low number of tests created for this table. With a test set of 50 or more you should see a better match between a value's usage probability and its frequency in the test set.

Just to reinforce the fact that the Cleanroom combinatorial table method doesn't guarantee it will provide all test value pairs that are required for a pairwise combinatorial table, confirm that the pair Autolook Centering = Disabled and Crounch Behavior = Toggle is absent from Table 10.12. Now take a moment to see which other missing pairs you can find.

You will recall that pairwise combinatorial tables are constructed vertically, one column at a time. Until you complete the process for building the table you don't know what the test cases will be nor how many tests will result. Because Cleanroom combinatorial tables are constructed horizontally—one line at a time—you get a completely defined test on the very first row, and every row after that for as many Cleanroom combinatorial tests as you choose to produce.

TFD Cleanroom Paths

Cleanroom TFD tests come from the same diagram you use for creating minimum, baseline, and expert constructed paths. Cleanroom test paths travel from state to state by choosing each subsequent flow based on its usage probability.

A usage probability must be added to each flow if the TFD is going to be used for Cleanroom testing. The probabilities of the set of flows exiting each state must add up to 100%. Figure 10.3 shows a flow with the usage probability after the action. If there is no action on the flow, then the usage probability gets added after the event.

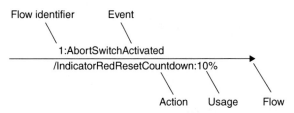

FIGURE 10.3 Example flow with usage probability.

Figure 10.4 shows an entire TFD with flow numbers and usage percentage amounts. Remember, the probabilities of flows exiting each state must add up to 100%. You might recognize this TFD from the templates provided in Appendix D. The flow numbers and usage percentages make this TFD ready for Cleanroom testing.

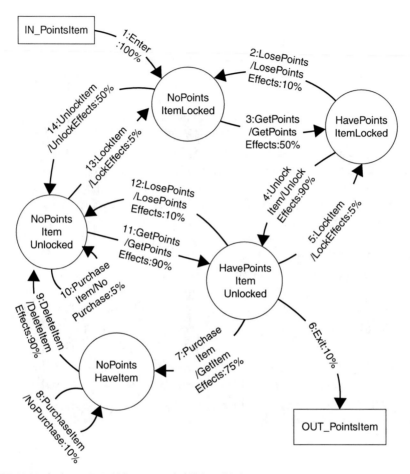

FIGURE 10.4 Unlock Item TFD with usage probabilities added.

TFD Cleanroom Path Example

With the usage information added to the TFD, generate random numbers to guide you around the diagram from flow to flow until you reach the OUT terminator. The resulting path defines a single test. Continue generating as many paths as you like, using new random number sets each time. Experience has shown that it is a good practice to always assign a 10% value to the Exit flow. A larger value will result in paths that exit too soon and a smaller value will cause too many paths that seem to go on forever before finally exiting. The 10% value provides a nice mix of long, medium, and short paths in your Cleanroom test set.

Each Cleanroom test case is described by the sequence of flow numbers along the Cleanroom path. Because the path length can vary from one test to another, you will not know ahead of time how many random numbers you need to generate for all of your paths. The result is that you could exit some tests after only a few flows, or you could travel around the diagram several times before reaching the OUT box. Normally you would generate the random numbers as you need them, but for your convenience the random number set for the example in this section is 30, 27, 35, 36, 82, 59, 92, 88, 80, 74, 42, and 13.

Generating a test case for the TFD in Figure 10.4 starts at the IN box. The only flow from there has a 100% usage, so there is no need to produce a random number—you must begin your test with this flow. Next, there are two possible ways out from the NoPointsItemLocked state: flow 3 and flow 14. Each of those flows has the usage probability of 50%. Assign them each a random number range according to their numerical order. Use flow 3 if the random number is 1–50 and use flow 14 if it is 51–100. Get the random number 30 from the list above and take flow 3 to HavePointsItemLocked. The test path so far is 1, 3.

There are two flows exiting state HavePointsItemLocked. Flow 2 has a 10% usage and flow 4 has a 90% usage. The range for flow 2 is 1–10 and for flow 4 it's 11–100. Use 27 as the random number for this flow. That sends the test along flow 4 to HavePointsItemUnlocked. The test path at this point is 1, 3, 4.

HavePointsItemUnlocked is the most interesting state so far, with four flows to choose from for the next step in your test. Flow 5 has a 5% usage, flow 6 has 10%, flow 7 has 75%, and flow 12 has 10%. The corresponding number ranges are 1–5 for flow 5, 6–15 for flow 6, 16–90 for flow 7, and 91–100 for flow 12. You anxiously await the next random number . . . and its . . . 35. Your test path now takes flow 7 to NoPointsHaveItem. The path is now 1, 3, 4, 7.

From NoPointsHaveItem there are two flow choices: flow 8 with a 10% usage and flow 9 with a 90% usage. You will take flow 8 if the random number is in the range 1–10 and flow 9 if it's within 11–100. Your new random number is 36, so take flow 9 to NoPointsItemUnlocked. The test path is currently 1, 3, 4, 7, 9.

Flows 10, 11, and 13 all leave NoPointsItemUnlocked. Flow 10's usage is 5% (1–5), flow 11 has a 90% usage (6–95), and flow 13 has a 5% (96–100) usage. Another random number is generated and it's 82. That's within the range for flow 11, so take that flow to HavePointsItemUnlocked. The path has grown to 1, 3, 4, 7, 9, 11, but you're not done yet.

You're back at HavePointsItemUnlocked and the next random number is 59. That fits in the 16–90 range for flow 7, taking you on another trip to NoPointsHaveItem. A usage of 92 here matches up with flow 9, going to NoPointsItemUnlocked. The test path is now 1, 3, 4, 7, 9, 11, 7, 9.

The next random number is 88. This takes you from NoPointsItemUn-locked to HavePointsItemUnlocked via flow 11. The 80 takes you along flow 7 for the third time in this path and the next number, 74, sends you to NoPointsItemUnlocked via flow 9. A 42 in the random number list chooses flow 11, which brings you once again to HavePointsItemUnlocked. These flows extend the path to 1, 3, 4, 7, 9, 11, 7, 9, 11, 7, 9, 11.

The next random number to use is 13. This falls within the 6–15 range, which corresponds to flow 6. That's the Exit flow, which goes to the OUT terminator. This marks the end of this test path. The completed path is 1, 3, 4, 7, 9, 11, 7, 9, 11, 7, 9, 11, 6.

Once a path is defined, create the test cases using the Data Dictionary techniques described in Chapter 11. To create an overview of this test, list the flows, actions, and states in the order they appear along the path. List the flow number for each step in parentheses at the beginning of each line, as follows:

```
IN_PointsItem
(1) Enter, NoPointsItemLocked
(3) GetPoints, GetPointsEffects, HavePointsItemLocked
(4) UnlockItem, UnlockEffects, HavePointsItemUnlocked
(7) PurchaseItem, GetItemEffects, NoPointsHaveItem
(9) DeleteItem, DeleteItemEffects, NoPointsItem
Unlocked
(11) GetPoints, GetPointsEffects, HavePointsItem
Unlocked
(7) PurchaseItem, GetItemEffects, NoPointsHaveItem
(9) DeleteItem, DeleteItemEffects, NoPointsItem
Unlocked
(11) GetPoints, GetPointsEffects, HavePointsItem
Unlocked
```

```
(7) PurchaseItem, GetItemEffects, NoPointsHaveItem
(9) DeleteItem, DeleteItemEffects, NoPointsItem
Unlocked
(11) GetPoints, GetPointsEffects, HavePointsItem
Unlocked
(6) Exit, OUT_PointsItem
```

Generating this path provided some expected results. The path starts with the IN and ends with the OUT, which is mandatory. Flows with large percentages were selected often, such as flows 9 and 11, which each have a 90% usage probability.

Did anything surprise you? Some flows and states didn't appear in this path at all. That's okay for a single path. When you create a set of paths you should expect to explore a wider variety of flows and states.

Was the flow longer than you expected? Flows 7, 9, and 11 appeared multiple times in this path. This is not what you would expect from minimum or baseline path sets. It's also interesting to note that those three flows form a loop. They were used three times in a row before finally exiting and ending the path.

Was the path longer than you wanted it to be? Is this a path you would have chosen on your own? Because this technique is based on a process rather than the ideas or preconceptions of a particular tester, the paths are free of bias or limitations. Cleanroom paths also highlight the fact that the game is not played one operation at a time and then turned off. These paths will test realistic game-use scenarios if your percentages are reasonably correct. As a result, your Cleanroom tests will have the ability to reveal defects that are likely to occur during extended or repeated game use.

Flow Usage Maintenance

There will come a time when you will need to move one or more flows around on your TFD. This could perhaps affect your usage values. When a flow's destination (arrowhead end) changes, you are not required to change its usage. Conversely, if you change a flow to originate from a new state, you must re-evaluate the usage values for all flows coming from both the new state and the original one.

Figure 10.5 shows an updated version of the Unlock Item TFD. Flow 9 on the left side of the diagram now goes all the way back to NoPointsItemLocked instead of NoPointsItemUnlocked. The usage percentage for flow 9 does not have to change. The percentages for all the flows coming from NoPointsHaveItem still add up to 100: 10% for flow 8 and 90% for flow 9.

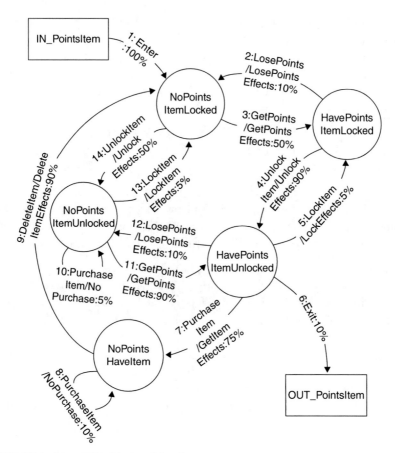

FIGURE 10.5 Unlock Item TFD with altered flow 9.

Figure 10.6 includes a second update to the Unlock Item TFD. Flow 6 originally started at HavePointsItemUnlocked, but now it goes from NoPointsHaveItem to the OUT box. For this case, all flows coming from both HavePointsItemUnlocked and NoPointsHaveItem were re-evaluated to add up to 100% from each originating state.

For HavePointsItemUnlocked, one or more percentages need to increase because that state lost a flow. You can give flow 12 the 10% that used to be allocated to flow 6. That would not overly inflate the usage for flow 7, and it keeps flow 5's usage small. As Figure 10.6 shows, flow 12 now has a 20% usage instead of its original 10% value.

Additionally, one or more flows coming from NoPointsHaveItem must now be reduced to make room for the new flow. Because flow 6 is an Exit flow, it must have a 10% usage. Two other flows come from NoPointsHaveItem: flow 8 with a 10% usage and flow 9 with a 90% usage. Reducing flow 8 by 10% will put it at 0%, meaning it will never be selected for any Cleanroom paths for this TFD. Instead, take away 5% from flow 8 and 5% from flow 9. The new percentages for these flows are reflected in Figure 10.6. Alternatively, you could

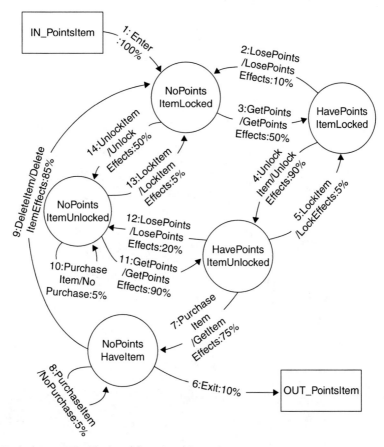

FIGURE 10.6 Unlock Item TFD with altered flows 6 and 9.

have taken 10% away from flow 9 and left flow 8 at 10%. Your choice depends on what distribution you think best reflects the expected relative usage of these flows according to the game player, mode, or data you are trying to model.

Flow Usage Profiles

You might want to have multiple usage profiles to choose from when you create TFD Cleanroom paths. One way to accomplish this is to create copies of the TFD and change the usage numbers to match each profile. Another solution is to do what you did for combinatorial profiles: produce a mapping between each test element and its usage probability for one or more game users, types, or modes. In this case, usage numbers should not appear on the TFD. Figure 10.7 shows the Unlock Item TFD without usage percentages on the flows.

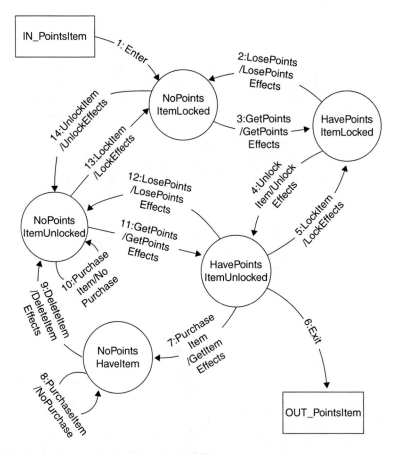

FIGURE 10.7 Unlock Item TFD without usage probabilities.

Table 10.13 shows how one profile's probabilities map to the flows on the TFD. Document the random number range that corresponds to each flow's usage. For example, because flows 3 and 14 go out from NoPoints-ItemLocked, flow 3 gets the range 1–50 and flow 14 gets 51–100. When you edit the TFD to add, remove, or move flows, you must revisit this table and update the usage and range data.

TABLE 10.13 Casual Player Usage Table for Unlocked Item TFD Flows

Flow	Casual
1	100
2	10
3	50
4	90
5	5
6	10
7	75
8	10
9	90
10	5
11	90
12	10
13	5
14	50
TOTAL	600

The total at the bottom of the flow probability table is a good way to check that your percentages add up correctly. The total should be equal to 100 (for the Enter flow) plus 100 times the number of states on the diagram (flows exiting each state must add up to 100%). The TFD in Figure 10.6 has five states, so 600 is the correct total.

Generate your Cleanroom tests from the flow usage table similarly to the way you do when the flow usage is on the diagram. The only difference is the extra step to look up the flow's range in the table. If you are creating an automated process or tool to construct TFD Cleanroom paths, this table could be stored in a database or exported to a text file.

> *Admittedly, keeping track of flow usage in a table presents some problems. Because the flow numbering does not have to be related to the way flows appear on the diagram, it takes a little more work to identify the flows coming from each individual state. For example, the flows coming from NoPointsItemLocked—3 and 14—are at opposite ends of the flow list. This wrinkle can become more of a problem when many flows are added, moved, or removed to adapt to changes in the game software. Just be careful and check your numbers when you are faced with this situation.*

!
TIP

INVERTED USAGE

Inverted usage can be applied when you want to emphasize the less frequently used functions and behaviors in the game. This creates a usage model that might reflect how the game would be used by people trying to find ways to exploit or intentionally crash the game for their own benefit. It also helps draw out defects that escaped earlier detection because of the very fact that the game is rarely, if ever, expected to be used in this way.

Calculating Inverted Usage

Inverted usage is calculated using a three-step process:

1. Calculate the reciprocal of each usage probability for a test parameter (combinatorial) or for all paths exiting a state (TFDs).

2. Sum the reciprocals.

3. Divide each reciprocal from step 1 by the sum of the reciprocals calculated in step 2. The result is the inverted probability for each individual usage value.

For example, say there are three values A, B, and C, with the usage 10%, 50%, and 40%, respectively.

Apply step 1 of the inversion process to get reciprocal values of 10.0 for A ($\frac{1}{0.10}$), 2.00 for B ($\frac{1}{0.5}$), and 2.50 ($\frac{1}{0.40}$) for C.

Add these reciprocals to get a sum of 14.5. The reciprocals are divided by this sum to get the inverted values of 69.0% ($\frac{10}{14.5}$) for A, 13.8% ($\frac{2}{14.5}$) for B, and 17.2% ($\frac{2.5}{14.5}$) for C. These can be rounded to 69%, 14%, and 17% for test generation purposes.

One characteristic of this process is that it inverts the proportions between each probability compared to its companions for a given set of usage values.

In the preceding example, B is used 5 times more frequently than A ($\frac{50}{10}$) and 1.25 times more frequently than C ($\frac{50}{40}$).

The relationship between inverted A and inverted B is $\frac{69\%}{13.8\%}$, which is 5.00.

Likewise, the relationship between inverted C and inverted B is 1.25 ($\frac{17.2\%}{13.8\%}$).

For any case where there are only two usage values to invert, you can skip the math and simply reverse the usage of the two values in question. You will get the same result if you apply the full process, but why bother when you could use that time to do more testing?

If an item has a 0% usage, then the first step in the inversion process will cause a divide by zero situation. Keep that from happening by adding 0.01% to each value before doing the three-step inversion calculation. This will keep the results accurate to one decimal place of precision in the results and maintain the relative proportions of usages in the same set.

Combinatorial Table Usage Inversion

Table 10.1 showed a set of usage probabilities for the *HALO Reach* Look Sensitivity test values of 1, 3, and 10. Construct a table of inverted values starting with the Casual player profile. The three usage probabilities in that column are 10, 85, and 5. These are percentages, so the numerical values of these probabilities are 0.10, 0.85, and 0.05.

Apply step 1 and calculate $\frac{1}{0.10} = 10$.

Do the same for $\frac{1}{0.85}$, which is 1.18, and $\frac{1}{0.05}$, which equals 20.

Add these numbers according to step 2. 10 + 1.176 + 20 = 31.176. Finish with step 3.

Dividing 10, which is the reciprocal of the usage probability for Look Sensitivity = 1, by 31.18, which is the sum of all three reciprocals, gives an inverted probability of 0.321. Because the numbers in the table are percentages, this gets entered as 32.1. Likewise, divide 1.18 by 31.18 to get the second inverted usage result 0.038, or 3.8%. Complete this column by dividing 20 by 31.18 to get 0.641 and enter 64.1 as the inverted usage for Look Sensitivity = 10.

Comparing the inverted usage values to the original ones confirms that the relative proportions of each usage value have also been inverted. Originally, the usage for Look Sensitivity = 1 was 10% versus 5% for Look Sensitivity = 10: a 2 to 1 ratio. In the inverted table, the Look Sensitivity = 10 value is 64.2—twice that of the 32.1% usage for Look Sensitivity = 1. You can examine the values for each parameter to confirm that this holds true for the other values within each column.

The complete inverted Look Sensitivity usage for all player profiles is provided in Table 10.14.

TABLE 10.14 Inverted Usage Percentages for the Look Sensitivity Parameter

Look Sensitivity	Casual	Achiever	Explorer	Multiplayer
1	32.1	99.9	60.9	75.9
3	3.8	0.0	8.7	5.1
10	64.1	0.0	30.4	19.0
Total	100	100	100	100

The "normal" and inverted usage tables for all of the HALO Reach Advanced Controls parameters are provided in an Excel spreadsheet file on the book's DVD. There are separate worksheets for the Normal and Inverted usages. You can change the values on the Normal Usage sheet and the values on the Inverted Usage sheet will be calculated for you.

TFD Flow Usage Inversion

The TFD Enter and Exit flows present special cases you must deal with when inverting usages. Because these are really "test" operations versus "user" operations, the usage percentage for these flows should be preserved. They will keep the same value in the inverted usage set that you assigned to them originally. Table 10.15 shows the Unlock Item TFD's inverted Casual player usage table initialized with these fixed values.

TABLE 10.15 Inverted Flow Usage Table
Initialized with Enter and Exit Flow Data

Flow	Casual
1	100
2	
3	
4	
5	
6	10
7	
8	
9	
10	
11	
12	
13	
14	

Complete the table by performing the inversion calculation process for the flows leaving each state on the TFD. Go from state to state and fill in the table as you go along. Start at the top of the diagram with the NoPoints-ItemLocked state. Do inversion calculation for flows 3 and 14. Because these flows have the identical value of 50%, there's no need to do any math. The inverted result in this case is the same as the original. Put 50s in the table for these flows, as shown in Table 10.16.

TABLE 10.16 Fixed Usage Added for
Flows Leaving NoPointsItemLocked

Flow	Casual
1	100
2	
3	50
4	
5	

(*Continued*)

TABLE 10.16 Continued

Flow	Casual
6	10
7	
8	
9	
10	
11	
12	
13	
14	**50**

Moving clockwise around the diagram, do the inversion for flows 2 and 4 coming from HavePointsItemUnlocked. There are only two values, so you can swap values without having to do a calculation. Table 10.17 shows the 90% inverted usage for flow 2 and the 10% inverted usage for flow 4 added to the table.

TABLE 10.17 Inverted Usage Added for Flows Leaving HavePointsItemLocked

Flow	Casual
1	100
2	**90**
3	50
4	**10**
5	
6	10
7	
8	
9	
10	
11	
12	
13	
14	50

The next state on your trip around the TFD is HavePointsItemUn-locked. This is the state that has the Exit flow, which is already recorded as 10% in the inverted table. The trick here is to invert the other flows from this state while preserving the total usage of 100% when they are all added up, including the Exit flow. Have you figured out how to do this? For step 1, calculate only the reciprocals of flows 5 (5%), 7 (75%), and 12 (10%). These would be 20, 1.33, and 10, respectively. The sum of the reciprocals (step 2) is 31.33. Divide each reciprocal with the sum (step 3) to get 0.638, 0.042, and 0.319. Because it has already been established that flow 6 (Exit) accounts for 10% of the usage probability total for HavePointsItemUnlocked, then these other three flows must account for the remaining 90%. Multiply the inverted usages for flows 5, 7, and 12 by 0.9 (90%) to account for that. The final result for flow 5 is 0.574 (57.4%), for flow 7 is 0.038 (3.8%), and for flow 12 is 0.287 (28.7%). Table 10.18 shows these numbers included with the results for the other flows usages calculated so far.

TABLE 10.18 Inverted Usage Added for Flows Leaving HavePointsItemUnlocked

Flow	Casual
1	100
2	90
3	50
4	10
5	57.4
6	10
7	3.8
8	
9	
10	
11	
12	28.7
13	
14	50

Go to the next state, which is NoPointsHaveItem. This is another situation with only two flows to invert. Swap the usage values for flow 8 and flow 9. Table 10.19 shows flow 8 added to the table with a 90% inverted usage and flow 9 with a 10% inverted usage.

TABLE 10.19 Inverted Usage Added for Flows Leaving NoPointsHaveItem

Flow	Casual
1	100
2	90
3	50
4	10
5	57.4
6	10
7	3.8
8	90
9	10
10	
11	
12	28.7
13	
14	50

NoPointsItemUnlocked is the last state to account for on the diagram. Three flows leave this state, so you have to do some calculations. Flow 10 has a 5% usage, so its reciprocal is 20. Flow 11 has a 90% usage. Its reciprocal is 1.11. Flow 13 has the same usage as flow 10 and, therefore, the same reciprocal of 20. Now do step 2 and add up the reciprocals. 20 + 1.11 + 20 = 41.11. Find the inverted usage of each flow by dividing their reciprocals by this total.

For flows 10 and 13, calculate $\frac{20}{41.11}$, which results in 0.486, or 48.6%.

Calculate flow 11's inverted usage as $\frac{1.11}{41.11}$, which is 0.027, or 2.7%. Enter these values to the table to get the completed version shown in Table 10.20.

TABLE 10.20 Completed Table with Inverted
Usage for NoPointsItemUnlocked

Flow	Casual
1	100
2	90
3	50
4	10
5	57.4
6	10
7	3.8
8	90
9	10
10	**48.6**
11	2.7
12	**28.7**
13	**48.6**
14	50

With these inverted percentages you can produce TFD Cleanroom paths and test cases in the same way you did earlier from the normal usage probabilities.

One technique that makes it a little easier to keep track of the number ranges associated with each percentage is to add a Range column to the usage table. Table 10.21 shows how this looks for the Unlock Item TFD inverted usages. This column can be especially helpful when the flows from a state are scattered around, such as flows 3 and 12 coming from NoPoints-ItemLocked.

TABLE 10.21 Inverted Casual Player Usage
and Ranges for Unlock Item TFD

Flow	Casual	
	Usage	**Range**
1	100	1–100
2	90	1–90

(Continued)

TABLE 10.21 Continued

Flow	Casual	
	Usage	**Range**
3	50	1–50
4	10	91–100
5	57.4	1–57
6	10	58–67
7	3.8	68–71
8	90	1–90
9	10	91–100
10	48.6	1–49
11	2.7	50–52
12	28.7	72–100
13	48.6	53–100
14	50	51–100

Summary

Game players have tendencies and patterns of use that can be incorporated into game tests for the purpose of testing the game the way players play the game. The point of doing that is to find and remove the bugs that would show up when the game is played in those ways. If you are successful, those players will not find any bugs in your game. That's good for them and good for you.

When you sell millions of copies of your game, "rare" situations can show up a number of times over the life of a title. Tests based on inverted usage profiles can emphasize and expose those rare defects in your game.

Exercises

1. What type of player are you? If you do not match any of the types listed in this chapter, give your type a name and describe it. Now think of someone else you know and find their player type. Describe a scenario where you would expect you and your friend to play the game differently. How are the game functions, features, and elements used differently by your two styles?

2. Identify and list each pair of values that is missing from the Cleanroom combinatorial table in Table 10.12. Explain why they are not necessary and why they might not even be desirable in this application.

3. Is it possible to have the same exact test case appear more than once in a Cleanroom test set? Explain.

4. Create a set of tables with the inverted Casual profile usage probabilities for each of the *HALO Reach* Advanced Settings parameters.

5. Generate six Cleanroom combinatorial tests from the inverted usage tables you produced in Exercise 4. Use the same random number set that was used to generate the combinatorial tests shown in Table 10.12. Compare the new tests to the original ones.

6. Modify the TFD from Figure 10.4 to incorporate the inverted usages in Table 10.21. Round the usage values to the nearest whole percentage. Make sure the total probabilities of the flows exiting each state add up to 100. If not, adjust your rounded values accordingly.

7. Generate a path for the TFD you produced in Exercise 6. List the flows, actions, and states along your path using the same format shown earlier in this chapter. Compare the new path to the original one.

CHAPTER 11

TEST TREES

In This Chapter

- Test case trees
- Tree feature tests
- Test tree designs

Test trees can be use for three different purposes in game testing:

1. *Test case trees* document the hierarchical relationship between test cases and game features, elements, and functions.

2. *Tree feature tests* reflect the tree structures of features and functions designed into the game.

3. *Test tree designs* are used to develop tests that systematically cover specific game features, elements, or functions.

TEST CASE TREES

In this application of test trees, the tests have already been developed and documented. The tree is used each time the game team sends a new release to the testers. The test lead can determine which tests to execute based on which defect fixes or new abilities were introduced in the release. Such an organization could also reflect the way the game itself is structured.

Take, for example, a tree of tests for *Warhammer 40,000: Dawn of War*, which is a real-time simulation (RTS) game for the PC. In this game, up to eight players can compete against one another and/or computer AI opponents. Players control and develop their own race of warriors, each of which has its own distinct military units, weapons, structures, and vehicles. Games are won according to various victory conditions, such as taking control of a location, defending a location for a given amount of time, or completely eliminating enemy forces.

At a high level, the *Dawn of War* tests can be organized into Game Options tests, User Interface tests, Game Mode tests, Race-specific tests, and Chat capability tests. The Option tests can be grouped into Graphics, Sound, or Controls options. The User Interface tests can be divided between the Game Screen UI and the in-game Camera Movement. Additionally, there are three major Game Modes: Campaign, Skirmish, and Multiplayer, and four Races that players can choose from: Chaos, Eldar, Orks, and Space Marines. The Chat capability is available when connected via LAN, Online, or Direct Link. Figure 11.1 shows these top two levels of organization arranged as a tree.

During game development, each bug fix can affect one or more areas of the game. With the test case tree, you can easily target which tests to run by finding them under the tree nodes related to the parts of the game affected by the new code. Some fixes could have to be re-checked at a high level, such as a change in the Chat editor font that applies to all uses of chat. Other fixes might be more specific, such as a change in the way Chat text is passed to the online chat server.

It is also possible to define the tree in finer detail in order to make a more precise selection of tests. For example, the Skirmish Game Modes tests could be further organized by which Map is used, how many Players are active in the match, which Race is chosen by the player, what Game

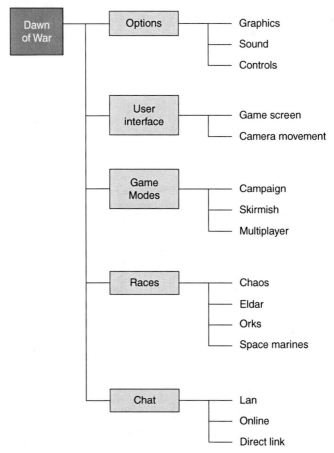

FIGURE 11.1 *Dawn of War* two-level test case tree.

Options are selected, and which Win Conditions are applied. Figure 11.2 shows the further breakdown of the Skirmish branch.

Revealing the additional details of the Skirmish mode is important because it exposes another set of tests that should be run if changes are made to any game assets or functions that are specific to one or more of the Races. Whether your tests are stored in a regular directory system, configuration management repository, or test management tool, you can organize them to match the tree hierarchy of the game's functions. This is an efficient way to find the tests you want to run once you map them to the code changes in each release you test.

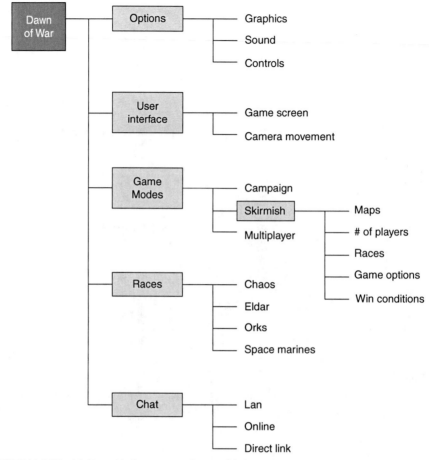

FIGURE 11.2 Skirmish Game Mode test case sub-tree added.

TREE FEATURE TESTS

A second application of test trees is used to reflect the actual tree structure of features implemented in the game. *Dawn of War* has such structures for the tech trees of each race. These trees define the dependency rules for which units, vehicles, structures, and abilities can be generated. For example, before the Eldars can produce Howling Banshee units, they must first construct an Aspect Portal and upgrade the structure with the Howling Banshee Aspect Stone. Other units can be produced immediately, such as the Rangers. These trees can be quite complex, with dependencies between multiple structures, upgrades, and research items. Test these trees by following the various paths to successfully construct each item. Also check that attempted "shortcuts" will **not** produce the intended result, such as trying to produce Warp Spider units without the Warp Spider Aspect Stone. Be thorough and examine all the ways this might be attempted— such as from a menu, command line, or by clicking an icon. Figure 11.3 shows the Aspect Portal tech tree for the Eldar race.

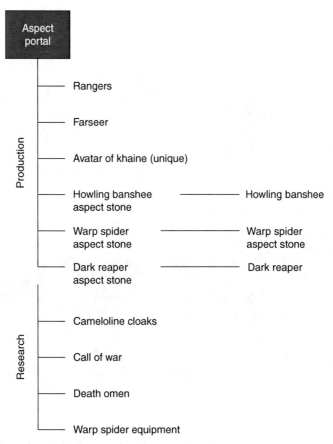

FIGURE 11.3 *Dawn of War* technology tree for Eldar Aspect Portal.

Another example of this type of tree is the job, or skill, tree typically defined for RPG games, such as the *Final Fantasy* or *Dragon Age* series. Characters might be required to develop skills up to a certain level before new skills or abilities become available. In some cases, the skill and role choices are dictated by the choice of character race, occupation, and/or faction. Each successive choice will perhaps narrow the options available for the remaining choices. For these kinds of trees, think of the string of lights on a Christmas tree. If one light is faulty, the remaining connected lights will also be off. In this case, some Classes or Backgrounds won't be available if the preconditions (required combinations of previous choices) aren't met. As a tester, you'll want to test each possible result by leaving out the necessary preconditions, one at a time; plus, you'll test for the case where all of the necessary conditions are met. See Figure 11.4 for an example of how this is portrayed in the game screen for a Male Dwarf in *Dragon Age: Origins*.

FIGURE 11.4 Male Dwarf character generation in *Dragon Age: Origins*.

Selecting the "Male" gender reveals the Race choices that are available. In this case, any of the three races—Human, Elf, or Dwarf—can be chosen. Choosing the Dwarf race limits your choice of class to Warrior or Rogue. Selecting the Rogue class for the Dwarf Male limits you to two of the six Background possibilities available: Commoner or Noble.

When the character tree isn't already drawn for you on the game screen, go ahead and construct your own. As you progress through the tree, check that the allowed roles and skills are available at the end of the tree, and also check that choices that should be unavailable are blocked along the way.

Job trees are another construct built into many popular games. Take a moment to look at Figure 11.5 which shows a tree diagram for the mage jobs available to Hume characters in *Final Fantasy Tactics A2: Grimoire of the Rift* (FFTA2).

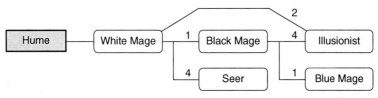

FIGURE 11.5 Hume Mage job tree for *FFTA2*.

Before he can take on the role of an Illusionist, the player's character must master two White Mage abilities and four Black Mage abilities. The diagram also shows that the character must master one White Mage ability before he can even take on the role of Black Mage, in order to begin mastering Black Mage abilities.

NOTE   *The entire job tree structure for* FFTA2 *can be seen at* http://finalfantasy.wikia.com *[WIKIA 10]. Complete access information is provided in the references for Chapter 11, in Appendix E.*

Define the tree feature tests for a particular job by providing the test values for each of the nodes along the tree branches. You can keep the tests to a minimum by checking only the "edges" of the values that determine whether a skill, job, or ability is unlocked. For example, there are no tests for White Mage mastery = 2 nor Black Mage mastery = 1 or 2. It's sufficient to know that the Illusionist job is still not unlocked when only 3 Black Mage abilities are mastered in test case 2, and then establish that it's properly unlocked when Black Mage proficiency reaches 4. Table 11.1 shows the test cases that should result from the tree in Figure 11.5.

TABLE 11.1 Hume Mage Illusionist Job Tree Tests

Test	White Mage	Black Mage	Illusionist Enabled
1	1	4	No
2	2	3	No
3	2	4	YES

Trees can also define and limit which areas or locations within a game can be accessed by the player at any given time. Figure 11.6 shows the progression of battlegrounds that become available to players of the *Battleheart* RPG for iOS devices. Check marks indicate locations conquered, skulls represent unconquered locations that are available to the player, and padlocks indicate locations that are not accessible.

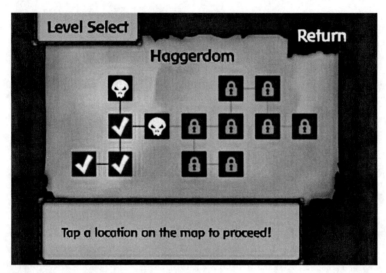

FIGURE 11.6 *Battleheart* battleground selection tree.

Yet another example is the Energy Path mission tree for the North Las Vegas location in the *Mafia Wars* game on Facebook®. Players must complete the "Blackmail A Car Dealer" mission to access the "Steal A Truckload Of Slots" on the left side branch and the "Secure Some Wheels" mission on the right. The tooltip for the "Steal A Truckload Of Slots" mission also reveals that completing the mission gives the player access to purchase the "Slots" property, accessed on the player's "My Casino" screen. See Figure 11.7 for the structure of this tree as shown in the game.

Many other feature trees exist across a wide variety of games. Here's a list of some places you might find them:

- Technology trees

- Progressing through tournament brackets

- Game option menu structures

FIGURE 11.7 *Mafia Wars* Energy Path mission tree for the North Las Vegas territory.

- Adding or upgrading spells, abilities, or superpowers

- Increasing complexity and types of skills needed to craft or cook items

- Earning new ranks, titles, trophies, or medals

- Unlocking codes, upgrades, or power-ups

- Unlocking new maps, battlegrounds, environments, or race courses

- Unlocking better cars, outfits, or opponents

One situation that's especially interesting to test is when different menu trees or tree paths can affect the same value, ability, or game element. Such values should be set and checked by all the possible means (paths) provided by the game. For example, the *Dawn of War* Game Options that are set in Skirmish mode also become the values used in the Multiplayer, LAN, Online, and Direct Host modes.

TEST TREE DESIGNS

Thus far, this chapter has dealt with intentionally organized paths and patterns built into the game for progression, improvement, or advancement of various aspects of video games. At the other end of the spectrum, some features can seem incredibly chaotic. Take, for example, card battle games. In these games, players take turns playing cards from a deck they have assembled, which perhaps must also meet certain specifications imposed by the game rules. Winning the card battle usually involves eliminating the opponent, his creatures (army, players, etc.), or both. A card will perhaps have a special behavior that is defined by the type of card and/or additional instructions printed on the card. Some cards can affect other players or cards. There are cards for offensive and defensive purposes. Hundreds of different cards can potentially interact and affect each other in unexpected or undesirable ways. More and more cards become available over time, creating new and sometimes unexpected interactions. Remember Rule #1: Don't Panic! You can create a test tree design to define a set of tests for special card capabilities.

Magic: The Gathering® is a popular CCG (collectible card game) which is available in video game form as downloadable content on the XBOX and PS3. *Magic: The Gathering, Duels of the Planeswalkers*™ game includes a "Challenge" mode in which the player has a single turn to defeat the opponent who seems to have an insurmountable advantage. Only a specific combination of cards, played in the correct order and put to proper use, will result in victory.

In a *Magic: The Gathering* duel, cards are played that provide energy ("mana") of various types (red, blue, green, white, black, or colorless) which are used to summon creatures or power spells and abilities. Assigning the right types of mana to each card played is key to enabling subsequent spells or abilities to be played in the same turn.

Challenge 5 has you playing against Liliana with only 2 life points left to your name. Somehow you have to figure out how to damage Liliana for 13 points or more in one turn if you are going to win. You have 6 cards in your hand, plus 5 creatures in play, and 6 mana—3 green (G) and 3 black (B)—on the table to power your cards. The cards and their costs are as follows:

Overrun – 2GGG

Elvish Champion –1GG

Imperious Perfect – 2G

Elvish Warrior – GG

Elvish Eulogist – G

Eyeblight's Ending – 2B

You can organize the possible sequences of played cards into a tree structure, accounting for all of the choices remaining after each subsequent play. This will reveal which sequences (paths) will lead to defeat and which (at least one) should result in success. As an alternative to laying out trees in a graphical format, you can use a spreadsheet to organize and visualize the structure and relationships between game options, player choices, and the results for each branch.

Start defining the paths, using the most expensive card to play. This reduces the amount of mana left with which to play subsequent cards so it should be one of the simpler branches in the tree/table. In this scenario, the Overrun card has the highest cost of 2GGG, which means the player has to pay 3 green colored mana and 2 additional mana of any color (green included) to play this spell. Once that has been played, only one black mana is left. This is not enough to pay for any of the remaining cards. Attacking after playing this card and applying any of the effects available to your other cards in play will not result in a victory; so this is a losing path. See Table 11.2 for the representation of this branch of the test tree in a tabular (spreadsheet) format. Because each path is a test case, they should be numbered for easy reference.

TABLE 11.2 Overrun Card Branch for the Liliana Challenge

Test	1st Card	Payment	2nd Card	Payment	Result
1	Overrun (2GGG)	BGGG	N/A	N/A	Lose

The next most restrictive card is Elvish Champion, which costs 1GG—two green mana and one other mana of any color. Some rows for this branch end with no 2nd card played, because a player could choose to complete their turn even if they haven't used up all of their available mana. Also, because the "1" means any type of available mana could be paid, there needs to be a separate sub-branch for when green mana is used for the "1" and another for when black mana is used. These choices will provide different constraints on which cards could possibly be played with the remaining mana available. A key to creating a thorough table is to recognize that different action "payment" combinations for each node in the tree must all be accounted for. Additional sub-branches are necessary in order to represent the various options for playing a second card. See Table 11.3 for the Elvish Champion branch of the test tree. Take note that in the last branch of this table, you will still have two black mana available after paying a total of BGGG, but no further move is possible because there are no cards in your hand which can be played for that cost.

TABLE 11.3 Elvish Champion Card Branch for the Liliana Challenge

Test	1st Card	Payment	2nd Card	Payment	Result
2	Elvish Champion (1GG)	GGG	None	N/A	Lose
3			Eyeblight's Ending (1BB)	BBB	Lose
4		BGG	None	N/A	Lose
5			Eyeblight's Ending (1BB)	BBG	Lose
6			Imperious Perfect (2G)	BBG	Lose
7			Elvish Eulogist (G)	G	Lose

NOTE
Sometimes it's a tip-off to the player that all of the resources provided, such as mana, must be used in order to solve a problem or win a challenge. While this is not a bug per se, but a tester you should point this out when it's to the detriment of the game, such as when there's only one way to spend the resources and, °surprise!° That's the winning move!

Next is the branch for playing the Imperious Perfect card first. This card costs 2G to play—one green mana plus two more of any color. With the mana available for the challenge, the possible costs for this card are GGG, BGG, and BBG. Here you encounter a greater number of restrictions as certain colors of mana are used up, such as the inability to play the Elvish Champion card (1GG) when paying BGG for the Imperious Perfect. Table 11.4 maps out the card play sequences available when starting your turn with the Imperious Perfect card.

TABLE 11.4 Imperious Perfect Card Branch for the Liliana Challenge

Test	1st Card	Payment	2nd Card	Payment	RESULT
8	Imperious Perfect (2G)	GGG	None	N/A	Lose
9			Eyeblight's Ending (2B)	BBB	Lose
10		BGG	None	N/A	Lose
11			Eyeblight's Ending (2B)	BBG	Lose
12			Elvish Eulogist (G)	G	Lose
13		BBG	None	N/A	Lose
14			Eyeblight's Ending (2B)	BGG	Lose
15			Elvish Champion (1GG)	BGG	Lose
16			Elvish Warrior (GG)	GG	Lose
17			Elvish Eulogist (G)	G	Lose

Continue by building out the Elvish Warrior card branch. This card costs only two mana (GG), so there might be opportunities for more than two cards to be played, depending on how the mana is spent. Once the Elvish Warrior card is followed by Elvish Eulogist, you choose not to play any more cards, but are still capable of paying for Eyeblight's Ending with the three black mana that remain. Additional columns need to be added to the test tree table to accommodate the possible "3rd card nodes" of the test tree. Table 11.5 shows the table for the Elvish Warrior card, which provides not just one, but TWO winning branches.

TABLE 11.5 Elvish Warrior Card Branch for the Liliana Challenge

Test	1st Card	Payment	2nd Card	Payment	3rd Card	Payment	Result
18	Elvish Warrior (GG)	GG	None	N/A	N/A	N/A	Lose
19			Imperious Perfect (2G)	BBG	N/A	N/A	Lose

(Continued)

TABLE 11.5 Continued

Test	1st Card	Payment	2nd Card	Payment	3rd Card	Payment	Result
20			Elvish Eulogist (G)	G	None	N/A	Lose
21					Eyeblight's Ending (2B)	BBB	**WIN**
22			Eyeblight's Ending (2B)	BBG	N/A	N/A	Lose
23				BBB	None	N/A	Lose
24					Elvish Eulogist (G)	G	**WIN**

Keep in mind that to win this challenge, you have to do more than just put the proper cards into play. When Eyeblight's Ending is played, you need to target (destroy) the opponent's Nightmare card, which is her only creature with the Flying ability. After the Elvish Eulogist is played, you need to "tap" the Immaculate Magistrate card—which was already in play at the start of the challenge—to increase the amount of damage that will be done by the Elven Riders card. With the Nightmare out of the way, your Elven Riders cannot be blocked, so when you attack, you deliver 13 points of unblocked damage to defeat Liliana.

At this point, two more main branches remain to be explored. The Elvish Eulogist card is the last one that requires a green mana cost, as shown in Table 11.6. Two more winning sequences are revealed.

TABLE 11.6 Elvish Eulogist Card Branch for the Liliana Challenge

Test	1st Card	Payment	2nd Card	Payment	3rd Card	Payment	Result
25	Elvish Eulogist (G)	G	None	N/A	N/A	N/A	Lose
26			Elvish Warrior (GG)	GG	N/A	N/A	Lose

(Continued)

TABLE 11.6 Continued

Test	1st Card	Payment	2nd Card	Payment	3rd Card	Payment	Result
27					Eyeblight's Ending (2B)	BBB	**WIN**
28			Imperious Perfect (2G)	BGG	N/A	N/A	Lose
29				BBG	N/A	N/A	Lose
30			Eyeblight's Ending (2B)	BGG	N/A	N/A	Lose
31				BBG	N/A	N/A	Lose
32				BBB	N/A	N/A	Lose
33					Elvish Warrior (GG)	GG	**WIN**

The last tree to construct starts when Eyeblight's Ending is played first. This opening move produces the largest table for this challenge. This time the player is prevented from accessing the two winning branches in this portion of the tree because the game will not let you pay three black mana (BBB) for the Eyeblight's Ending card. Instead, it automatically pays two black mana and one green mana (BBG).

TABLE 11.7 Eyeblight's Ending Branch for the Liliana Challenge

Test	1st Card	Payment	2nd Card	Payment	3rd Card	Payment	Result
34	Eyeblight's Ending (2B)	BGG	None	N/A	N/A	N/A	Lose
35			Elvish Eulogist (G)	G	N/A	N/A	Lose
36		BBG	None	N/A	N/A	N/A	Lose

(*Continued*)

TABLE 11.7 Continued

Test	1st Card	Payment	2nd Card	Payment	3rd Card	Payment	Result
37			Elvish Champion (1GG)	BGG	N/A	N/A	Lose
38			Imperious Perfect (2G)	BGG	N/A	N/A	Lose
39			Elvish Eulogist (G)	G	N/A	N/A	Lose
40		BBB	None	N/A	N/A	N/A	Lose
41			Elvish Champion (1GG)	GGG	N/A	N/A	Lose
42			Imperious Perfect (2G)	GGG	N/A	N/A	Lose
43			Elvish Warrior (GG)	GG	N/A	N/A	Lose
44					Elvish Eulogist (G)	G	WIN*
45			Elvish Eulogist (G)	G	N/A	N/A	Lose
46					Elvish Warrior (GG)	GG	WIN*

As you play through the card sequences in this final portion of the tree, you should notice that when you play the Eyeblight's Ending card as your first card, the game automatically chooses to pay with BBG. At the time this book is being written, there is no mechanism in the game for the player to explicitly choose which lands (mana) are used to pay for each card as it's played, so the nodes on the test branch that require the player to pay BGG or BBG cannot be executed, preventing access to two winning branches in tests 44 and 46. Woe to the player who opens with Eyeblight's Ending, for he shall be thwarted!

There are also a number of losing plays which are blocked for the same reason, denying players the opportunity to explore those possibilities. For example, when playing Eyeblight's Ending after the Elvish Eulogist in tests 32 and 33, the game uses BBB and does not give the option to pay GBB as an alternative. This blocks tests 30 and 31. Looking back over the entire test tree, a total of 21 branches—nearly half of the tree—cannot be played:

- 2, 3 — cannot pay GGG for Elvish Champion

- 8, 9 — cannot pay GGG for Imperious Perfect

- 13, 14, 15, 16, 17 — cannot pay BBG for Imperious Perfect

- 28 — cannot pay BGG for Imperious Perfect

- 30 — cannot pay BGG for Eyeblight's Ending

- 31 — cannot pay BBG for Eyeblight's Ending

- 34, 35 — cannot pay BGG for Eyeblight's Ending

- 40 through 46 — cannot play BBB for Eyeblight's Ending

These tests should still remain in your test design, but they could be grayed out and/or designated as "blocked" until the AI is updated to either utilize the mana differently or provide a way for players to explicitly determine how mana is spent for each card.

NOTE

The mana AI issue has been a topic on discussion boards so it has perhaps been taken care of by the time you are reading this book. You can follow some of the online discussions regarding this problem for both the XBOX 360 and PS3 versions at www.gamefaqs.com [NOWAY 10; HOWDOYOU 09] and www.gamespot.com [ISTHERE 10]. Complete access information is provided in the references for Chapter 11 in Appendix E of this book.

Summary

Well, that was a good mental workout! Tree structures are useful for organizing test cases so that the proper set of tests can easily be selected for a given set of changes to the game. Each downstream node represents a set of tests with a more specific purpose and scope than the nodes above it. Additionally, tests can reflect tree-like relationships that exist between game functions and elements. The behavior of these structures is tested by exercising the values along the various possible paths from the start of the tree, through each branch, and ending when there are no more moves, decisions, or choices to make.

Finally, test trees can be designed to improve understanding of a complex game feature or problem to be solved, and to bring order to a seemingly chaotic or complex function. This is especially relevant when you need to explore the interaction of game rules, options, elements, and functions. A well-formed tree progressively decomposes the feature until the end nodes are reached, defining the specific actions to perform during testing. Don't forget to "prune" any branches that are not possible due to game limitations.

Exercises

1. From the test case tree in Figure 11.2, which test branch(es) should you re-run for a new release of the game that fixes a bug with the sound effect for the Orks "Big Shoota" weapon?

2. There are actually four multiplayer game modes in *Dawn of War*: LAN, Online, Direct Host, and Direct Join. Furthermore, the same choices available in Skirmish mode—Maps, # of Players, Race, Game Options, and Win Conditions—apply to the LAN and Direct Host multiplayer modes. Describe how you would update the test case tree in Figure 11.2 to include these additional choices.

3. Draw a test tree representing the following relationships between lessons and items in *The School of Wizardry*™ game for Facebook:

a. You can find a Disarming Spell by doing the "Discover that you possess wizard powers as well" lesson.

b. The "Get a wand of your own" lesson requires the Disarming Spell and can also give you the Flashlight Charm.

c. The "Go to your first day of nonwizard school" lesson requires one Flashlight Charm and can provide an Impeding Charm.

d. "Your first magic lesson with Uncle Mortimer—levitate an object"—requires one Impeding Charm and can give you a Confusion Spell.

e. The "Study the History of Magic" lesson requires two Confusion Spells and can provide a Cast Flame Charm.

f. The "Study potions with your uncle" lesson requires two Disarming Spells.

g. The "Escape the neverending path in the Mystical Forest" lesson requires three Cast Flame Charms.

h. The "Make it back home safely…" lesson requires five Cast Flame Charms.

4. Copy and edit the spreadsheet included in the Chapter 11 folder of the DVD provided with this book to update the "Liliana Challenge" tree table in order to show how it should look if the Imperious Perfect card were to cost 1G to play instead of 2G.

12

AD HOC TESTING AND GAMEPLAY TESTING

In This Chapter

- Free testing
- Directed testing
- Gameplay testing
- External testing

Although most of this book is designed to help you take a methodical, structured approach to testing a game, this chapter focuses on more chaotic, unstructured—yet no less crucial—approaches to game testing.

Ad hoc testing, sometimes referred to as "general" testing, describes searching for defects in a less structured, more intuitive manner. *Gameplay* testing describes playing the game to test for such subjective qualities as balance, difficulty, and the often elusive "fun factor."

AD HOC TESTING

Ad hoc is a Latin phrase that can be translated as "to this particular purpose." Ad hoc testing is, in its purest form, a single test improvised to answer a specific question.

Despite the most thorough and careful test planning and test design, or the most complex test suite you might have developed, even after being reviewed carefully by other test leads or the project manager, there is always something you (and they) might have missed.

Ad hoc testing allows you, as an individual tester, to explore investigative paths that perhaps occurred to you, even subconsciously or unconsciously, in the course of performing structured test suites on the game. During the course of testing a game you will, almost daily, have thoughts along the lines of "I wonder what happens if I do…?"

Ad hoc testing gives you the opportunity to answer those questions. It is the mode of testing that best enables you to explore the game, wandering through it as you would a maze.

There are two main types of ad hoc testing. The first is *free testing*, which allows the professional game tester to "depart from the script" and to improvise tests on the fly. The second is *directed testing*, which is intended to solve a specific problem or to find a specific solution.

Free Testing Comes From the Right Side of Your Brain

Because it is a more intuitive and less structured form of testing, free testing is sometimes called "right-brain testing." Nobel prize-winning psychobiologist Roger W. Sperry asserted that the two halves of the human brain tend to process information in very different ways. The left half of the brain is much more logical, mathematical, and structured. The right half is more intuitive, creative, and attuned to emotions and feelings. It is also the side that deals best with complexity and chaos.

For a good summary of Sperry's ideas on this topic, especially as it applies to creative thinking, see Chapter 3 of Drawing on the Right Side of the Brain, *by Betty Edwards [EDWARDS 89].*

As the video game industry continues to grow, there is continued pressure for "bigger, better, and more" in every aspect of a game's design—more features, more user customization, more content, more genre-blending, and more complexity. At its best, ad hoc testing allows you as a tester to explore what, at times, can appear to be an overwhelmingly complex game design.

Ad hoc testing also presents you with an opportunity to test the game as you would play it. What type of gamer are you? Do you like to complete every challenge in every level and unlock every unlockable? Do you like to rush or build up? Do you favor a running game or a passing game? Do you rabbit through levels or explore them leisurely? Ad hoc testing allows you to approach the game as a whole and to test it according to whatever style of play you prefer. (For an expanded discussion of player types, see Chapter 10, "Cleanroom Testing.")

"Fresh Eyes"

Fatigue, carelessness, and apathy are all enemies of good game testing. Those testers who must exercise the same part of a game repeatedly are most at risk, but over the course of a long project, sooner or later each team member is likely to suffer from one condition or another. It's very easy for testers to become "snow blind," a state in which you've been looking at the same assets for so long that you can no longer recognize anomalies as they appear. You need a break.

Ad hoc testing can allow you to explore modes and features of the game that are beyond your primary area of responsibility. Depending on the manner in which your project is managed, you as a tester will perhaps be assigned to one specific area, mode, feature, or section of the game. All the test suites you perform on each build might focus on that specific area. Ad hoc testing allows you to move beyond to other areas, and allows other testers to explore your area, without a test suite to guide them.

This method can include the following:

- Assigning members of the multiplayer team to play through the single-player campaign

- Assigning campaign testers to skirmish or multiplayer mode

- Assigning the config/compatibility/install tester to the multiplayer team

- Assigning testers from another project entirely to spend a day (or part of a day) on your game

- Asking nontesters from other parts of the company to play the game (see the section "Gameplay Testing" later in this chapter)

The sidebar "Who Turned the Lights On?" tells about a case in point.

Who Turned the Lights On?

A venerable PC games publisher operated a handful of test labs in its various studios around the country, and the local test managers often would send builds of their current projects to each other for ad hoc testing and "idiot checking."

When one test manager handed the latest build of another studio's Formula One-type racing game to two of his testers, he was surprised to see them back in his office minutes later. "Crashed it already!" they proudly reported.

"How?" the manager cried. "You've barely had time to get past the main menu!"

"We turned the headlights on!"

As you might expect, the default time in the default track in the default mode was "day." When the two testers started their race in this mode, they turned their car's headlights on "just to see what happens." The game crashed instantly.

Needless to say, this counterintuitive pair of settings (time = day and headlights = on) was added to the combinatorial tables by the chastened, but wiser, test lead.

By performing ad hoc testing, you can put fresh eyes on various parts of the game to find previously overlooked issues; and using ad hoc testing early will quickly help to reveal any lingering deficiencies in your test plans, combinatorial tables, and test flow diagrams.

The "fresh eyes" concept is applicable to structured testing as well. It's wise to have testers rotate the specific suites they're responsible for periodically—even every build.

Directed Testing Makes Order Out of Chaos

Ad hoc testing is a natural complement to structured testing, but it is by no means a substitute for it. Whether you have been given a specific assignment by your test lead or you're playing through the single-player campaign "just to see what happens," your testing should be documented, verifiable, and worthwhile.

Set Goals and Stick to Them

Before you begin, you should have a goal. It need not (and should not) be as complex or as well thought out as the test cases and test suites discussed earlier. You need to know where you're going so you don't waste your (and the project's) time, however. Briefly write out your test goal before you launch the game.

Whether you actually achieve the goal of your free testing is less important. If, in the course of trying to reach your goal, you stumble upon a defect you hadn't intended to find, that's great. That is what free testing is all about.

This goal can be very simple, but it must be explicit. Here are some examples:

- How far can I play in story mode?

- Can I play a full game by making only three-point shots?

- Is there a limit to the number of turrets I can build in my base?

- Can I deviate from the strategy suggested in the mission briefing and still win the battle?

- Is there anywhere in the level I can get my character stuck?

If you're leading a multiplayer test, let all the other testers know the purpose of the game session before it starts. Successful multiplayer testing requires communication, coordination, and cooperation, even if it seems that the testers are merely running around the level trying to shoot each other. In most circumstances, one tester should direct all of the other players in order to reach an outcome successfully, which can often be "as difficult as herding kittens." If one tester in a multiplayer test loses sight of the aim of the test, the amount of time wasted is multiplied by the number of testers in the game. Don't let your team fall into this trap.

In your testing career, avoid the use of the verb "to play" when you refer to game testing. This will help to counter the widely held notion that your department "just plays games for a living." It will also help to reinforce to your test team that your work is just that, work. Remember: the first time you play through a game, you're playing. The fortieth time, you're working.

If You're Not Recording, You're Not Testing

You should continually take notes as you're testing through the game. Game designer Sid Meier (*Civilization*) has said that good games are made up of "interesting choices." It is imperative that you keep track of these choices—writing down which options you choose, paths you take, weapons you equip, plays you call, and so on—in a very meticulous and diligent manner. In so doing, when you encounter a defect, you will be better able to come up with a reproducible path.

Documentation could be difficult when you're in the middle of a 12-trick chain in a *Tony Hawk*-style stunt game. That's where video capture becomes an almost indispensable test tool. The easiest means of accomplishing this—although the equipment might seem antiquated—is with videotape. Looping a VCR into your hardware configuration, and giving each tester a number of blank VHS tapes, will allow them to have a visual record of every move they make in the game. PC games can be captured with such third-party tools as Fraps (*www.fraps.com*) or Camtasia Studio (*www.techsmith.com/camtasia/*). The drawback to using video capture software rather than videotape is that you run the risk of taxing system resources during the game's runtime, thereby creating defects or lower performance benchmarks than you would normally experience without video capture software running simultaneously on the system.

Testing video should not become a crutch, or an excuse for less-than-diligent work on the part of the tester. It should serve as a research tool and a last-resort means of reporting a defect. Use the following steps as a guide:

1. Start the VCR (or capture software) and press the record button before you start the game. (It's too easy to forget, otherwise.)

2. When you come to a defect you can't reproduce, rewind the tape, study the tape, and then show it to your test lead and colleagues to discuss what could have caused the bug and whether anyone else has seen the same behavior in similar circumstances.

3. If you absolutely, positively, cannot reproduce the defect, copy a clip of the video to an .AVI file or other digital format. This will allow you to attach the video to a bug report, email it to the developer, or even keep it on your computer for reference.

4. Once you've filled up a VHS tape, replace it with a fresh one in your VCR. Keep the old tape in a safe spot for a couple of days, however, in case you need to refer to it. In the case of video capture files, which tend to be very large, you should establish some network backup protocol to prevent your local hard drive from filling up with gameplay captures.

5. It's generally safe to record over old VHS tapes, or to purge old capture files, once the next build enters test.

Free testing should have clear goals. The work done should be documented (via video) and documentable (through clear, concise, reproducible bug reports). It should also be worthwhile. The following are but a few of the common pitfalls you should avoid when free testing:

- Competing with other testers in multiplayer games. It's not about your individual score or win/loss record, it's about delivering a good product.

- Competing against the AI (or yourself) in single-player games.

- Spending a great deal of time testing features that could be cut. You might be made aware that a certain mode or feature is "on the bubble," that is, in danger of being eliminated from the game. Adjust your free testing focus accordingly.

- Testing the most popular features of the game. Communicate frequently with your test lead and colleagues so you can stay current with what areas, features, and modes have been covered (and re-covered) already. Focus your time on the "unexplored territory" of the game.

- Spending a disproportionate amount of time testing features that are infrequently used. You could be wasting time spending day after day exploring every nook and cranny of the map editor in your RTS, for example. Only about 15% of all users typically ever enter a map editor, and fewer than 5% actually use it to create maps. You want those players to have a good experience, but not if it places the other 85% of your players at risk.

Avoid Groupthink

Because ad hoc testing depends on the instincts, tastes, and prejudices of the individual tester, it's important as a test manager to create an environment in which testers feel free to think differently from one another.

Gamers are not a uniform, homogenous group; your test lab shouldn't be, either. If you've staffed your lab with nothing but self-identified "hardcore" gamers, you won't find all the bugs, nor will you ship the best product.

Groupthink is a term coined by social psychologist Irving Janis to describe a situation in which flawed decisions or actions are taken because a group under pressure often sees decay in its "mental efficiency, reality testing, and moral judgment" [JANIS 82]. One common aspect of group-think is a tendency toward self-censorship—where individuals within a group fail to voice doubts or dissent out of a fear of being criticized, ostra-cized, or worse. This is a danger in game testing because the majority of people who aggressively seek game tester jobs are men in their early 20s—young enough that pressure to conform to the peer group is still very strong. (For more information on groupthink, see *Groupthink: Psychological Studies of Policy Decisions and Fiascoes (Second Edition)*, by Irving Janis [JANIS 82].)

TIP

Turn your hardcore gamers into hardcore testers. Hardcore gaming is not the same as hardcore testing. So-called "hardcore" gamers are generally a masochistic lot—they willingly pay for games weeks and months before they're even released; they gladly suffer through launch week server overload problems; they love to download patches. Use the methods described in this book to get them to understand that bug-fixing patches should be the exception, rather than the rule. All it takes is careful test planning, design, and execution.

You perhaps will encounter attitudes in your test lab such as:

- "Everybody has broadband, so we don't need to test modem play."

- "Nobody likes the L.A. Clippers, so I won't test using them as my team."

- "Everybody played *StarCraft*, so we don't need to test the tutorial in our own RTS."

- "Nobody likes CTF (capture the flag) mode, so we don't need to spend much time on it."

- "Nobody uses melee weapons, so I'll just use guns."

Your job as a tester, and as a test manager, is to be aware of your and your team's pets and pet peeves, and to create an atmosphere in which a variety of approaches are discussed and respected freely and frequently. Cultivate and encourage different types of play styles. Recruit sports gamers. Recruit casual and nongamers. Foster diversity.

Testing as Detective Work

The second broad category of ad hoc testing is directed testing. You could best describe this method as "detective testing," because of its specific, investigative nature. The simplest form of directed testing answers very specific questions, such as:

- Does the new compile work?

- Can you access all the characters?

- Are the cut scenes interruptible?

- Is saving still broken?

The more complex type of directed testing becomes necessary when testers find a major defect that is difficult to seemingly impossible to reproduce. The tester has "broken the game," but can't figure out how she or he did it. As with a good homicide case, the tester finds himself with a body (the bug) and an eyewitness (himself or other testers). Unlike a homicide case, the focus is not on "whodunit." The perpetrator is a defect in the code. The focus is on "howdithappen?"

Directed testing commonly begins when one or more testers report a "random" crash in the game. This can be very frustrating, because it often delays running complete test suites and a significant amount of time could be spent restarting the application and re-running tests. Unstable code, especially in the later phases of the project, can be very stressful. Again, remember Rule #1: Don't Panic. You'll need your wits about you so that you can do your best detective work. Is your "random" crash a lone crime of passion, or have you found the work of a "serial killer"?

> *"Random" crashes are seldom truly random. Use directed testing
> and the scientific method in order to eliminate uncertainty along
> your path to being able to reproduce the bug often enough so that
> you can get the development team to find and fix it.*

!
TIP

How to Be a Repro Man (or Woman)

One of the most critical bits of information in any bug report is the *rate of reproduction*. In a defect tracking database, this field might be called (among other things) *frequency, occurrence rate, "happens,"* or *"repro" rate*. All these various terms are used to describe the same thing.

NOTE
Reproduction rate *can be defined as the rate at which, following the steps described in its bug report,* anyone *will be able to reproduce a defect.*

This information is generally expressed as a percentage ranging from 100% to "once," but this can be misleading. Assume, for example, that you find a defect during the course of your free testing. After a little research, you narrow down the steps to a reproducible path. You follow those steps and get the bug to happen again. You could, reasonably, report the defect as occurring 100% of the time—you tried the steps twice and it happened both times. It could be just as likely that the bug is only reproducible 50% of the time or less, however, and you just got lucky, as though you had flipped a penny and got it to land heads-up twice in a row.

For this reason, many QA labs report the repro rate as the number of observed occurrences over the number of attempts (for example, "8 out of 10"). This information is far more useful and accurate, because it allows your test lead, the project manager, and anyone else on the team to evaluate how thoroughly the bug has been tested. It also helps to keep you honest about the amount of testing you've given the defect before you write your report. How fair is it for you report that a crash bug happens "once" if you tried to reproduce it only once? If you want to maintain your credibility as a member of the test team, you won't make a habit of this.

On the other hand, with certain defects, even a relatively novice tester can be certain that a bug occurs 100% of the time without iterative testing. Bugs relating to fixed assets, such as a typo in in-game text, can safely be assumed to occur 100% of the time.

The word "anyone" is critical to the above definition of *reproduction rate*. A defect report is not very helpful if the tester who found the bug is the only one able to re-create it. Because videogame testing is often skill-based, it is not uncommon to encounter a defect in a game (especially a sports, fighting, platforming, or stunt game) that can only be reproduced by one tester, but that tester can reproduce the bug 100% of the time. In an ideal situation, that tester will collaborate closely with other members of the team so that they can zero in on a path that will allow others to recreate the bug.

If this is not possible due to time or other resource constraints, be prepared to send a video clip of the defect to the development team or, in worst cases, send the tester to the developer to do a live demonstration of the bug. This is very costly and time consuming because, in addition to any travel expenses, the project is also paying for the cost of having the tester away from the lab (and not testing) for a period of time.

In summary, the more reproducible a bug is, the more likely it is that it will be fixed. So always strive to be a "repro man."

The Scientific Method

It's no coincidence that the room where game testers work is often called a *lab*. Like most laboratories, it's a place where the *scientific method* is used both to investigate and to explore. The scientific method consists of the following steps:

1. Observe some phenomenon.

2. Develop a theory—a *hypothesis*—as to what caused the phenomenon.

3. Use the hypothesis to make a prediction; for example, *if I do this, it will happen again*.

4. Test that prediction by retracing the steps in your hypothesis.

5. Repeat steps 3 and 4 until you are reasonably certain your hypothesis is true.

These steps provide the structure for any investigative directed testing. Assume you've encountered a quirky defect in a PC game that seems very hard to reproduce. Perhaps a condition that breaks a script, gets your character stuck in the geometry of the level, causes the audio to drop out suddenly, or a complete crash to your PC's desktop. Here's what you do:

First, review your notes. Quickly jot down any information about what you were doing when the defect occurred, while it's still fresh in your mind. Review the video. Determine as best you can the very last thing you were doing in the game before it crashed.

Second, process all this information and make your best educated guess as to what specific combination and order of inputs could have caused the crash. Before you can retrace your steps, you have to determine what they were. Write down the input path you think most likely caused the crash.

Third, read over the steps in your path until you are satisfied with them. You guess that if you repeat them, the defect will occur again.

Fourth, reboot your computer, restart the game, and retrace your steps. Did you get the crash to occur again? If you did, great!

Fifth, write it up. If you didn't recreate the bug, change one (and only one) step in your path. Try the path again, and so on, until you successfully re-create the defect.

Unfortunately, games can be so complex that this process can take a very long time if you don't get help. Don't hesitate to discuss the problem with your test lead or fellow testers. The more information you can share, the more brainstorming you can do, the more "suspects" you can eliminate, and the sooner you'll nail the bug.

GAMEPLAY TESTING

Gameplay testing (or "play testing") is entirely different from the types of testing discussed so far in this book. The previous chapters have concerned themselves with the primary question of game testing: Does the game work? Play testing concerns itself with a different but arguably more important question: Does the game work *well*?

The difference between these two questions is obvious. The word "well" implies a substantial amount in a mere four letters. The answer to the first question is binary; the answer is either yes or no. The answer to the second question is far from binary because of its subjective nature. It can lead to many other questions:

1. *Is the game too easy?*

2. *Is the game too hard?*

3. *Is the game easy to learn?*

4. *Are the controls intuitive?*

5. *Is the interface clear and easy to navigate?*

And the most important question of all:

6. *Is the game* fun?

Unlike the other types of testing covered thus far, gameplay testing concerns itself with matters of judgment, not fact. As such, it is some of the most difficult testing you can do.

A Balancing Act

Balance is one of the most elusive concepts in game design, yet it is also one of the most important. Balance refers to the game achieving a point of equilibrium between various—usually conflicting—goals:

- Challenging, but not frustrating
- Easy to get into, but deep enough to compel you to stay
- Simple to learn, but not simplified
- Complex, but not baffling
- Long, but not too long

Balance can also refer to a state of rough equality between different competing units in a game:

- Melee fighters vs. ranged fighters
- Rogues vs. warlocks
- Sniper rifles vs. rocket launchers
- The Covenant vs. Humanity
- Ken vs. Ryu
- Plants vs. Zombies

The test team might be asked by the development team or project manager for balance testing at any point in the project life cycle.

It is often prudent to suggest delaying any serious consideration of balance until at least Alpha, because it is hard to form useful opinions about a game if key systems are still being implemented.

Once the game is ready for gameplay testing, it is important for test feedback to be presented in as specific, organized, and detailed a manner as any other defect report. Some project managers will perhaps ask you to report such balance issues as bugs in the bug database; others will perhaps ask the test lead to keep gameplay and balance feedback separate from defects. In either case, express your gameplay observations so that they are presented as based in fact, and hence, sound authoritative.

Let's examine some feedback collected from testers during balance testing on *Battles Realms*, a PC real-time strategy game (RTS) developed by Liquid Entertainment. It became clear very early in the course of play testing that the Lotus Warlock unit was overpowered. One tester wrote:

```
Lotus Warlocks do too much damage and need to be nerfed.
```

If you've spent any time on Internet message boards, comments like this should look very familiar. The tester is not specific. How much damage is too much? Relative to what? If *nerfed* means "made less powerful," how much less? 50%? 50 points? The development team is not very likely to take this comment seriously, thinking it's an impulsive, emotional reaction. (It so happens that it was. The tester had just been on the receiving end of a warlock rush.)

```
Lotus Warlocks should have a five-second cooldown added
to their attack.
```

This tester is overly specific. He has identified a problem (overpowered warlocks) and gone too far by appointing himself game designer and declaring that the solution is a five-second cooldown (that is, a delay of five seconds between the end of a unit's attack and the beginning of its next attack). This comment presumes three things: that the warlocks are indeed overpowered, that the designers agree that the best solution is to implement a cooldown, and that the code has been written (or can be written) to support a cooldown between attacks. The development team is likely to bristle at this presumption (even if it is a viable solution).

```
Lotus Warlocks are more powerful than the other three
races' highest-level unit. Their attack does approxi-
mately 10% more damage than the Dragon Samurai, Serpent
Ronin, and Wolf clan Werewolf. They get three attacks in
the same time it takes the other clans' heavy units to
do two attacks. Players who choose to play as the Lotus
Clan win 75% of their games, frustrating the non-Lotus
players.
```

This comment is specific and fact-based. It gives the producers and designers enough information to start thinking about rebalancing the units. It does not, however, suggest how the problem should be solved.

Interview

Determining what emotions a player is feeling during a game is a very important part of play testing, says Karen McMullan, who worked as a content designer on some of Ensemble Studio's biggest games (among them *Age of Mythology*, *Age of Empires III*, and *Halo Wars*).

 "The most useful thing for me as a designer is for you to tell me what you're feeling. What you're thinking about. What decisions you made, and why." Ms. McMullan suggests expressing gameplay feedback by "leading with a feeling and following it up with a reason. 'I was frustrated because my spearmen lost to chariots. Infantry are supposed to beat cavalry, right?' for instance." (Permission Karen McMullan)

"It's Just a Suggestion"

Play testing occurs constantly during defect testing. Because testers are not robots, they will always be forming opinions and making judgments, however unconscious, about the game they are testing. Occasionally, a tester will feel inspired to suggest a design change. In some labs, these are called "suggestion bugs," and are frequently ignored. Because bugs stress out programmers, artists, and project managers, they rarely appreciate the bug list being cluttered up with *suggestion bugs* or "severity S" defects.

A far more successful method of making your voice heard as a tester, if you're convinced you've got a valuable (and reasonable) idea for a design change, is the following:

1. Ask yourself whether this is a worthwhile change. "Zorro's hat should be blue," is not a worthwhile change.

2. Express your idea in the positive. "The pointer color is bad," is a far less helpful comment than, "Making the pointer green would make it easier to see."

3. Sleep on it. It might not seem like such a good idea in the morning.

4. Discuss it with your fellow testers. If they think it's a good idea, then discuss it with your test lead.

5. Ask your test lead to discuss it with the project manager or lead designer.

6. If your test lead convinces the development team that your idea has merit, at that point you might be asked to enter the suggestion into the defect database as a bug so that it can be tracked like any other change. Only do this if you are asked to do so.

Testers often have their suggested design tweaks incorporated into games by using this process—discussing the idea, getting the team to buy in, and communicating it to the developers outside of the bug database.

Making a Game Easy Is Hard Work

One element of game balance that becomes the most difficult to pin down late in the development cycle is, ironically, *difficulty*. Games take months and years to develop. By the time a game enters full-bore testing, the game testers will likely have completed the game more often than even the most ardent fan. The design and development team might have been playing the game for more than a year. Over the course of game development, the following take place:

- Skills improve with practice. If you couldn't grind a rail for more than 10 feet when you got the first test build of an action sports game, you can now grind for hours and pull off 20-trick combos without breaking a sweat.

- AI patterns, routes, and strategies are memorized. The behaviors of even the most sophisticated AI opponents become predictable as you spend weeks playing against them.

- Puzzles stop being puzzling. In adventure games or other types of games with hide-and-seek puzzle elements, once you learn how to solve a puzzle or where an item is hidden, it's impossible to unlearn it.

- Tutorials stop tutoring. It's very difficult to continue to evaluate how effective a lesson is if you've already learned the lesson.

- Jokes become stale.

- What was once novel becomes very familiar—almost boring. (See the discussion of "Fresh Eyes," earlier in this chapter.)

The upside of all this is that, on release day, the development and test teams are the best players of their own game on the planet. This won't last long, though, so you should enjoy "schooling" new players online while you can.

The downside is that you (and the rest of the project team) lose your ability to objectively evaluate difficulty as the game approaches release. Nothing of what is supposed to be fresh and new to a player seems fresh and new to you. That is why you need another set of fresh eyes: outside gameplay testers.

External Testing

External testing begins with resources outside of the test and development teams, but still inside your company. These opinions and data can come from the marketing department, as well as other business units. It's a good idea to have everyone who is willing, from the CFO to the part-time receptionist, gameplay test the game if there are questions that remain to be answered.

Here we must be careful to keep in mind Dr. Werner Heisenberg's warning that "The act of observing something changes the reality observed." Even small children are aware they're participating in a focus group or play test. Because they (or their adult counterparts) are often eager to please, they might tell you what they think you want to hear. Entire books have been written on how to manage this problem with consumer research.

(For more information on managing problems with consumer research, see Sudman and Wansink, *Consumer Panels* [SUDMAN 02].)

Although outside gameplay testing and opinion gathering is an effort typically initiated by the development or design teams, it is often implemented and managed by the test team.

Subject Matter Testing

If your game takes place in the real world, past or present, the development team will perhaps wisely choose to have subject matter experts review the game for accuracy. See the sidebar, "Testing for Realism," about how real-life input from experienced fighter pilots enhanced the development of a game.

Testing for Realism

During the development of the PC jet fighter simulator *Flanker*, producers at the publisher, SSI, used the Internet to pull together a small group of American and Russian fighter pilots who were given Beta builds of the game. Their feedback about the realism of the game, from the feel of the plans to the Russian-language labels on the cockpit dials, proved invaluable.

These experts posted their comments to a password-protected message board, and their feedback was carefully recorded, verified, and passed on to the development team. The game was released to very good reviews and was given high marks for its realistic creation of Soviet-era fighter planes.

Such an expert panel tends to be relatively small and easy to manage. It's much more challenging to manage a mass Beta test effectively.

External Beta Testing

External Beta testing can give you some very useful data. It can also give you a ton of useless data if the testing is not managed properly.

There are two types of Beta testing: closed and open. *Closed* Beta occurs first and is carefully controlled. Closed Beta testers are screened carefully and usually have to answer many questions before they are accepted into the Beta test. These questions can range from the technical specifications of their computer to which specific games they've played recently.

The simplest type of closed Beta testing occurs on console or other offline platforms. Testers are recruited and sent a Beta build of the game that is playable on consumer equipment. After the testers play the game, they are asked to complete an online questionnaire or to participate in a message board discussion. They could also be invited to report any bugs they might find.

Open Beta occurs after closed Beta concludes. Open Beta is open to all who are interested in participating. Although developers will still solicit some level of gameplay feedback from this much larger group, their role is to load test the network code and shake out such items as the login system, matchmaking, overall network stability, the in-game economy, and so on.

Although open Beta testers won't run test cases, they could report defects, in addition to providing gameplay feedback. Most Beta test managers will host a bug reporting site that allows Beta testers to report defects, make comments, and ask questions.

Besides playing the game the way it would "normally" be played, here are some other strategies you can adopt as an individual Beta tester:

- Try to create infinite point-scoring, money-making, or experience-producing strategies.
- Try to find ways to get stuck in the game environment, such as a pinball bouncing forever between two bumpers or an adventurer to falls into a river and can't get out.
- Spend some time in every feature, mode, or location provided in the game.
- Spend all of your time in one feature, mode, or location, and fully explore its options and functions.
- Try to find ways to access prohibited modes or locations.
- See what happens when you try to purchase, acquire, or use items and abilities that were designed for characters at a level much higher than yours.
- Try to accomplish something "first" in the game, such as becoming the first "maxed-out" character, the first to enter a particular town, the first to win a match, the first to form a clan, and so on.

- Wear, wield, and activate as many stat-increasing items as you can at one time, such as armor or power-ups.
- Try to be the player with the "most" of something in the game, such as wins, points, money, trophies, or vassals.

Likewise, you can conspire with other Beta testers to create situations that might not have been foreseen by the game developers, or which were impossible for them to test, such as:

- Get as many people as you can to show up in the same location in the game.
- Get as many people as you can to log into the game at the same time.
- Get as many people as you can to join the same match at the same time.
- Get as many people as you can to send you an in-game message at the same time.
- Create an in-game chat group with as many people as possible.
- Get multiple people to try to give you items at the same time.
- Get as many people as you can to stand within range of your "area of effect" spell.
- Get as many people as you can to cast stat increasing (or decreasing) spells on you.

Who Decides?

Ultimately, decisions that relate to changing the design, rebalancing, adding (or cutting) features, even delaying the release to allow more time for "polish" are not made by game testers. The testers' role is to supply the appropriate decision makers and stakeholders with the best facts and advice they can, so that the best decisions can be made.

Summary

Ad hoc testing is the mode of testing that best enables you to explore the game, wandering through it as you would a maze. There are two main types of ad hoc testing. The first is *free testing*, which allows the professional game tester to "depart from the script" and improvise tests on the fly.

The second is *directed testing*, which is intended to solve a specific problem or to find a specific solution. Gameplay testing focuses on the more subjective areas of player feelings and the "fun factor." External testing can be conducted for a variety of reasons, including gameplay feedback, but external testers—being nonprofessionals—should be monitored closely and their feedback scrutinized carefully so that only the best and most useful information is surfaced to the development team.

Exercises

1. It's a good idea to keep the same tester performing the same test cases for the length of a project. True or False?

2. Why is it unwise for game testers to refer to the work they do as "playing?"

3. Discuss the differences (in both method and results) between free testing and gameplay testing.

4. What are two methods of expressing a defect's reproduction rate?

5. You and seven other testers jump into a deathmatch session of the online shooter you're testing. Once the game starts, it's a free-for-all, with each tester competing to win the session. Is this gameplay testing or ad hoc testing? Why?

6. You've been assigned to test the gameplay of a *Marvel vs. Capcom*-type fighting game and suspect that one of the fighters seems significantly weaker than the others. What ad hoc tests can you perform in order to confirm and quantify your suspicion?

CHAPTER 13

DEFECT TRIGGERS

In This Chapter

- Game operating regions
- Six types of defect triggers
- Classifying defects
- Adding defect triggers to test designs

Orthogonal Defect Classification (ODC) includes a set of Defect Triggers to categorize the way defects are caused to appear. These same triggers can be used to classify tests as well as defects. Test suites that do not account for each of the triggers will be incapable of revealing all of the defects in the game.

OPERATING REGIONS

Game operation can be broken down into three stages: Game Start, In-Game, and Post-Game. These regions don't just apply to the game as a whole. They can also be mapped to discrete experiences within the game, such as new missions, seasons, or levels. There is also a Pre-Game region in which the game environment—hardware, operating system, and so on—is operational but the game has not been started. Figure 13.1 shows the relationship of these operating regions.

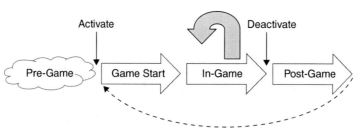

FIGURE 13.1 Game software operating regions.

Pre-Game Operating Region

The Pre-Game region represents the period that precedes the use of the game. For consoles, this would be the time prior to inserting the game disk, or while browsing in the lobby to choose which game to play. On PCs and mobile phones, this is the period in time before you launch the game app. Cartridge-based handhelds will also have an operational mode that is used prior to the insertion of the game cartridge. In each of these cases, the user can change settings and do things with the device that will potentially impact the subsequent operation of your game.

Game Start Operating Region

The Game Start region accounts for operations that are performed from the time the player starts the game until the time the game is actually ready to be played. Some activities that take place during this time can be interrupted, such as cinematic sequences that provide an introduction or highlights of the game's features. Other activities, such as a screen displaying the "loading" progress, cannot be accelerated or interrupted. The game software also performs activities that are essential to the proper operation of the game but are not visible to the player. At the very end of this process, the game could be in a "ready" state, during which it is waiting for the player to hit a button or key in order to enter the game.

In-Game Operating Region

The In-Game region covers all of the actions you could possibly make when playing the game. Some functions can be performed only once during the course of the game, whereas others can be repeated throughout the game. There are also functions that depend on the player meeting some condition before they can occur. Games that incorporate nonplayer characters (NPCs) also manage and control these resources during this operating period.

Post-Game Operating Region

The player can end the game or a gaming session a number of ways. Quitting without saving requires less processing than when saving. The player is often given the opportunity to save character data and progress before the game terminates itself. Games played on portable devices can be ended by turning off the device. If the device's Off switch is under software control, the game software can perform save and shutdown operations prior to killing power.

Story-based games treat the user to a final cinematic sequence and roll credits when users reach the end of the story. Some games unlock new experiences for the player who reaches the end so he can continue to enjoy the game when going back through it a second time. This could activate code that is not exercised at all until the first time the game is completed.

THE TRIGGERS

Six Defect Triggers span the four game operating regions. These triggers describe ways to cause distinct categories of game defects to show up during testing. Together, these triggers account for all of the possible defects that can occur.

The Configuration Trigger

Some game configuration takes place in the Pre-Game region, prior to running the game. This includes device or environment settings that are established before running the game, such as game platform software versions. Date and time, screen resolution, system audio volume, operating system version, patches, and language settings are all examples of Configuration triggers. Figure 13.2 shows the many video configuration settings available for *Mass Effect 2* on the PC.

Mass Effect 2 Configuration Utility

File   Mass Effect 2   System   Help

Mass Effect 2

Video

This page contains the Mass Effect 2 video settings.

Windowed	Fullscreen
Window Mode	Normal
Aspect Ratio	Normal (4:3)
Resolution	800 x 600
High Quality Bloom	Off
Film Grain	Off
Motion Blur	Off
Dynamic Shadows	Off
Light Environment Shadows	Off
Number Of Cinematic Lights	1
Use Spherical Harmonic Lighting	Off
Anisotropic Filtering	Default

Mass Effect 2
- Welcome
- Video
- Audio
- Game
- Save Games

System
- Summary
- System
- Storage
- Display
- Sound
- Network
- Platform

Welcome to the Mass Effect 2 Configuration Utility!

FIGURE 13.2 *Mass Effect 2* PC Video Configuration settings.

Configuration also involves external devices that can be used with the game platform. Game controllers, keyboards, mice, speakers, monitors, and network connections are all parts of the test configuration. These devices typically connect to the game console's I/O (Input/Output) ports through various connectors or wireless receivers. An XBox 360 example is shown in Figure 13.3.

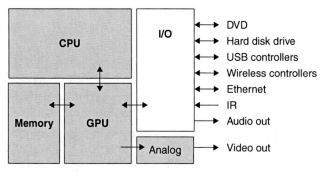

FIGURE 13.3 XBox 360 I/O Interfaces.

NOTE *To learn more about the interfaces and overall architecture of the Xbox 360 system, an article is available online at the IEEE Digital Library [IEEE 06].*

The nature of these external devices is that they each have their own settings, properties (for example, version), and physical connection. Even game controllers can have additional devices attached to them. A Nintendo Wii remote can be used in conjunction with a Nunchuck, guitar controller, Balance Board, WiiWheel™ or MotionPlus accessory.

Disconnecting one or more devices during gameplay is a type of configuration change. Unfortunately for developers, the game software is unable to do anything to prevent the user from connecting or disconnecting external devices during gameplay, or from changing settings or software versions on the game platform. Configuration changes can occur in any of the game software operating regions.

Connecting a device could be done to correct an accidental disconnection ("The dog kicked the wireless router plug out of the wall!"), replace batteries, change out a faulty device, or add a new capability, such as a headset for voice control. These scenarios should be anticipated by the game design and incorporated into the game tests.

Configuration possibilities shouldn't be excluded from testing just because your initial response is "Why would anyone ever do that?" Recognize, when you have this kind of reaction, that you should test that area vigorously. It is likely that other people would have reacted similarly and didn't bother to find out what would happen in that case.

Configuration failures might show up immediately as a result of the configuration operation or at some later time when a game operation relies on the new configuration. Seemingly unrelated capabilities might also fail as a side-effect of a configuration change.

The Startup Trigger

The Startup trigger is utilized by attempting operations while some game function is in the process of starting up, or immediately after that while code values and states are in their initial conditions. This could be a highly noticeable activity, such as a "Loading please wait…" screen or something that's behind the scenes, such as loading data for a room you've just entered.

Particular code vulnerabilities exist during the startup period. These do not present themselves at any other time in the game. Code variables are being initialized. Graphics information is being loaded, buffered, and rendered. Information is read from and/or written to disk.

As an example, here is a summary of the events that take place in *Unreal Engine 3* in order to start up a new level [UNREAL 11]:

1. The GameInfo's *InitGame()* event is called

2. The GameInfo's *SetGrammar()* event is called

3. All Actors' *PreBeginPlay()* events are called

4. All Actors' zones are initialized

5. All Actors' *PhysicsVolumes* are initialized

6. All Actors with *bScriptInitialized=false* have their *PostBeginPlay()* functions called

7. The *SetInitialState()* function is called on all actors with *bScriptInitialized=false*

8. Actors are "Attached" based on their *AttachTag, bShouldBaseOnStartup, Physics,* and world collision settings.

Startup defects are triggered by operations that take place during the Game Start period. These operations can be user-initiated or can be caused by the game platform. Interrupting any part of this sequence could mean that some essential operation will not complete its work or might not get to run at all. The Startup trigger accounts for bugs that will show up only as a result of the initial conditions that result from the game's initialization and startup processes. That means that defects that occur the very first time you use a game capability, such as a new map, item, power-up, or spell, should also be classified as Startup defects.

The Exception Trigger

Special portions of the game code are exercised by the Exception trigger. Exception handling in a game is normally recognized by the player. Audio "bonks" or alert boxes are common ways in which an in-game problem is communicated. Some exceptions are under the control of the game, such as restricting user input choices. Other exceptions are caused by external conditions that are not under the control of the game software, such as network connection problems. Figure 13.4 shows the special alert you get when trying to play *Godville*™ if the mobile device is not connected to the Internet. Exceptions can occur in any of the game operating regions.

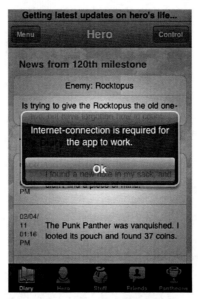

FIGURE 13.4 *Godville* connection exception alert.

The Stress Trigger

The Stress trigger tests the game under extreme conditions. These could be conditions imposed on either hardware or software resources. Memory, screen resolution, disk space, file size, and network speed are all examples of game conditions that could be stressed by users or through testing. Simply reaching a limit does not constitute a stress condition. Once stressed, the resource must be used or operated in some way for the stress behavior to reveal itself.

The Normal Trigger

Normal game operation takes place in the In-Game operating region. This refers to using the game apart from any stress, configuration, or exception conditions, similar to the way you would script a demo or describe in the user manual how the game should be played. The "normal" code is distinct from the code that handles the exceptions, the code that processes configuration changes, and the code that takes over under stressful conditions.

Most of the testing that is done uses Normal triggers. That's fine, because that is how the game will be used the vast majority of the time; testing is not just about finding defects, it also demonstrates that the game functions the way it is supposed to. Testing that uses Normal triggers almost exclusively, however, is only training the code to follow a script. It will not detect many user faults that will occur in real-life situations.

The Restart Trigger

The Restart trigger classifies a failure that occurs as a result of quitting, ending the game, turning off the game device, ejecting the game disk, or terminating the game's operation in any other way. Some games are nice about this and prompt you to save vital information before allowing you to exit a game scenario, mission, level, or ongoing battle. When ending the game, some information needs to be remembered and some forgotten. If either is done incorrectly, the player can gain an advantage or lose precious progress.

Sometimes you can notice the effects of a Restart defect during the End Game period, or you might have to wait until the next time you use the game. This is illustrated by a couple of bugs reported for the tower defense game Revenge of the Titans:

```
"When I restart level 13 (Sinus edam) (after
failing) and I click on factory, there seems to be
some sort of a bug there, and then I get a "level
failed" dialog"[REVENGE 10].
```

NOTE

```
"I've been encountering this bug, usually happens
when I restart a level many times, one time it
happened when the boss killed my base and then
died right after, or other times it just happens
out of nowhere: the level refuses to spawn any
titans, the thread level is forever low, and the
level selection has red dots but they can't be
played" [STEAM 11].
```

You can "restart" under various conditions, such as when a game takes you back to a level selection screen, or when you load a saved game after failing. Be sure to explore each of the different restart methods available for the game you are testing, and follow through by playing the game for a while, after the reloads, in order to detect any undesirable effects of the restart.

CLASSIFYING DEFECTS

You don't have to wait for your next project to start using Defect Triggers in your tests. Use keywords to help classify new or existing tests and defects. With that information you can identify where the defects are coming from and what testing is missing. Not surprisingly, many bugs that get released belong to Defect Triggers that received little attention, if any, during game testing.

When defects of a certain trigger start to show up, that's your cue to beef up the tests to use that trigger even more often.

Table 13.1 provides lists of keywords you can use to classify your defects and tests according to each of the six defect triggers.

TABLE 13.1 Defect Trigger Keywords

Trigger	Keywords
Configuration	configure, model, type, version, environment, add, remove, setup
Startup	startup, initial, first, uninitialized, creation, boot, warm-up, wake-up, loading, transition
Exception	exception, error, violation, exceeds, NULL, unexpected, recover, prevented, blocked, prohibited, unavailable
Stress	stress, load, rate, slowest, fastest, low, high, speed, capacity, limit, long, short, few, many, multiple, empty, full
Normal	normal, typical, common, usual, expected, planned, basic, default, out-of-the-box, allowed, available
Restart	restart, reset, reload, cleanup, eject, power down, ctrl-alt-del, quit

Following are some examples taken from a list of updates for *The Elder Scrolls IV: Oblivion [ELDER 11]*. Remember, missing capabilities are defects as well as game functions that don't work properly.

> "Fixed issue where stolen items would lose their stolen status if the player character was female."

Because the character gender is established prior to entering the game world, this should be identified as a Configuration issue.

> "Fixed a crash with stealing an object, exiting and immediately re-entering an interior."

In this situation, the problem only manifests when the interior location is re-entered. This should be considered a Restart fault.

> "Fixed memory leak with sitting in a chair multiple times."

The Stress keyword "multiple" is used here and it is in reference to a problem that occurs when trying to sit in a chair over and over again, so this is a Stress defect.

> "Player can no longer fast travel when paralyzed."

Fast Travel is a map-based way of traveling between landmarks in the Elder Scrolls world. Being paralyzed is not a configuration because it is a situation that occurs after the character has been configured and is active in the game world (the In-Game operating region). Neither is the fast travel ability a result of a particular configuration. This is simply a Normal defect.

> "Fixed issue where lock/unlocked states on doors would occasionally be stored incorrectly in a saved game."

In this context, locking and unlocking is the door's "life cycle" in the game world. Loading the saved game data "restarts" the player's character and the state of all of the game assets. This restart loses track of the door's proper state. The defect has been revealed by a Restart trigger.

"Improved LOD visual quality for landscape."

Problems don't just have to happen in game logic to be considered bugs. Here the level of detail of the rendered landscape was improved. The solution is not related to a particular condition or configuration of the game. This is a Normal defect.

"Fixed issue with LOD not loading in properly when entering/exiting worldspaces."

Game maps can also have a life cycle: Start Map–Use Map–Change/ Restart Map and so on. The worldspace is rendered with an undesir- able level of detail as a result of the map restart. Therefore, this defect is triggered by that Restart.

"Pickup sound effects no longer play during the loading screen."

Yet another "life cycle" reveals itself here. The cycle of examining an item: select the item to examine, pick it up, examine it, then keep it or drop it. Because the problem is tied to the "loading" screen, map this to the Startup trigger.

"Fixed an occasional crash with NPCs who were not loaded going into combat"

This is a case where the game is referencing one or more "unavailable" resources. This is an Exception trigger defect.

"In Light the Dragonfires, fixed issue where improper journal would appear if you closed the Oblivion gate."

Don't confuse a game mission or quest with "configuration." Think of a quest as a feature or function of the game. Even though this bug only appears in a particular quest, the problem was in the In-Game operating region and not dependent on any configuration. It is another Normal trigger defect.

Sometimes you will come across defects that perhaps seem to belong to more than one trigger category. An example might be the case where an exception is not handled properly during startup. What you must resolve is which situation was primarily responsible for triggering the defect. If the situation is considered only an "exception" during startup, then it is the exception that is triggering the fault. The rationale is that there is a particular piece of code that should exist to handle the exception during startup. The exception condition causes that code to execute and finds that it is missing or faulty. Conversely, if the handling of that exception is common throughout the game, and it fails to operate properly only during startup, then it is the fact that you tried it at startup that triggered the exception code not to run or to run improperly. Your responsibility as a tester is to test the handling of this exception in all operating regions of the game in order to help make this kind of determination.

DEFECT TRIGGERS AND TEST DESIGNS

Each element in the test design represents one of the Defect Triggers. Using one or more test design techniques will not by itself guarantee that all of the Defect Triggers will be sufficiently represented in your tests. It takes an explicit effort to identify appropriate triggers and to incorporate them into whatever type of test designs you produce. All of the Defect Triggers should be included either in a single test design or a set of test designs related to a specific game feature, function, or capability. If you have data from previous projects, see which triggers have been effective at finding defects and include those in your designs, as well as any others you can think of.

The effectiveness of each trigger can be measured in terms of defects per test. You can also think of this as the sensitivity of the game code to each trigger. A large defects/test number relative to other triggers tells you how to find bugs economically and could also hint at an underlying flaw in the game platform design or implementation. If you only have time or resources to run a given number of tests, running the tests for the most effective triggers will yield more defects than running the tests for the trigger that produces the fewest defects per test (usually the Normal trigger). As you continue to create and run more tests for the most effective triggers, you will saturate them and will no longer be able to find new bugs. Repeat this process to establish saturation for all of the triggers.

TUTORIAL

Combinatorial Design Trigger Examples

Let's go back to the *HALO Reach* Controller menu combinatorial table, shown in Chapter 8, "Combinatorial Testing" (Table 8.24), to see if any triggers need to be added. Look Sensitivity is tested for its default, minimum, and maximum values. The minimum and maximum values could be considered Stress values because the game is supposed to respond ("process") as slowly or as quickly as it can to the movement of the joystick. The remaining parameters have values that determine whether a capability is either on or off. None of these address a particular configuration or a situation that would apply to Startup, Restart, Exception, or Stress conditions. As a result, the majority of test values represent Normal behavior. For this test to be more effective, incorporate the missing triggers as well as any other possible Stress values.

Start by identifying Configuration resources related to the Controller options. Online players typically use a headset in conjunction with the game controller. This affects where game audio is routed—to your headset or to your game console's audio output. By design, some audio sources will continue to be routed to your main speakers and others to the headset. The controllers themselves can be wireless or wired. Each controller is sequentially assigned to unique slots on the game console. It is also possible to remove a controller during the process of selecting the options, and subsequently re-connect it in the same position or in a different one. Wireless controllers "disconnect" when going out of range from the console's wireless receiver, when their batteries run out of power, or when the player intentionally removes the batteries. Disconnecting a controller connected to an accessory could have unintended consequences, such as resetting calibration values on a racing wheel. These possibilities suggest new parameters and values to add to the combinatorial table.

The updated table is shown in Table 13.2. Because of the added complexity introduced by the new parameters and values, the Allpairs tool was used to generate this table.

TABLE 13.2 Controller Settings Combinatorial Table with Configuration Triggers

Test	Look Sensitivity	Look Inversion	Autolook Centering	Crouch Behavior	Clench Protection	Remove Controller	Replace Controller	Headset Equipped	Controller Connection
1	1	YES	YES	HOLD	ENABLE	1	1	YES	WIRED
2	3	NO	NO	TOGGLE	DISABLE	1	2	NO	WIRELESS
3	3	NO	YES	HOLD	DISABLE	2	1	YES	WIRELESS
4	1	YES	NO	TOGGLE	ENABLE	2	2	NO	WIRED
5	10	NO	YES	TOGGLE	ENABLE	3	3	YES	WIRED
6	10	YES	NO	HOLD	DISABLE	3	4	NO	WIRELESS
7	1	NO	NO	HOLD	DISABLE	4	3	YES	WIRELESS
8	3	YES	YES	TOGGLE	ENABLE	4	4	NO	WIRED
9	10	NO	NO	TOGGLE	ENABLE	1	1	NO	WIRELESS
10	10	YES	YES	HOLD	DISABLE	2	2	YES	WIRED
11	3	YES	NO	HOLD	ENABLE	3	3	NO	WIRED
12	1	NO	YES	TOGGLE	DISABLE	3	4	YES	WIRELESS
13	10	YES	NO	TOGGLE	DISABLE	4	1	YES	WIRED
14	1	YES	YES	HOLD	DISABLE	1	3	NO	WIRELESS
15	3	NO	NO	HOLD	ENABLE	2	4	YES	WIRED
16	1	NO	YES	HOLD	ENABLE	4	2	NO	WIRELESS
17	10	NO	YES	TOGGLE	ENABLE	2	3	NO	WIRELESS
18	10	YES	NO	HOLD	DISABLE	1	4	YES	WIRED
19	3	YES	YES	TOGGLE	DISABLE	3	1	NO	WIRELESS
20	1	NO	NO	TOGGLE	ENABLE	3	2	YES	WIRED

As an alternative, create a separate table to cover the configuration-related parameters and value pairs. This approach enables you to use the mostly "Normal" table as a "sanity test" and then switch over to the tables for the other triggers once the game passes the sanity tests. The Controller settings configuration table is shown in Table 13.3.

TABLE 13.3 Controller Actions Configuration Table

Test	Remove Controller	Replace Controller	Headset Equipped	Controller Connection
1	1	1	YES	WIRED
2	1	2	NO	WIRELESS
3	1	3	YES	WIRELESS
4	1	4	NO	WIRED
5	2	1	NO	WIRELESS
6	2	2	YES	WIRED
7	2	3	NO	WIRED
8	2	4	YES	WIRELESS
9	3	1	YES	WIRED
10	3	2	NO	WIRELESS
11	3	3	YES	WIRELESS
12	3	4	NO	WIRED
13	4	1	NO	WIRELESS
14	4	2	YES	WIRED
15	4	3	NO	WIRED
16	4	4	YES	WIRELESS

The next step is to seek out Exception trigger opportunities. Because the option values are selected by scrolling, there is no opportunity to enter a "wrong" value. It is perhaps possible to disrupt the selection mechanism itself, however. The A and B buttons are used for accepting the options or going back to the previous screen. Try holding down X, Y, the Left Trigger ("L"), or Right Trigger ("R") during the selection of the test values. Again, one of your options is to add a column for these values, plus the "None" choice, into a single table, as shown in Table 13.4. Although the table has grown again, these 28 cases represent pairwise coverage of 15,360 total possible combinations of these values!

TABLE 13.4 Controller Settings with Configuration and Exception Triggers (*Continued*)

Test	Look Sensitivity	Look Inversion	Autolook Centering	Crouch Behavior	Clench Protection	Remove Controller	Replace Controller	Headset Equipped	Controller Connection	Simultaneous Key
1	1	YES	YES	HOLD	ENABLE	1	1	YES	WIRED	NONE
2	3	NO	NO	TOGGLE	DISABLE	2	2	NO	WIRELESS	NONE
3	10	YES	NO	TOGGLE	ENABLE	1	2	NO	WIRED	X
4	1	NO	YES	HOLD	DISABLE	2	1	YES	WIRELESS	X
5	3	NO	YES	HOLD	ENABLE	3	3	NO	WIRED	Y
6	10	YES	YES	TOGGLE	DISABLE	4	4	YES	WIRELESS	Y
7	1	NO	NO	TOGGLE	ENABLE	3	4	YES	WIRELESS	L
8	3	YES	NO	HOLD	DISABLE	4	3	NO	WIRED	L
9	10	NO	NO	HOLD	DISABLE	1	3	YES	WIRELESS	R
10	3	YES	YES	TOGGLE	ENABLE	2	4	NO	WIRED	R
11	10	YES	NO	TOGGLE	DISABLE	3	1	NO	WIRELESS	Y
12	1	NO	YES	HOLD	ENABLE	4	2	YES	WIRED	L
13	1	YES	YES	TOGGLE	DISABLE	1	3	NO	WIRELESS	NONE
14	10	NO	NO	HOLD	ENABLE	2	4	YES	WIRED	NONE
15	3	NO	YES	TOGGLE	ENABLE	3	1	YES	WIRELESS	X

TABLE 13.4 Continued

Test	Look Sensitivity	Look Inversion	Autolook Centering	Crouch Behavior	Clench Protection	Remove Controller	Replace Controller	Headset Equipped	Controller Connection	Simultaneous Key
16	1	NO	NO	HOLD	DISABLE	1	2	YES	WIRED	Y
17	3	YES	NO	TOGGLE	DISABLE	1	1	NO	WIRED	L
18	1	NO	NO	TOGGLE	ENABLE	4	1	NO	WIRELESS	R
19	10	YES	YES	HOLD	DISABLE	3	2	NO	WIRED	X
20	10	YES	NO	HOLD	ENABLE	2	3	YES	WIRED	R
21	10	NO	YES	HOLD	DISABLE	2	4	NO	WIRELESS	L
22	3	NO	NO	TOGGLE	ENABLE	4	3	YES	WIRELESS	X
23	1	YES	NO	TOGGLE	DISABLE	3	2	YES	WIRELESS	R
24	3	YES	YES	HOLD	ENABLE	1	4	YES	WIRELESS	Y
25	10	YES	NO	HOLD	DISABLE	4	4	NO	WIRED	NONE
26	1	NO	YES	TOGGLE	ENABLE	3	3	NO	WIRED	NONE
27	1	YES	NO	TOGGLE	DISABLE	2	4	NO	WIRED	X
28	3	NO	YES	TOGGLE	ENABLE	2	2	NO	WIRELESS	Y

A potential danger in doing this is that most of your test cases will result in an exception behavior that might prevent you from observing the effects of the other test values. In Table 13.4 only six tests—1, 2, 13, 14, 25, and 26—avoid a possible input exception. A way around this is to create a separate table to isolate the exception effects, as shown in Table 13.5. The "NONE" value for the Simultaneous Key parameter is not included because it is not an Exception trigger, and it is already implicitly represented in the nonexception table for this feature.

TABLE 13.5 Controller Settings Table with Only Exception Triggers Added

Test	Look Sensitivity	Look Inversion	Autolook Centering	Crouch Behavior	Clench Protection	Simultaneous Key
1	1	YES	YES	HOLD	ENABLE	X
2	3	NO	NO	TOGGLE	DISABLE	X
3	1	NO	YES	TOGGLE	ENABLE	Y
4	3	YES	NO	HOLD	DISABLE	Y
5	10	YES	YES	TOGGLE	DISABLE	L
6	10	NO	NO	HOLD	ENABLE	L
7	1	YES	NO	TOGGLE	DISABLE	R
8	3	NO	YES	HOLD	ENABLE	R
9	10	YES	YES	HOLD	DISABLE	X
10	10	NO	NO	TOGGLE	ENABLE	Y
11	1	NO	NO	HOLD	DISABLE	L
12	3	YES	YES	TOGGLE	ENABLE	L
13	10	YES	NO	HOLD	ENABLE	R

The extreme Look Sensitivity values were identified as Stress triggers, but is there any other "stressful" operation that can be done during option selection? For this particular game, both the left analog stick and the D-Pad on the game controller can be used to scroll through the options (vertically) and choices (horizontally). Operating them simultaneously could produce interesting results. Add this to the test table by defining the Scroll Control parameter with the values of LEFT STICK, D-PAD, and BOTH. Follow the same rationale as for the previous triggers when deciding whether to add these parameters and values to a single table for this screen versus creating a separate table for this trigger.

All that's left to do now is to identify Startup and Restart triggers for your Controller settings. These particular settings are tied to individual player profiles. This presents the opportunity to test the settings for a brand new profile versus one that has already been in use. The new profile behavior is your Startup trigger. Add this to the tests as a "Profile" parameter with NEW (Startup) or EXISTING (Normal) choices.

The Controller setting selection process can be restarted in a variety of ways: go back to the previous screen without saving, eject the game disk from the console, or turn the console off. Follow up these operations by going back into the Advanced Controls screen to check for any abnormalities. Because these settings can be stored in either internal or removable memory, another way to do a "restart" is to load information previously saved to external memory back on top of your internally saved modified values. Represent these possibilities in your table with a "Re-Enter" parameter that has a possible value of NONE for the Normal trigger and BACK, EJECT, OFF, and LOAD EXTERNAL for the Restart trigger.

TFD Trigger Examples

TFD triggers are located along the flows. The Ammo TFD template, provided in Appendix D, will be used to illustrate how to incorporate all of the defect triggers into a TFD. It has a few more flows than the TFD you constructed in Chapter 11, but is it "complete" in terms of triggers? Use it in one of the *Unreal Tournament* game titles, and see what you can find.

To begin with, the template includes several Normal trigger flows, such as GetGun and GetAmmo when you have neither (NoGunNoAmmo). The same event can represent different triggers, however, depending on its context with respect to the states it's leaving and entering. For example, GetAmmo when you already have the maximum amount is a case of performing a function when a resource (ammo) is at its maximum. This qualifies as a Stress trigger. Shooting a gun with no ammo falls on the other end of the spectrum where the ammo resource is at a minimum (0). Figure 13.5 shows the Ammo TFD template with these Stress triggers highlighted.

Now how about adding a Startup trigger? The TFD Enter flow jumps right to the point where the player is active in the match. In reality, there is a "pre-game" period where the player can run around the arena before hitting the "fire" button (usually the left mouse button) to initiate the match. This is relevant to the purpose of the test because a player who runs over weapons or ammo during this time should not accumulate any items as a result.

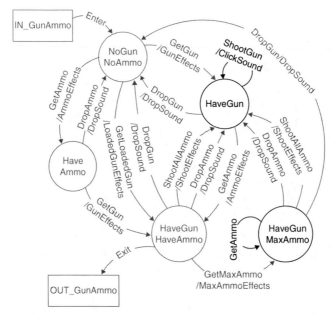

FIGURE 13.5 Ammo TFD template with Stress flows highlighted.

Represent this startup process on the TFD by performing "mitosis" on the "NoGunNoAmmo" state. That is, split it into two connected states. One state retains the original name and connections (except for the Enter flow) while the other captures the dry run and countdown behavior. Figure 13.6 shows the process of splitting this portion of the TFD.

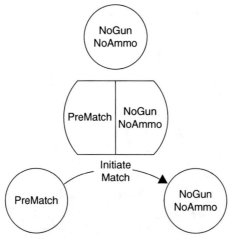

FIGURE 13.6 NoGunNoAmmo state mitosis.

The new PreMatch state can be introduced to the TFD. Start by disconnecting the Enter flow from NoGunNoAmmo and attaching it to PreMatch. Then add flows to attempt GetAmmo and GetGun during the PreMatch period. These flows are Startup triggers, as shown in Figure 13.7.

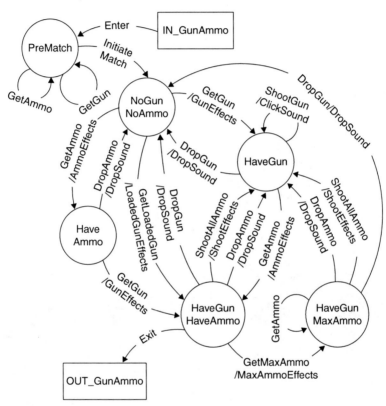

FIGURE 13.7 PreMatch state and Startup trigger flows added to Ammo TFD.

Next, add the Restart trigger to the diagram. It's possible to change your status to Spectator in the middle of a match and then join back in as a participant. Spectator mode takes your character out of the game and lets you follow players in the game while you control the camera angle. Any guns or ammo picked up prior to entering Spectator mode should be lost when you join the same match that is still in progress. Rejoining the game from Spectator mode is done instantly without the countdown timer that you get when you start the match for the very first time. Suspending and rejoining can be done at any time during the match after the initial countdown timer has expired. Add a SpectateAndJoin flow from each of the in-game states on the TFD and tie it back to NoGunNoAmmo. Don't forget the loop flow from NoGunNoAmmo back to itself. A TFD with these updates is shown in Figure 13.8.

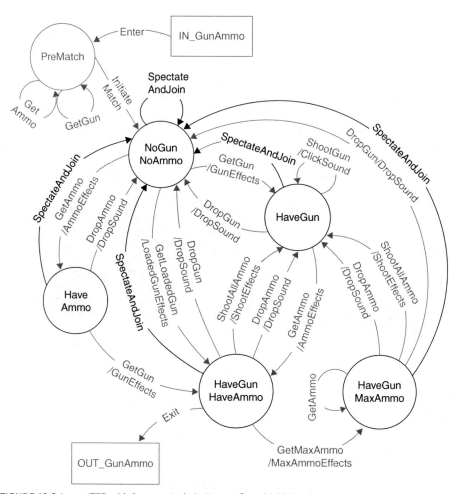

FIGURE 13.8 Ammo TFD with SpectateAndJoin Restart flows highlighted.

Note that more "pressure" is being put on the NoGunNoAmmo state with all of the flows entering and exiting. It's like a busy intersection; they tend to be much more dangerous than the ones that aren't so busy. This reflects the importance of this state to the well-being of the feature and its potential sensitivity to changes.

The TFD is getting cozy, but there are a still a few more triggers to consider. For the Exception trigger, there is an operation available to use a weapon's alternate-fire mode. Typically, the left mouse button is used for normal firing and the right mouse button for alternate firing. Some weapons, such as the Grenade Launcher, do not have an alternate firing mode. They should not fire nor decrement their ammo count when the user attempts alternate firing. This is something you can use as an Exception trigger. Because this "UnsupportedAltFire" operation will not change the ammo status of the weapon, add it as a loop on the TFD states where there is both a gun and ammo. Your result should resemble the diagram in Figure 13.9.

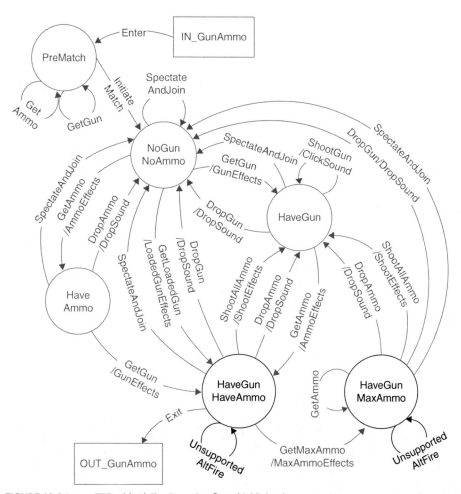

FIGURE 13.9 Ammo TFD with AltFire Exception flows highlighted.

Finally, the Configuration must be included. One of the weapon settings in the game allows the player to select an older style rendering of
certain weapons. Although this is appealing to players who owned earlier
titles in this series, it also creates an additional test responsibility. You can
check that changing the weapon rendering while the game is in progress
does not affect the amount of ammo loaded in that weapon nor produce
unwanted artifacts, such as unexpected audio or "shadow" (duplicate)
weapons. Add a ToggleWeaponSkin flow at all of the states where the player
has the weapon. Because this should not affect the ammo, these flows will
loop back into the states from which they originated. Figure 13.10 shows
the TFD with these Configuration flows.

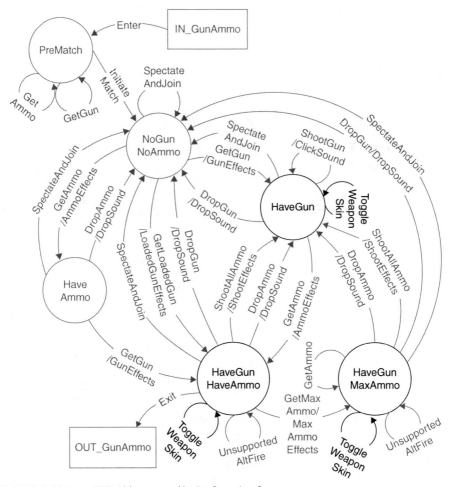

FIGURE 13.10 Ammo TFD with weapon skin Configuration flows.

Now the TFD is getting really crowded! Just remember that the same option that was presented for combinatorial tests is applicable to TFDs, test tree designs, or any other formal or informal means you use to come up with test cases. You can incorporate the triggers into a single design or create companion test designs that work together as a suite of tests to provide the trigger coverage you need.

You might also find it useful to document the intended triggers for each test element. One easy way is to provide a letter code in parentheses after the event name on each TFD flow, parameter value for combinatorial tests, or branch node for test tree designs. You can count the number of times each letter appears to see how many times each trigger is being used. It also helps you classify defects you find when running the tests. Just be aware that this carries a maintenance burden to reevaluate the trigger designation whenever you move or add new test elements to the design.

Summary

What a difference the extra triggers make in the test design! Is it more work? Yes. It's also better. You have improved the capability of this test to find defects, and you will have more confidence in your game when it passes tests that use all of the triggers. Defect Triggers were not created with any one particular test methodology in mind. They are effective whether you are testing at the beginning or the end of the project and whether you have meticulous test designs or you are just typing in test cases as you go along. If you choose not to use them, you are adding to the risk of important defects escaping into your shipping game.

Exercises

Having come this far in the book, you should be well equipped to offer your own suggestions and to contribute to your team's test strategies. The following exercises are designed to give you some practice at that.

1. Which is your favorite Defect Trigger? Why? Which one would be the most difficult for you to include in your tests, both in terms of test execution and test design?

2. Earlier in this chapter it was mentioned that both the D-Pad and Analog joystick on the game controller could be used to make the *HALO Reach* option selections. Describe how you would incorporate these choices into your test suite. Do you prefer adding them to a large single table for the feature or creating a separate smaller table focused on the option selection means? Be specific about which factors would cause you to change your answer.

3. It could be interesting to start an *Unreal Tournament* match while standing on one of the gun or ammo items. The game automatically snaps you back to the original starting point after a 3-second countdown before the action starts. Describe how you would update the Ammo TFD to include this possibility, including what effects you would check for and why.

4. Again, for the Ammo TFD, describe how you would add or change flows to represent someone playing from a PC who can fire her gun using either a joystick or the left mouse button. Treat this as a case where both the mouse and joystick are connected during the game. Also indicate which triggers are represented by this possibility.

5. Texas Hold 'Em poker has become very popular and many video games on various platforms have popped up to take advantage of the level of interest in this card game. Make a list or outline of how you would include each trigger in your testing of a hypothetical or actual Texas Hold 'Em video game. Don't stop at one example—list at least three values, situations, or cases for each of the non-Normal triggers. Remember to include tests of the betting rules—not just the mechanics and winning conditions for the hand. If you are not familiar with the rules of this card game, do a search online and read a few descriptions before you build your trigger lists.

CHAPTER 14

REGRESSION TESTING AND TEST REUSE

In This Chapter

- Distributing tests
- Defect modeling
- Test design patterns
- Combinatorial expansion

REGRESSION TESTING

*R*egression Testing is a strategy for deciding which tests to run against each version of the game. This applies to code that is under development as well as to bug-fix releases. It gets its name from the need to determine if any of the code has "regressed" (gone backward in progress) due to changes introduced in the latest build. A good strategy will minimize the number of tests you run and will still be able to help you catch newly introduced and remaining errors.

Chapter 6, "The Game Testing Process," describes the important role regression testing plays in distributing a good release. Once testing is under way, you need to be able to react in real time as the game code or assets become updated in response to bugs or change requests. You also need to be able to adjust your tests to cover new changes in the code or specs.

A-B-Cs

Regression testing needs to do more than re-run tests that have previously failed. The rationale for this is best described in "Does Code Decay? Assessing the Evidence from Change Management Data," by Alvaro Navarro. "Implicit decay is caused by changes, but code that is not changed could also decay because it's affected by changes in other code parts of the software" [NAVARRO 05, slide 7]. Every time you get handed new code to test, you're getting a combination of code that hasn't been touched, code that has intentionally changed, and code that perhaps was unintentionally affected by the changes.

One approach for dealing with code decay is to break your tests in thirds, executing a new third every time you get new code. Rather than breaking up your entire test suite into top, middle, and bottom thirds, it's better to slice each major function or feature into thirds. This helps re-establish that each feature is working correctly in every build, demonstrates that the code has not decayed, and keeps your test results from getting stale.

NOTE *For more information about decaying code see "Software Rot" at Wikipedia.com [SOFTWAREROT 11].*

Here's an example of how you could distribute your tests across a mobile card battle game where you have one screen for purchasing cards, another for assembling your deck, and another for battling with an AI opponent and determining a winner.

In this imaginary test suite, there are 40 combinatorial test cases for purchasing cards, two TFDs with a total of 20 paths for assembling your deck, and one TFD with 6 paths and 15 tests written manually to test the card battle process. Table 14.1 shows how these can be distributed into three test sets called A, B, and C.

TABLE 14.1 A-B-C Distribution of Card Battle Tests

Card Battle Feature	Test Type	"A" Tests	"B" Tests	"C" Tests
Purchase Cards	Combinatorial	13	13	14
Deck Forming	TFD	7	7	6
Resolve Battle	TFD + Manual	7	7	7

To distribute the tests even more efficiently, break them down by each design. If the three Purchase Cards combinatorial designs generate 12, 12, and 16 test cases respectively, then the "A" tests should use four tests from the first combinatorial table, four from the second, and five from the third. If the two Deck Forming TFD designs have 11 and 9 paths, respectively, then use four from the first TFD and three from the second one. Follow suit for the Resolve Battle tests. Then repeat the process for the "B" and "C" cycles so that all of the test cases are scheduled to be run across all three cycles. Table 14.2 shows a detailed breakdown and A-B-C distribution of the Purchase Cards combinatorial test cases generated by separate designs for selecting a pack to purchase, paying for the cards, and updating the card inventory.

TABLE 14.2 Detailed Distribution of Purchase Cards Combinatorial Test Cases

Test Design	A Cycle	B Cycle	C Cycle
SelectPack	Test1		
	Test2		
	Test3		
	Test4		
		Test5	
		Test6	
		Test7	
		Test8	
			Test9
			Test10
			Test11
			Test12
PayForCards	Test1		
	Test2		
	Test3		
	Test4		
		Test5	
		Test6	

(*Continued*)

TABLE 14.2 Continued

Test Design	A Cycle	B Cycle	C Cycle
		Test7	
		Test8	
			Test9
			Test10
			Test11
			Test12
UpdateInventory	Test1		
	Test2		
	Test3		
	Test4		
	Test5		
		Test6	
		Test7	
		Test8	
		Test9	
		Test10	
			Test11
			Test12
			Test13
			Test14
			Test15
			Test16

A good procedure to follow whenever you get a release with bug fixes is to run the tests that previously failed plus any new tests you created for that bug, regardless of which cycle you are on. Following that, run the tests you identified for the current cycle to maintain your confidence in the quality of the remaining features.

Defect Modeling

Besides deciding which tests to run, regression testing can also involve the modification of existing tests or the creation of new tests. When you don't have specific tests for new issues or tweaks that pop up in Alpha, Beta, post-release, or patches, you can provide very targeted test designs that model specific bugs or changes. Like the tests you created earlier in the project, the new tests should be run in cycles in order to establish that the changes continue to work as intended. As an example, we'll create a test to model this defect that was fixed in a patch for *Gears of War 2*:

```
An issue that could cause players' Look Sensitivity to
be changed to their Zoom sensitivity while zooming in,
zooming out, and firing. [UPDATE2 11]
```

Gears of War 2 gives the player the ability to configure three independent weapon-wielding sensitivity parameters. The *Look Sensitivity* affects how quickly your player can turn back and forth when looking around the environment with his weapon at his side. *Target Sensitivity* determines how fast you can swivel your weapon when it is raised and you are looking through the gun sight for targets to shoot. The *Zoom Sensitivity* value determines how quickly your player can turn when your weapon is raised and zoomed in to magnify your target. For example, when wielding a sniper rifle, you might want to be able to look around quickly to find something to shoot at, have some more control when you're picking out a distant target, and slowly guide the crosshairs to get a precise shot when you zoom in with the scope. In that case, you would have *Look Sensitivity* = High, *Target Sensitivity* = Medium, and *Zoom Sensitivity* = Low. When the defect changes the Look Sensitivity to the Zoom Sensitivity, that will slow down your ability to scan and notice incoming enemies when you're not aiming at anything, contrary to the your original setup.

To get this TFD started, draw bubbles and connecting lines that exactly match the different states of the game that are described in the bug report. The report explicitly mentions three events: zooming in, zooming out, and firing. It's logical to model this with a "zoomed in" state and a "zoomed out" state. Events like "FireWeapon" and "ZoomIn" provide transitions and loops. Figure 14.1 shows a first cut at the sensitivity regression scenario.

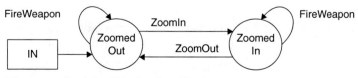

FIGURE 14.1 First stage of Look Sensitivity bug-fix verification TFD.

This is a good start, but so far the design doesn't have any states or flows related to the use of the *LookSensitivity* parameter, which is the part that was broken prior to the patch. Because *LookSensitivity* affects the player's turning speed when their weapon is lowered, this test needs a NotAiming state. That will serve as a place to start the failure verification scenario and a place to return to in order to check that *LookSensitivity* behaves according to the player's setting once he lowers his weapon. The NotAiming state is also a good place to connect the OUT box because it will force the *LookSensitivity* to be checked at the end of each test.

Finally, this TFD needs to take into account what should be verified when arriving at each zoomed state. The tests generated from this design must check that the appropriate sensitivity setting is applied to each zoomed state. That checking can be done each time the test arrives at the ZoomedIn or ZoomedOut by performing a "look" so the data dictionary definitions for those states must instruct the tester to look and check that the appropriate sensitivity is used—the Zoom Sensitivity value for the ZoomedIn state, the Target Sensitivity for the ZoomedOut state, and the Look Sensitivity for the NotAiming state.

Figure 14.2 shows the full verification TFD with actions, flow numbers, and the OUT state added to the diagram.

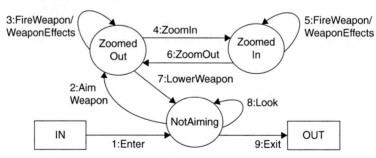

FIGURE 14.2 Complete Look Sensitivity bug-fix verification TFD.

Once the diagram and checks are in place, you need to come up with a set of paths to test. The situation here is slightly different from when you create a fresh new TFD for something you haven't tested yet. In this case, you must test the specific path that matches the failure scenario described in the bug report. If there was more than one way to cause the failure, each of those paths must be defined for this test. Once that's been done, define additional paths to ensure each flow is tested at least once. For the current design, the defect verification paths should include the zoom in/zoom out/ fire sequence, which corresponds to flows 4, 6, and 3, plus doing the "Look" after lowering your weapon to make sure *LookSensitivity* has not changed. This makes the basic bug verification path 1, 2, 4, 6, 3, 7, 8. This path should also function as the baseline path for this TFD.

Beyond the baseline, you need to have at least one path that includes flow 5, but also consider what other paths will do a thorough job of ensuring that the original defect is not still lurking in the code. Be sure to define one or more paths with loops, cycle through the baseline, and a take a long path or two. Some paths that would be appropriate for the current example are as follows:

Loops—a) Fire your weapon multiple times when zoomed in, then zoom out, and lower the weapon to check *LookSensitivity*. b) Follow the baseline to the ZoomedIn state, then ZoomIn and ZoomOut multiple times before firing from the ZoomedOut state. c) After entering, look multiple times from the NotAiming state before proceeding with the rest of the baseline.

Baseline Cycling—Follow the baseline and return to the NotAiming state, but instead of exiting from there, go back through the baseline a second time.

Long Path—Go through each flow three times in different sequences.

The benefit of modeling the defect and doing a new design instead of running a existing test that "sort of" covers the defect scenario is that you will do a better job of revealing manifestations of related defects that could exist but were not found during the initial testing, or new defects that were introduced by the code changes that were made to fix the bug. The purpose is to create a safety net of tests that will increase your confidence that the original issues are fixed and no new issues were introduced by the fixes.

Time Keeps on Ticking

Some games seem as though they have been played almost forever. Successful sports titles in particular can evolve and grow over a course of many years by updating rosters, uniforms, schedules, stadiums, and so on. You can play one version of the game over many seasons or purchasing the newer editions of the game. When the same part of a game is exercised over and over again, unintended side effects could show up. Rather than clearing memory and deleting saved files each time you re-run a test, have a machine or drive that keeps saved files so you can accumulate information in order to age the game to the point where things start to break down.

Take a moment to stop and think about detrimental situations that could result from playing or testing a game over a long period of time…

Have you thought about it? Some plausible examples are:

- The weapon shop runs out of inventory.

- The game won't allow you to plant any more trees.

- Your player accumulates money or points until there are no more digits left to represent an increase in the amount.

- All vehicles are damaged so badly that they can't be used, preventing access to the next area or zone.

- Your stats are maxed out so buffs and bonuses have no effect.

A real-life example of an aging problem shows up in *FIFA 11* after you take your Virtual Pro through many seasons. New players are generated to simulate what happens in real life when the original players don't have their contracts renewed or they retire from the game. The new players receive newly generated names and are incorporated into each of the teams over time. One impact of the newly minted players is that there are no audio assets for the pronunciation of their names, so the in-game announcers continue to use the audio for the original player's name at that roster spot. An additional side effect occurs where some new players are assigned empty names. This manifests itself in many places where the player's name is blank on various game screens and reports. Figure 14.3 shows an exhibition match lineup screen where the left center midfielder (LCM) for the Bohemians club has a blank name. Wherever the game UI would normally make reference to the player's name, such as when the player scores a goal or receives a yellow card, you see only a blank space or just the player's jersey number. Looking across all of the teams in the game reveals that many other teams exhibit the same problem and some have more than one player without a name. The big lesson here is that if you end your testing after only one season, or never play through the game multiple times, you can miss faults that occur and accumulate over time.

FIGURE 14.3 *FIFA 11* match lineup with nameless player.

Expanding Possibilities

Regression testing also applies to checking original game features in the presence of new additions, such as expansion packs or items added to an online store. Integrating them with existing tests might not always be possible. The *Gears of War 2* "All Fronts" expansion pack added 19 maps, a new single player chapter, and 13 new achievements. Some of the achievements have requirements that combine original *Gears 2* features or achievements with the new content. For example, the "Be Careful What You Wish For" achievement requires you to have reached level 8 in multiplayer and completed waves 1 through 10 on the Highway map in Horde. A player who had previously reached level 8 or higher should be able to earn the achievement by completing the 10 waves. Players who bought the game and the expansion together, however, would have to satisfy both requirements before receiving the achievement. It's possible for the player to reach the required level before completing the 10th Horde wave, and it's also possible for the player to complete the 10th wave before reaching level 8. A player who is already at level 8 before installing the expansion pack only has to worry about completing the 10th wave on the new map. This situation turns out to be a good time to use a test tree to represent the various ways to fulfill the conditions of the achievement.

Figure 14.4 shows a test tree for the "Be Careful What You Wish For" achievement. The tree accounts for what level the player is at with respect to the goal (level 8), when the target level or target wave criteria is met—and also accounts for both being met simultaneously and which criteria is reached after the first one is met. Reaching any of the terminal nodes in the tree should result in successful completion of the achievement.

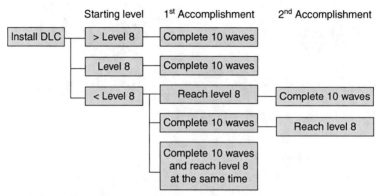

FIGURE 14.4 Highway map wave achievement tree.

TEST REUSE

Test Reuse is a strategy to create tests that are designed and structured to expand and adapt to the evolution of the game. The effort you put into the development of a test design or script can be used over and over again for more than one feature, more than one version, more than one game or all of the above. To be successful, you need to think about reuse from the time you begin designing your tests.

TFD Design Patterns

As you gain experience testing games, you'll be able to recognize recurring situations within each game, as well as common situations that appear across multiple genres and titles. This provides an opportunity to optimize the way you produce new test designs. Many of these situations can be represented by two or three major game states, with a few transitions between each state. Test Flow Diagrams are a good vehicle for turning out tests based on these patterns. Each new test can be created by changing the state names and flows without having to rethink the structure of the diagram each time. Figure 14.5 shows the skeleton for a two-state pattern.

FIGURE 14.5 Two-State TFD design pattern.

Here's how to use the pattern for testing weapon swapping in a first-person shooter. State1 becomes the state where you are wielding the default weapon, so you can call that state Weapon1. State2 is where you are using an alternate weapon instead of the default. You get from State1 to State2 by swapping weapons, and likewise to get from State2 back to State1. This pattern also can be used for swapping weapons from your inventory or having to drop your weapon in order to pick up a new one. Figure 14.6 shows the weapon swap scenario implemented using the two-state pattern.

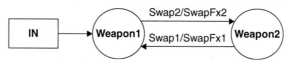

FIGURE 14.6 Weapon Swap using the two-state design pattern.

To reuse this pattern for the same game running on different platforms, you need to account for platform-specific events. For example, game controls can be very different for a version that's published for consoles, versus the same game running on PCs or mobile devices. Swapping weapons might be accomplished by a single controller button hitting a keypad number or tapping on the screen. The differences can be reflected in the name you give to each Event, or you can use a generic name for each event and have the flexibility to define whether it's the same button used for each, or a different type of control altogether. A simple table can provide the separate event and action definitions for each supported platform without requiring you to make any new diagrams. Table 14.3 provides some example definitions for swapping weapon 1 on those various platforms:

TABLE 14.3 Swap1 Event Definitions for Various Platforms

Platform	Swap1 event definition
PC	Press the 1 key on the numeric keypad
Console	Press the X button on the controller
Mobile	Tap the "1" icon in the lower left corner

Similarly, the actions resulting from each swap could vary due to different animations and/or sound effects designed for each weapon type and/or platform. Keep in mind that this doesn't just apply to weapons—you can take the same approach if you are swapping kittens, skee balls, or golf clubs. Use the patterns to get started quickly and turn them into well-designed TFDs by adding related flows and states that are particular to your game and the intended purpose of the test. Additional techniques described in previous chapters, such as expert paths and flow usage profiles will help you round out your design. Complete the TFD by adding the OUT state, numbering the flows, and providing percentages for each flow if you are doing usage-based testing. Once you generate your paths, your new test is ready to go. Figure 14.7 illustrates some example scenarios that fit into the two-state pattern. This is not an exhaustive list but is meant to encourage you to recognize situations where you can use these patterns to test your game features more efficiently. Note that some scenarios begin with a negative state (e.g., NotPoisoned) and others with a positive one (HasBall). Where you start the test depends entirely on the initial state of the situation you want to model—either by your choice as a test designer, or to reflect the

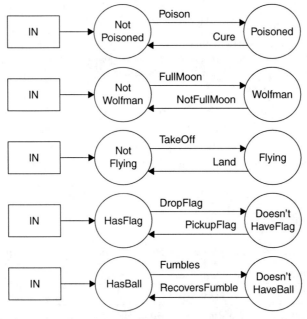

FIGURE 14.7 Example two-state scenario starter diagrams.

natural progression of the game. For example, in the Wolfman example, the game story begins with the hero in human form and the moon not yet full.

There are also game situations that can be tested using a three-state pattern. The principle is the same as for the two-state patterns. An extra twist to the three-state template is that one of the states has a transition in only one direction and another always has two flows going back to the starting state. This might not apply 100 percent of the time, but start with the basic pattern and force yourself to discover what information can be put on each of the flows. After establishing the basic pattern, provide the additions or subtractions that will make your test complete and correct, while keeping it relatively simple. Figure 14.8 shows the template for the three-state TFD pattern.

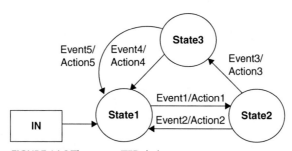

FIGURE 14.8 Three-state TFD design pattern.

As with the two-state patterns, you can have different event, action, or state definitions for the same game running on different platforms, but you don't have to change the diagram to accommodate that. Figure 14.9 shows the three-state pattern applied to a few generic game scenarios.

None of the two-state or three-state pattern lists are exhaustive, and the patterns themselves by no means represent every game scenario you will encounter. As you progress through your career as a tester, pay attention to the patterns that emerge from your own test designs and add them to your pattern collection. Reuse them and evolve them to get more and more mileage for your effort. At the same time, resist the temptation to be satisfied with a pattern-based test that might not be the best test for the situation at hand. Treat the pattern as a starting point rather than an endpoint. It's not meant to constrain you but to get you going quickly with the basic stuff so you can direct your energy at including all the special parts that make the test uniquely yours.

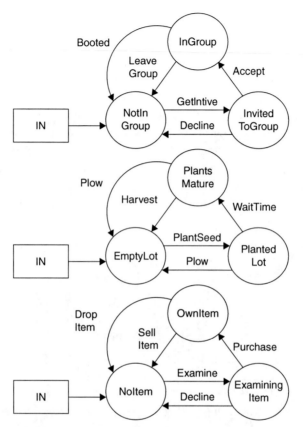

FIGURE 14.9 Example three-state scenario starter diagrams.

Looking Back and Forth

Looking back at the TFD created for the *Gears of War* sensitivity bug, doing a thorough and efficient job of testing means reusing that one design to test each of the five weapons in the game that have zoom capabilities: Hammerburst Assault Rifle, Longshot Sniper Rifle, Boltok Pistol, Gorgon Pistol, and Snub Pistol. An efficient way to handle this without making edits, creating additional diagrams, or adding paths is to repeat the tests for each zoomable weapon. When the test is reused in this way, each variant needs to show up as a separate item in your test inventory so that you can track results and include each of them in your A-B-C execution cycles. It's also best in this case to mix weapons and paths into each of the cycles so you're not blind to a fault that occurs for an individual weapon or path.

Table 14.4 shows how this might look if you've defined three paths for your Look Sensitivity TFD.

TABLE 14.4 Look Sensitivity Test Scheduling for Zoomable Weapons

Test Design: LookSensitivity		
A Cycle	**B Cycle**	**C Cycle**
Path1 - Hammerburst		
Path 2 - Longshot		
Path 3 - Boltok		
Path 1 - Gorgon		
Path 2 - Snub		
	Path 3 – Hammerburst	
	Path 1 - Longshot	
	Path 2 - Boltok	
	Path 3 - Gorgon	
	Path 1 - Snub	
		Path 2 - Hammerburst
		Path 3 - Longshot
		Path 1 - Boltok
		Path 2 - Gorgon
		Path 3 - Snub

Earlier in this chapter, a test tree was used to provide a design for testing a particular achievement added to *Gears of War 2* via an expansion pack. Even though this happened after your main test development campaign, you can still benefit from taking a reusable approach. The expansion pack has a total of seven new achievements with similar requirements, varying by what level the player achieves, how many waves must be cleared, and which map must be used. Instead of creating seven similar test trees, produce a single generic version that can be understood and run by testers according to the different data requirements for each achievement. Figure 14.10 shows a generic test tree to accommodate existing and future achievements that are structured the same way.

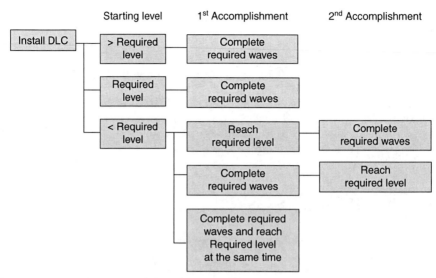

FIGURE 14.10 Generic wave completion achievement tree.

NOTE *For details about the achievements that are part of the All Fronts Collection, see* Gears of War 2 All Fronts *Official Achievement List at* http://xbox360.ign.com/articles/986/986572p1.html.

Combinatorial Expansion

Games will grow in complexity as they evolve and get updated. Redoing your tests from scratch is not a productive strategy. Because combinatorial tests can absorb new parameters and values with minimum growth of your test inventory, they're a great way to evolve your tests to keep up with new or updated features.

Electronic Arts' FIFA series has been around for a long time, providing more capabilities each year to keep up with soccer fans' growing expectations. *FIFA 2007* for XBox 360 provides the following choices on the Game Settings–Visual screen:

Time/Score Display: OFF, ON

Camera: Dynamic, Dynamic V2, Tele, End-to-End

Radar: 2D, 3D, OFF

Match Intro: ON, OFF

These values can be reduced to 12 tests using a combinatorial design generated by the *allpairs* tool, as shown in Table 14.5.

TABLE 14.5 *FIFA 2007* Visual Settings Combinatorial Table

	Camera	Radar	TS Display	Match Intro
1	Dynamic	2D	OFF	OFF
2	Dynamic	3D	ON	ON
3	DynamicV2	2D	ON	OFF
4	DynamicV2	3D	OFF	ON
5	Tele	OFF	OFF	OFF
6	Tele	2D	ON	ON
7	EndToEnd	OFF	ON	ON
8	EndToEnd	3D	OFF	OFF
9	Dynamic	OFF	OFF	ON
10	DynamicV2	OFF	ON	OFF
11	Tele	3D	ON	OFF
12	EndToEnd	2D	OFF	ON

For the 2008 edition, the Match Intro setting was removed and two new settings, HUD and Indicator, were added. HUD choices are "Player Name Bar" and "Indicator." Indicator choices are "Player Name" and "Player Number." Also, the Camera choices were moved to the Game Settings–Camera screen and a "Pro" camera choice was added. Separate Camera setting choices can be made for different game modes—Single Player, Multiplayer, Be a Pro, and Online Team Play, but for the purposes of this example we will treat them as a single setting. When it's time to test, go through the table for each of the different modes, taking advantage of yet another way to reuse this test design.

The 2008 version of the table can be constructed from scratch, but it's easier to just make the changes to the 2007 file you ran through *allpairs* and regenerate a new table. Listing 14.1 shows the *FIFA 2008* data for the *allpairs* input file and Table 14.6 shows the new visual settings combinatorial table generated for *FIFA 2008*. One hundred and twenty combinations are now reduced to 16 test cases.

LISTING 14.1 Allpairs *File for* FIFA 2008 *Visual Settings Changes*

Camera	Radar	TS-Display	HUD	Indicator
Dynamic	2D	OFF	NameBar	Name
DynamicV2	3D	ON	Indicator	Number
Tele	OFF			
EndToEnd				
Pro				

TABLE 14.6 *FIFA 2008* Visual Settings Combinatorial Table

	Camera	Radar	TS Display	HUD	Indicator
1	Dynamic	2D	OFF	NameBar	Name
2	Dynamic	3D	ON	Indicator	Number
3	DynamicV2	2D	ON	NameBar	Number
4	DynamicV2	3D	OFF	Indicator	Name
5	Tele	OFF	OFF	NameBar	Number
6	Tele	OFF	ON	Indicator	Name
7	EndToEnd	2D	OFF	Indicator	Number
8	EndToEnd	3D	ON	NameBar	Name
9	Pro	2D	ON	Indicator	Name
10	Pro	3D	OFF	NameBar	Number
11	Dynamic	OFF	OFF	Indicator	Name
12	DynamicV2	OFF	ON	NameBar	Number
13	Tele	2D	OFF	NameBar	Name
14	Tele	3D	ON	Indicator	Number
15	EndToEnd	OFF	OFF	Indicator	Number
16	Pro	OFF	ON	NameBar	Name

The files for all of the FIFA combinatorial update examples are included on the book's DVD in the folder for this chapter.

FIFA 2009 made only one small addition to the visual settings: a "Broadcast" choice for the Camera option. This is easily incorporated into an additional row in the *allpairs* input file shown in Listing 14.2, which produces the tests shown in Table 14.7. Adding the Broadcast value was inexpensive, costing only three more tests.

LISTING 14.2 Allpairs *File for* FIFA 2009 *Visual Settings Changes*

Camera	Radar	TS-Display	HUD	Indicator
Dynamic	2D	OFF	NameBar	Name
DynamicV2	3D	ON	Indicator	Number
Tele	OFF			
EndToEnd				
Pro				
Broadcast				

TABLE 14.7 *FIFA 2009* Visual Settings Combinatorial Table

	Camera	Radar	TS-Display	HUD	Indicator
1	Dynamic	2D	OFF	NameBar	Name
2	Dynamic	3D	ON	Indicator	Number
3	DynamicV2	2D	ON	NameBar	Number
4	DynamicV2	3D	OFF	Indicator	Name
5	Tele	OFF	OFF	NameBar	Number
6	Tele	OFF	ON	Indicator	Name
7	EndToEnd	2D	OFF	Indicator	Number
8	EndToEnd	3D	ON	NameBar	Name
9	Pro	2D	ON	Indicator	Name
10	Pro	3D	OFF	NameBar	Number
11	Broadcast	OFF	OFF	Indicator	Name
12	Broadcast	2D	ON	NameBar	Number
13	Dynamic	OFF	ON	NameBar	Number
14	DynamicV2	OFF	OFF	NameBar	Name
15	Tele	2D	OFF	Indicator	Number
16	Tele	3D	ON	NameBar	Name
17	EndToEnd	OFF	ON	Indicator	Number
18	Pro	OFF	OFF	NameBar	Name
19	Broadcast	3D	OFF	Indicator	Number

Because only the Camera parameter list was expanded for *FIFA 09*, an alternative to producing an entirely new table would be to "tack on" additional rows to the table, which will cover the combinations necessary for the added Broadcast choice. The advantage of doing this is that you can continue to use the tests you've already produced so you don't have to update your test management system or redo the automation for those tests. The test suite will grow based on which parameter acquired the additional value. In this case, the new Camera parameter added only three more tests because that was the highest number of choices for any of the other parameters. To form the required pairs, the new choice has to be combined with each of the choices for the other parameters in the test. If a new value was added to the HUD instead of the Camera, then five new tests would be required to pair the new HUD value with each of the five Camera choices: Dynamic, DynamicV2, Tele, EndToEnd, and Pro. Table 14.8 shows test cases 17-19 tacked onto the end of the *FIFA 2008* table.

TABLE 14.8 *FIFA 2009*–Visual Settings Appended to *FIFA 2008* Table

	Camera	Radar	TS-Display	HUD	Indicator
1	Dynamic	2D	OFF	NameBar	Name
2	Dynamic	3D	ON	Indicator	Number
3	DynamicV2	2D	ON	NameBar	Number
4	DynamicV2	3D	OFF	Indicator	Name
5	Tele	OFF	OFF	NameBar	Number
6	Tele	OFF	ON	Indicator	Name
7	EndToEnd	2D	OFF	Indicator	Number
8	EndToEnd	3D	ON	NameBar	Name
9	Pro	2D	ON	Indicator	Name
10	Pro	3D	OFF	NameBar	Number
11	Dynamic	OFF	OFF	Indicator	Name
12	DynamicV2	OFF	ON	NameBar	Number
13	Tele	2D	OFF	NameBar	Name
14	Tele	3D	ON	Indicator	Number
15	EndToEnd	OFF	OFF	Indicator	Number
16	Pro	OFF	ON	NameBar	Name
17	**Broadcast**	**2D**	**OFF**	**NameBar**	**Name**
18	**Broadcast**	**3D**	**ON**	**Indicator**	**Number**
19	**Broadcast**	**OFF**	**OFF**	**NameBar**	**Name**

FIFA 10 retained the same choices as *FIFA 09* so you get to keep those tests without any changes. Now let's take a look at what changed in *FIFA 11*. First, the "Indicator" visual setting was renamed "Player Indicator" and a "Gamertag Indicator" On/Off setting was added. Second, a "Net Tension" setting was added, allowing you to choose between Default, Regular, Loose, or Tight tension. Lastly, the "Dynamic V2" Camera setting was renamed "Co-Op." When you update the allpairs input file, make sure each row has a total of seven columns (six tabs) to account for the two added parameters. Listing 14.3 shows the *allpairs* input data for the *FIFA 11* visual settings.

LISTING 14.3 Allpairs *File for* FIFA 2011 *Visual Settings Changes*

Camera	Radar	TS-Display	HUD	Player Indicator	Gamertag Indicator	Net Tension
Dynamic	2D	OFF	NameBar	Name	OFF	Default
Co-Op	3D	ON	Indicator	Number	ON	Regular
Tele	OFF					Loose
EndToEnd						Tight
Pro						
Broadcast						

This time the change has a more significant impact on the test suite. Table 14.9 shows that six more tests are required, so now the table has grown to more than double the size of that which was first produced for *FIFA 2007*. You also need to consider that the time to setup, run, automate, and check the results of these tests has become more complicated because of the additional parameters that have to be accounted for.

TABLE 14.9 *FIFA 2011* Visual Settings Combinatorial Table

	Camera	Radar	TS-Display	HUD	Player Indicator	Gamertag Indicator	Net Tension
1	Dynamic	2D	OFF	NameBar	Name	OFF	Default
2	Dynamic	3D	ON	Indicator	Number	ON	Regular
3	Co-Op	3D	ON	NameBar	Number	OFF	Default
4	Co-Op	2D	OFF	Indicator	Name	ON	Regular

(Continued)

TABLE 14.9 Continued

	Camera	Radar	TS-Display	HUD	Player Indicator	Gamertag Indicator	Net Tension
5	Tele	OFF	ON	NameBar	Name	ON	Loose
6	Tele	OFF	OFF	Indicator	Number	OFF	Tight
7	EndToEnd	2D	ON	Indicator	Number	OFF	Loose
8	EndToEnd	3D	OFF	NameBar	Name	ON	Tight
9	Pro	OFF	ON	Indicator	Name	ON	Default
10	Pro	2D	OFF	NameBar	Number	OFF	Regular
11	Broadcast	3D	OFF	Indicator	Name	OFF	Loose
12	Broadcast	2D	ON	NameBar	Number	ON	Tight
13	Dynamic	OFF	ON	NameBar	Name	OFF	Regular
14	Co-Op	OFF	OFF	NameBar	Number	ON	Loose
15	Tele	2D	OFF	Indicator	Number	ON	Default
16	Tele	3D	ON	NameBar	Name	OFF	Regular
17	EndToEnd	OFF	OFF	Indicator	Number	OFF	Default
18	Pro	3D	ON	Indicator	Name	OFF	Tight
19	Broadcast	OFF	ON	NameBar	Name	ON	Default
20	Dynamic	~3D	OFF	Indicator	Number	ON	Loose
21	Co-Op	~2D	ON	Indicator	Name	OFF	Tight
22	EndToEnd	~OFF	ON	NameBar	Name	ON	Regular
23	Pro	~2D	OFF	NameBar	Number	ON	Loose
24	Broadcast	~3D	OFF	Indicator	Number	OFF	Regular
25	Dynamic	~OFF	OFF	NameBar	Number	ON	Tight

Summary

It's very expensive to run all of your tests for every incremental change to a game, so choosing the right set of tests to run can make a big difference in how fast your team can retest and re-certify the new code. Good regression testing is a combination of safety, history, and intuition. The right formula will balance higher quality with a shorter time frame for getting your product out to your avid customers.

Tests that are constructed in a consistent and rational manner make it easier for testers to maintain, update, and execute their tests efficiently. Like well-built durable objects in the real world, reusable tests should last a long time, be useful in many situations, and require little or no maintenance to continue functioning.

Exercises

1. Create a bug-fix TFD for the following *Gears of War 2* issue:

> "An issue where players couldn't chainsaw enemy meatshields if the meatshields were already damaged."

2. Use a 2-bubble TFD pattern to provide tests for at least three scenarios you might find in a vampire role-playing game. Consider situations from both the vampire's perspective and the perspective of other characters who might appear in the game.

3. The DVD that comes with this book contains video excerpts of a match played by the two teams shown in Figure 14.3. Write down all of the situations you can find on the video where the left center midfielder's (LCM) name should appear but is not shown.

4. Update Table 14.9 to account for a "3DTV" Gamertag Indicator value, adding the minimum number of new test cases needed to maintain full pairwise coverage.

15

CAPTURE/PLAYBACK TESTING

In This Chapter

- Capture/playback automation overview
- Implementing capture/playback test automation
- Working with capture/playback tests

Test automation enables you to get more testing done in the precious time allotted to you. By leaving repetitive testing tasks to machines, testers can spend more time creating new test designs, improving existing tests, and keeping up with the game code as it changes throughout the project life cycle. Choosing the right projects, people, and automation tools will prevent individual frustration and organizational rejection. Automation should be considered a regular part of a tester's job.

Some automated test solutions involve special hardware, software, programming languages, or all three. These are not always a good fit for testers who might not have heavy hardware and/or software engineering backgrounds. These solutions also tend to be expensive because of their special-purpose nature. An alternative approach is one that is light on programming and keeps the tester focused on the art and science of testing. Capture/playback testing provides access to visual assets and game data. It's entirely compatible with the tests produced by the methodologies taught earlier in this book, and many useful tests can be produced and executed without the need for special hardware or extra software compiled with the game code.

CAPTURE/PLAYBACK AUTOMATION OVERVIEW

Capture/Playback testing is an automation approach that you can begin working with right away. It's like using a digital video recorder while you test. Your inputs are recorded as you play the game and you designate various points where screen images are captured for comparison whenever you "replay" the test in the future. This is well suited to the graphical nature of video games. Capture/Playback test automation is not very effective for making subjective assessments of a game, however. Automated tests excel at comparing stored information against what occurs during the test, but they cannot judge ease of use, playability, or how fun a game is.

Most off-the-shelf test automation solutions are not suited for random events such as mob spawns, AI opponents, or dealing shuffled cards. To support capture/playback automation in these cases you need access to tools that give you control of the random number seed(s) or other mechanisms that drive the random behavior in a deterministic and repeatable manner. For example, a value can be provided in the game data file for testers to specify which seed to use for the AI, or a special pop-up in-game control panel can be provided for the same purpose. This kind of support needs to be identified in your test plan, or through some other means, early in the project in order that your automated tests can be developed in time for test execution.

Another use for capture/playback is to record ad hoc and directed play testing. The test can't detect problems it's not programmed to look for, but you can pause at any time to capture interesting windows or screen images in order to show them to skeptical developers. The recording can be used to see what steps got you to the problem spot. This is similar to the airplane black box recorder that's always on, so that when an accident occurs, analysts can work backward from the data to draw conclusions about what caused the accident.

Here are some other benefits to utilizing capture/playback automation:

- Retesting is faithfully repeated exactly as it was done the first time. You will discover intentional and unintentional changes to software this way.

- Problems get noticed and recorded every time, no matter how late in the day it is, nor how long the test machine has been working.

- Automated tests produce documentation of the test results every step along the way, every time the test is run. Typically, other pertinent information is recorded as well, such as date, time, and identification of the software build being tested.

- Different automated tests can run concurrently on multiple computers. One person can easily manage two machines running automated tests.

- Automated tests can be run during nonworking days and hours. In some game projects there is no such thing as "nonworking days and hours," but perhaps automated testing can reintroduce that concept to your project.

On the other hand, capture/playback testing has some limitations and drawbacks:

- Capture/playback automation requires some overhead to keep automation scripts up to date with the game code.

- Capture/playback automation won't notice if something goes wrong apart from what it is specifically checking for. A test that is checking one part of the UI might not notice when your health suddenly goes to zero or your sword disappears.

- You can't just grab anyone who says they do testing and expect them to be immediately successful at capture/playback test automation. Programming training and experience will make a difference in how quickly a new test automator will get up to speed.

The scope of off-the-shelf capture/playback test tools is quite broad, supporting PC, Web, Flash, and mobile games. Achieving even modest automation goals can have a big impact. If you expend the effort to get just 20% of your tests automated, that will earn back an extra productive work day every week for each tester.

CAPTURE/PLAYBACK TEST PLANNING

Capturing a test for later playback should add only a slight overhead to running the test manually. At various points during the capture process you will need to guide the test tool to capture the specific game data and screen elements that must be checked by the test. This investment is returned when you can automatically play back the tests every time after that. Keep in mind that maintaining the captured tests is expensive when the game features being tested are unstable. Time can be wasted on implementing, reviewing, and managing changes that are good for only a few test runs. In that situation, consider postponing automation until at least two of the three factors—the requirements, design, and code—are more stable. In an agile development environment, you can provide automated tests to verify the deliverables from each sprint. As more functionality is added in each sprint, the automated tests can keep pace by expanding existing tests or capturing new ones.

TestComplete™ is a commercial capture/playback tool that will be the focus for the remainder of this chapter. The TestComplete "getting started" guide "Automated Test Performance Tips," [SMARTBEAR 11] recommends the following approach to planning your tests:

- **Define the test goal** and decide which application functionality should be tested. The clearer the goal and the simpler the test, the better. Large tests that deal with various aspects of the application's behavior are hard to create and maintain. It is better to create a simple test that is aimed at one objective only. Once you create several simple tests, you can always organize them into a one larger test.

- **Plan testing steps** and decide which actions the test will perform. The testing steps depend on the test purpose and the nature of the application under test. Testing steps could include actions that prepare the application for the test (that is, they put the application to some initial state). Also, testing steps could feed corresponding input to the application.

- **Plan checking actions.** Typically, after the application has performed some actions, something changes in that application: data in an application window can be changed or rearranged, a new window could be created, and a file can be created on, or deleted from, your hard disk. You must determine what criteria should be used to pass or fail a test and which checkpoints will be used to verify these criteria.

- **Log the result.** The test results can be logged in different ways; for instance, your tests can save the full test results to a file or show a message notifying you that the test run is over.

Now, follow along as we apply various automated test techniques and strategies to the *Mass Effect 2* Video Configuration settings mentioned in Chapter 13, "Defect Triggers." These are shown again for reference in Figure 15.1.

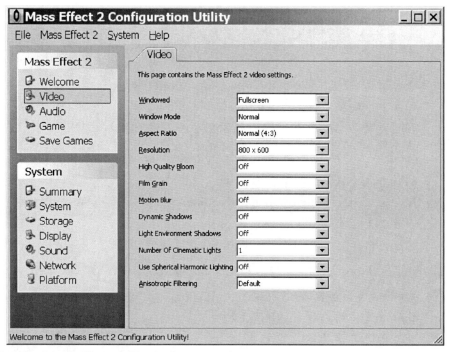

FIGURE 15.1 *Mass Effect 2* PC Video Configuration settings.

Defining the Test Goals

You should have some idea of what you are going to record and test for before you start automating. You can use tests that are produced by the various design methodologies described elsewhere in this book or test scripts that have been in your family for years. In either case, you need to define or plan ahead of time which screen or window elements you are going to check (capture) in order to establish that the game is working correctly. For the *ME2* Video settings, this could mean checking that updated values can be saved and will show up correctly the next time you pull up the settings window. It's also important to decide how far you want to go to verify the changes you make to the game. Perhaps early in the game development cycle you have only the Video settings Configuration Utility to work with, so a visual check is adequate. Later in the project, you will perhaps need to verify the effects of the settings by playing the game on different environments: video cards, monitors, laptops, and operating system versions.

Planning the Test Steps

Here's an example of an "early stage" plan for testing some of the user interface elements of the Video tab of the *Mass Effect 2* Configuration Utility for PCs.

1. Change the Aspect Ratio from Normal (4:3) to Widescreen (16:9). This change has the additional effect of automatically changing the Resolution from 800 × 600 to 1088 × 612, so you need to compare both changes as the result of the single field change.

2. Change the Resolution to 1280 × 720. This demonstrates that the Resolution can still be changed manually after the automatic change that occurred in step 1.

3. Change Light Environment Shadows from Off to On.

4. Save a Report file in the My Documents folder (File>Save Report…).

5. Save the updated video Settings (Mass Effect 2>Save Settings).

Planning Checking Actions

1. Check that the Aspect Ratio can be changed from Normal (4:3) to Widescreen (16:9) from a pulldown list. This has the additional effect of automatically changing the Resolution from 800 × 600 to 1088 × 612, so you need to confirm both fields as the result of the single change.

2. Check that the 1280 × 720 Resolution is available from the pulldown and is shown as the new value after it has been selected.

3. Check that Light Environment Shadows are changed to On.

4. Check that the settings recorded in the Report file are saved in the My Documents folder. The settings recorded in this file should reflect the °original° values because at this point the changes made during the test have not been saved.

5. Check that the Settings were saved in the settings file. This can be accomplished by exiting the Configuration Utility, starting it up again, and examining the Aspect Ratio, Resolution, and Light Environment Shadows values; or the file contents can be directly examined or compared to a known good reference.

Logging the Results

Because we are using an automation tool here, this is the part we expect to be handled behind-the-scenes. Some tools will provide images and most will provide some form of a textual log file. If you put the right tools together, you can even get the tests and test results automatically deposited into your test management and defect tracking tools. Just be careful not to trade off the quality and usefulness of the test automation tool for a little bit of documentation convenience.

CAPTURING TESTS

Test recording starts with the click of a button. It's typical for capture/playback test tools to provide a Record Bar window like the one shown in Figure 15.2. The recording will capture the screen contents as you perform the steps that you planned for your test. From left to right, the basic controls are Record, Stop recording, Pause, and a pulldown menu for adding Checkpoints. Various types of elements can be subject to comparison, such as graphic elements, data in fields, or file contents. You can mix different kinds of elements into a single test, capturing the entire screen, a specific window, a region, or individual items.

A Checkpoint is used to perform a comparison between a specific game element and the "expected" value or result of an operation. A Manual Checkpoint is used to specify steps that a tester must perform manually in order to verify that part or all of

FIGURE 15.2 Recording panel with test controls.

a test result was correct. This is a way to "fill in the blanks" for capabilities that aren't normally accessible by the testing software—such as checking that your phone received an instant message reporting that one of your online game worlds reached its maximum player capacity.

Additional arrow icons might appear in the recording panel. They expand the control to reveal more advanced options, such as inserting your own comments into the test.

Figure 15.3 shows how TestComplete records the test steps defined by an Item, the Operation performed on that item, a Value associated with the item, and a Description of how the operation and value were utilized or affected by each test step. You can see that the test begins with launching *Mass Effect 2*, followed by a series of clicks that altered some of the original settings. Further down you can see that the settings were Saved to a file before some additional operations were performed.

When you save the *ME2* Config Report file, the game appends the date to the end of the file name. You need to provide a consistent file name here in order to check the contents during every playback, so during your test capture session, replace the date portion of the file name with the word "New" to save the file as "MassEffectConfigReportNew."

Item	Operation	Value	Description
Run TestedApp	MassEffect2Launcher	...	Runs the "MassEffect2Launcher" tested application.
MassEffect2Config			
wndAfx			
ComboBox	ClickItem	"Widescreen (16:9)"	Selects the 'Widescreen (16:9)' item of the 'ComboBox' com
ComboBox1	ClickItem	"1280 x 720"	Selects the '1280 x 720' item of the 'ComboBox1' combo-box.
ComboBox2	ClickItem	"On"	Selects the 'On' item of the 'ComboBox2' combo-box.
Afx	Click	28, 17	Clicks at point (28, 17) of the 'Afx' object.
wndAfx1	Click	56, 12	Clicks at point (56, 12) of the 'wndAfx1' object.
dlgSaveAs	SaveFile	"C:\Documents and Settings\H	Saves the 'C:\Documents and Settings\HP_Administrator\M
wndAfx			
Afx	Click	101, 20	Clicks at point (101, 20) of the 'Afx' object.
wndAfx1	Click	63, 12	Clicks at point (63, 12) of the 'wndAfx1' object.

FIGURE 15.3 *Mass Effect 2* Video Configuration test steps.

TestComplete also provides screen captures for each test step. These are shown in a "gallery" and are individually highlighted to match the test step that is highlighted in the Test Step view. Figure 15.4 shows the first two screens captured. These correspond to the "ComboBox" and "ComboBox1" items listed in the Test Steps. Both the test steps and screen captures provide great artifacts to attach to the issues you log in your project's defect tracking system. It saves developers analysis time and reduces the number of times you have to reiterate the same test to collect a specific piece of data.

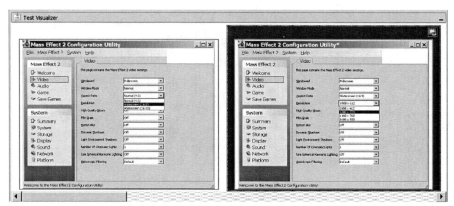

FIGURE 15.4 The first two *Mass Effect 2* Video Configuration test screen captures.

TEST PLAYBACK AND ANALYSIS

Playing back a recorded or coded test typically produces a report and possibly one or more log files. When something fails, it could be due to a legitimate error in the game or it could be caused by an improper test. Debugging automated game tests is similar to debugging the game code. You can isolate the area that fails into its own independent test to see if the result was perhaps affected by the test steps that preceded the one that failed. Look at what came in and what went out. In some cases, the test might have failed due to your test environment. This includes the test machines, operating system, console hardware, settings, controllers, accessories, and files that are being tested. The automation tool also imposes its own settings, which can affect the test results.

When you play the test back, the game needs to be in the same initial state that you established when the test was recorded. The captured content will be compared to results that you originally specified as the "good" values and content. As shown in Figure 15.5 it's a tester's duty to expect the unexpected. After returning the video settings to their initial state and running the *ME2* video configuration test, something went wrong. According to the Test Log, there was an unexpected window when trying to Save the report file.

Time to investigate. Your next step should be to check the images captured during the test run. Figure 15.6 shows the picture that was captured for the step that failed. When we captured the test, there was no existing

Type	Message	Time	Priority	Has Picture	Link
ⓘ	The application "C:\Program Files\Mass Effect 2\MassEffect2Launcher.exe" started.	19:16:30	Normal		
✅	The combo box item 'Widescreen (16:9)' was selected.	19:16:32	Normal	🖼	
✅	The combo box item '1280 x 720' was selected.	19:16:33	Normal	🖼	
✅	The combo box item 'On' was selected.	19:16:35	Normal	🖼	
✅	The window was clicked with the left mouse button.	19:16:37	Normal	🖼	
✅	The window was clicked with the left mouse button.	19:16:37	Normal	🖼	
✅	The file 'MassEffectConfigReport2011-04-17' was selected in the Save dialog.	19:16:39	Normal	🖼	
❌	Unexpected window	19:16:50	Normal	🖼	
❌	The test execution was interrupted.	19:16:51	Normal	🖼	

Test Log — filters: ⊗ ☑ Error   ⚠ ☑ Warning   ⓘ ☑ Message   ● ☑ Event   ☑ Checkp(Search)

FIGURE 15.5 *Mass Effect 2* Video Configuration test log.

report file. Now that the test is attempting to save the values again, the game is prompting the user with an alert dialog requiring that the user confirm that the existing file should be replaced. Chalk this problem up to incomplete preparation of the test environment before re-running the test. How you correct this is in your hands. You could add "teardown" steps at the end of the test to delete any files created and restore all settings to their default or original values. Alternatively, you can do those steps at the beginning of the test.

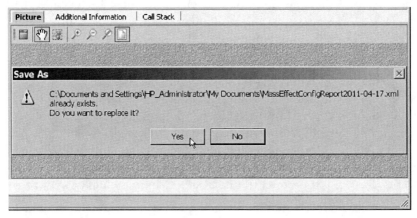

FIGURE 15.6 "Save As" dialog for existing *ME2* report file.

Further Confirmation

Now you've experienced how capture/playback can confirm what's happened on the screen, but what about issues that occur behind the scenes, like confirming the contents of the files the game generates? The *Mass Effect 2* Config Report file that was saved during step 4 of our captured test records information in XML format. XML stands for eXtensible Markup Language and is prevalent in Web pages and communication between applications and Web sites over the Internet. It's a human-readable format so take a look at Listing 15.1, which shows the data that corresponds to the video settings that were saved prior to updating the file in the last step of our test. The data relevant to our test results is the section following the CDATA (Character DATA) identifier. There are actually three sections within the CDATA block, but the one that pertains to our test is labeled [SystemSettings]. Inside of that section you can see the names and values of each parameter that was available for examination in the Report file.

LISTING 15.1 Mass Effect 2 *Configuration Report File Settings Excerpt*

```
- <settings>
    - <configfile name="GamerSettings.ini">
  <![CDATA[ [SystemSettings]
    Resolution=_800x600
    ResX=800
    ResY=600
    BorderlessWindow=False
    Fullscreen=True
    QualityBloom=False
    DynamicShadows=False
    LightEnvironmentShadows=False
    MaxCharacterCinematicLightingPasses=1
    EnableLightEnvSHLights=False
    MotionBlur=False
    FilmGrain=False
```

```
[SaveGames]

Location=

[AppCompat]

MeasuredCPUScore=773.589355

CompatLevelComposite=0

CompatLevelCPU=5

CompatLevelGPU=0

GPUVendorID=4318

GPUDeviceID=465

]]>

</configfile>

</settings>
```

There are actually three different sets of data within the *configfile* CDATA section. The section labeled [SystemSettings] is the one that applies to our current test. Each SystemSettings entry has the name of a parameter followed by the value that is stored for that parameter. These are known as *name-value pairs*. In the graphical view of this data, which we captured in our test recording, the "name" refers to the title of each field that is displayed and the "value" refers to the data that is stored for each field. Remember, at the point in our test where we saved this data, the information on the screen differed from the values that have actually been stored in the file. If you want to compare the stored settings in the file contents after saving the updated values, an additional operation must be added to the test.

NOTE   *For more information about XML, check out the Web page "A Beginners Guide to Creating and Displaying Your First XML Document." [DEVGURU 05]*

Pre- and Post-Testing

A good practice for when you have many similar tests performing operations on a particular screen or feature is to create a test that you run prior to your "real" test. This pre-test takes care of your preparation steps apart from the main test logic. A suitable post-test can also be added to do common cleanup tasks such as deleting temporary files or resetting the player's location in the game. Design your pre- and post-tests to be reused in combination with different "main" tests so that you don't have to duplicate many of your test steps every time. The result will be fewer items to manage when the feature changes or when functions or scenes are added and removed as the game evolves throughout the project.

Here's how pre-test steps can work for *ME2* video configuration testing:

1. Launch *Mass Effect 2*.

2. Click Configure.

3. Click on Video in the *Mass Effect 2* section of the screen.

So how does this help? Maybe during the course of the project, or as an update, a "Controller" configuration choice gets added or the text "Video" gets changed to "Visual." Now you won't have to march through your inventory of tests making changes to each and every one just to keep your old tests working. Just update the pre-test to account for the new choices and names.

Do likewise for the post-test. After the values have been changed and the files were stored (report file and saved settings) and verified, you might want the report file removed so you don't accumulate an overabundance of files on your hard drive from running the test over and over again. You will also want the saved settings file removed after it's been verified so you can avoid getting unexpected dialogs like the one in Figure 15.6. A concise post-test might go something like this:

1. Delete Report files.

2. Put the settings back to their default values.

3. Save the Settings file (now with the default values).

4. Close the Configuration Utility window.

An alternative to doing steps 2 and 3 would be to replace the Settings file that was saved during the test with a Settings file that's already loaded with the default values. Then, you could choose whether you prefer to load the default settings file together with the "factory defaults" in the pre-test and skip doing it here. For safety's sake, you could do both the pre-test delete and the post-test restore, which could increase the ability to reuse your pre- and post-tests across other *ME2* configuration tests.

One last point is that there is **no checking** being done in the pre- or post-test. Anything that needs to be checked should be part of the main test case. If a file isn't available when the post-test tries to delete it, it shouldn't be treated as a defect. Some of your main scenarios are possibly intentionally designed to skip the step where you save that file.

Playback Options and Control

Playback options are independent of the recorded test file. This allows you to "turn the knobs" for the tests you've already recorded without having to change the test code or recapture the results.

When you have a large number of tests to run and every minute counts, the following values in the Playback properties can help you speed up TestComplete test execution:

Delay between events—Specifies the number of milliseconds to wait after the automated test script simulates any user action and before it continues with the next action. A large time value means slower test execution.

Key pressing delay—Specifies the number of milliseconds to wait after each keystroke is simulated. Use larger values to slow down the keystroke simulation.

Dragging delay—Specifies the number of milliseconds it takes the mouse cursor to pass 20 pixels while performing a dragging operation during automated test playback. The higher this value is, the slower the dragging events simulation will be.

Mouse movement delay—Specifies the number of milliseconds it takes the mouse cursor to pass 20 pixels during automated test playback. The higher this value is, the slower the simulated mouse will move.

TestComplete also recommends that you check the values of the following options and consider decreasing them to achieve the fastest test playback speed. Before committing these new values throughout your test suite, try them out in practice to be certain they don't cause your test playback to produce false failures. For the fastest playback, use the following values:

- Delay between events = 0

- Key pressing delay = 0

- Dragging delay = 5 ms

- Mouse movement delay = 0

 See "Automated Test Performance Tips" [SMARTBEAR 11] for the full lowdown on squeezing the most time out of your test executions.

There are also times when you need to slow things down to ensure accurate testing. Adding delays can give processes, actions, and reactions more time to occur and can be properly matched to a previously captured reference. This is especially important to consider when any of the following situations could occur during your testing:

- Waiting for large file save to complete

- Waiting for a complicated process to complete

- Waiting for an online transaction to complete

- Waiting for a content or application update to download and/or install

If you have specific performance goals for key operations in your game, the delays should be closely tuned to those times, so that you are aware when they aren't being met. The feedback from these failed tests will help your developers improve the game experience—such as being aware of excess lag in certain zones of an MMORPG, excessive response times when bidding on virtual goods, or delay of game penalties occurring when a play is selected in time but received too late by the game server.

TestComplete provides a "delay" command as a miscellaneous option for your tests. The delay is specified in milliseconds, so for a 3-second delay you would specify 3000 milliseconds. You would typically insert this just before a "checking" operation takes place when there is uncertainty about the performance of the system. Some environmental issues that contribute to this uncertainty are whether the file is retrieved locally or from the Internet, what level of Internet service the user has, or which carrier a mobile gamer subscribes to.

Figure 15.7 shows a 10-second delay inserted after attempting to save a file. This is done in order to provide time for the request to be processed and the file confirmation dialog to be displayed before the next test step is executed.

Item	Operation	Value	Description
Afx	Click	29, 12, ...	Clicks at point (29, 12) of the 'Afx' object.
wndAfx1	Click	49, 17, ...	Clicks at point (49, 17) of the 'wndAfx1' object.
dlgSaveAs	SaveFile	"C:\Documents and ...	Saves the 'C:\Documents and Settings\HP_Admi...
File Checkp...	MassEffect...	"MassEffectConfigR...	Compares the MassEffectConfigReportGood Sto...
Delay		10000, ...	Delays the test execution for the specified time ...
MassEffect2Config			
dlgSaveAs			
btnYes	ClickButton		Clicks the 'btnYes' button.

FIGURE 15.7 Delay added between file save operations.

Yet another reason to adjust the playback speed is to check the game against potential user speed "profiles." Do elements of the game time out too soon if the player takes a long time to respond to a dialog or complete a mission? Do game input buffers overflow if they are bombarded with rapid clicks, buttons, or key presses? These can be real defects in the game code, which you can uncover by controlling playback speed and response delays.

TEST EDITING AND UPDATING

In the words of Yogi Berra, "It ain't over 'til it's over." You need to maintain and update your tests throughout the game project as well as for updated versions or annual releases of the same game title, such as those done for many sports games. The following are the most common categories of maintenance you are likely to deal with:

1. Correcting test mistakes

2. Keeping up with changes in specs

3. Adding more checks

4. Removing unnecessary checks

5. Accounting for expanded or downloadable content

The techniques in this section illustrate strategies and techniques to handle these situations.

Checkpoints

Checkpoints are places where your test explicitly looks for a result during test execution that can go beyond what's happening on the screen. For example, in the *ME2* Video Configuration test, checking the saved Report file contents can be added to your test using the File Checkpoint capability of TestComplete. It's selected from a host of Checkpoints selections, some of which are shown in Figure 15.8.

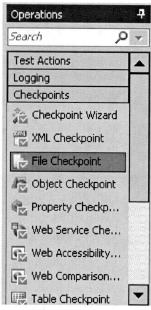

FIGURE 15.8 Selecting a File Checkpoint to insert into a recorded test.

As mentioned earlier, to verify that the Report file is correct, you need to provide a reference file for comparison. An easy way to do this is to create a reference file from the game, verify it by hand, and make a copy to use as a reference for other tests. Clearly identify the reference file, for example: MassEffect-ConfigReportGood. Now you can add a File Checkpoint to compare the test file with your reference. Indicate where the checkpoint belongs in your test sequence by positioning the checkpoint cursor immediately after the step that saves the file. Then, paste the full path to the file, for example, *C:\Documents and Settings\HP_Administrator\My Documents\MassEffectConfigReportGood.xml* into the File Checkpoint dialog box, as shown in Figure 15.9.

Create File Checkpoint   ✕

Select a file
Specify the file to be compared.

File name:
C:\Documents and Settings\HP_Administrator\My Documents\MassEffectConfigReportGood.xml   ...

FIGURE 15.9 Portion of dialog providing the checkpoint file path.

Finally, hit Next and Finish to confirm that this file will be used as your baseline (the "good" reference for comparison) every time this test is run. Figure 15.10 shows how this looks in TestComplete.

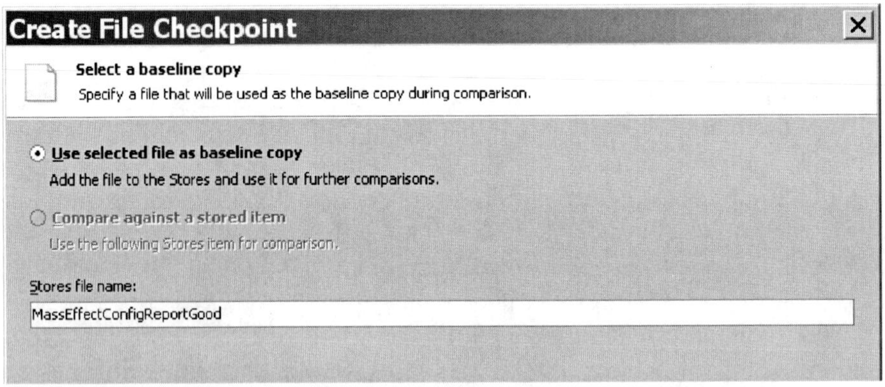

FIGURE 15.10 Portion of dialog confirming the use of the baseline file.

Because changing the Aspect Ratio to 16:9 is supposed to automatically change the Resolution to 1088 × 612, there should also be a checkpoint for that. This time we're checking a single value rather than an entire file, so use the Property Checkpoint to detect that change in the settings. This process lets you select an individual object (e.g., data field) to compare and specify what value or data should be contained in that item. Figure 15.11 shows the parameters you can choose from for the Resolution setting pull-down. We're expecting the wText value to match the 1088 × 612 resolution, so that gets entered in the Value box. When the test is played back, this extra check will be made before that value gets changed again by the test in the step that follows.

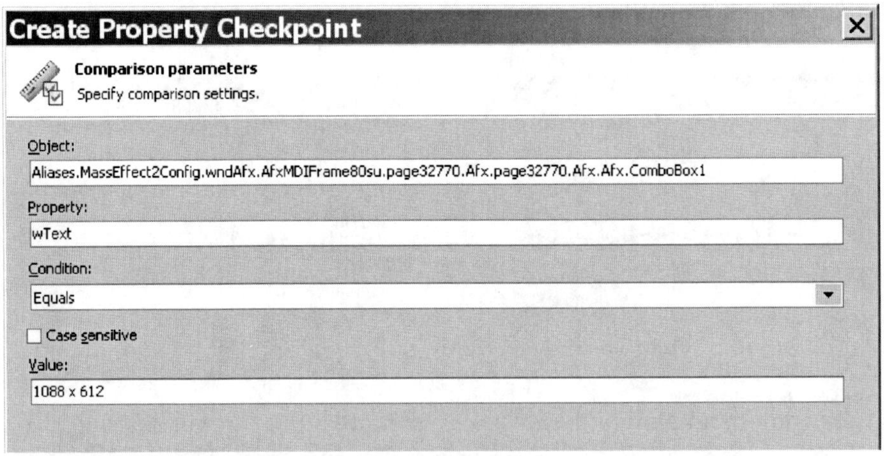

FIGURE 15.11 Portion of dialog specifying the 1088 × 612 Resolution checkpoint value.

Once the checkpoints are added, they appear in the test, as shown in Figure 15.12.

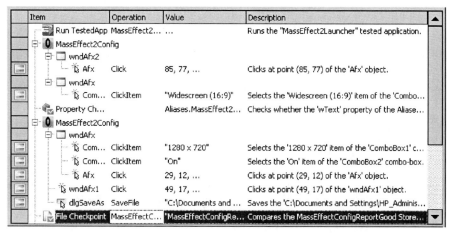

	Item	Operation	Value	Description	▲
	Run TestedApp MassEffect2...	...		Runs the "MassEffect2Launcher" tested application.	
	MassEffect2Config				
	wndAfx2				
	Afx	Click	85, 77, ...	Clicks at point (85, 77) of the 'Afx' object.	
	wndAfx				
	Com...	ClickItem	"Widescreen (16:9)"	Selects the 'Widescreen (16:9)' item of the 'Combo...	
	Property Ch...		Aliases.MassEffect2...	Checks whether the 'wText' property of the Aliase...	
	MassEffect2Config				
	wndAfx				
	Com...	ClickItem	"1280 x 720"	Selects the '1280 x 720' item of the 'ComboBox1' c...	
	Com...	ClickItem	"On"	Selects the 'On' item of the 'ComboBox2' combo-box.	
	Afx	Click	29, 12, ...	Clicks at point (29, 12) of the 'Afx' object.	
	wndAfx1	Click	49, 17, ...	Clicks at point (49, 17) of the 'wndAfx1' object.	
	dlgSaveAs	SaveFile	"C:\Documents and ...	Saves the 'C:\Documents and Settings\HP_Adminis...	
	File Checkpoint	MassEffectC...	"MassEffectConfigRe...	Compares the MassEffectConfigReportGood Store...	▼

FIGURE 15.12 File and Property checkpoints added to the test.

Now when the test passes, you can be certain that not only did the report file get saved, but the saved contents are exactly as you expected.

Editing Test Code

Some capture/playback tools store your test in an internal format while others give you an additional "code" view of your recorded test. Here's the code for a captured TestComplete test that makes changes to the *Mass Effect 2* video Resolution settings for the Widescreen (16:9) Aspect Ratio:

LISTING 15.2 Mass Effect 2 *Video Configuration Script Test*

```
Sub Test1

    Dim massEffect2Config

    Dim afxMDIFrame80su

    Dim afx

    TestedApps.MassEffect2Launcher.Run

    Set massEffect2Config = Aliases.MassEffect2Config

    Set afxMDIFrame80su = massEffect2Config.wndAfx.
AfxMDIFrame80su
```

```
Set afx = afxMDIFrame80su.Afx

Call afx.Click(95, 58)

Call afx.Click(84, 79)

Set afx = afxMDIFrame80su.page32770.Afx.page32770.
Afx.Afx

Call afx.ComboBox.ClickItem("Widescreen (16:9)")

Call afx.ComboBox1.ClickItem("1280 x 720")
```

End Sub

This is the kind of test you can easily edit to create new tests without having to go through the capture/playback process all over again. By changing one or more lines of code, you can expand the initial test to walk through all of the available choices, or quickly produce separate tests for each value.

To make a separate test for the 1368 × 768 resolution setting, start by copying the entire test and change its name to Test 2 or whatever you'd like to call it. Then change the line

```
Call afx.ComboBox1.ClickItem("1280 × 720")
```

to

```
Call afx.ComboBox1.ClickItem("1368 × 768").
```

To be complete, do the same and create a Test 3 for the remaining resolution choice, changing the third test to have the line

```
Call afx.ComboBox1.ClickItem("1600 × 900").
```

If you want to check all of the choices in a single test, copy the original line twice and change the resolution values to "1368 × 768" and "1600 × 1900." Also add Property checkpoints after each selection if you want to make sure the new values are retained after being selected. The "1088 × 612" value is supposed to occur automatically as a result of making the change from Normal to Widescreen, so a property check for that combo box needs to be added right after Widescreen is clicked. With those changes, the full test will look like Listing 15.3.

LISTING 15.3 All-Encompassing Widescreen Resolution Test Code

```
Sub Test3

    Dim massEffect2Config

    Dim afxMDIFrame80su

    Dim afx

    TestedApps.MassEffect2Launcher.Run

    Set massEffect2Config = Aliases.MassEffect2Config

    Set afxMDIFrame80su = massEffect2Config.wndAfx.
AfxMDIFrame80su

    Set afx = afxMDIFrame80su.Afx

    Call afx.Click(95, 58)

    Call afx.Click(84, 79)

    Set afx = afxMDIFrame80su.page32770.Afx.page32770.
Afx.Afx

    Call afx.ComboBox.ClickItem("Widescreen (16:9)")

    Call aqObject.CheckProperty(Aliases.MassEffect2Config.
wndAfx.AfxMDIFrame80su.page32770.Afx.page32770.Afx.Afx.
ComboBox1, "wText", cmpEqual, "1088 x 612", False)

    Call afx.ComboBox1.ClickItem("1280 x 720")

    Call aqObject.CheckProperty(Aliases.MassEffect2Config.
wndAfx.AfxMDIFrame80su.page32770.Afx.page32770.Afx.Afx.
ComboBox1, "wText", cmpEqual, "1280 x 720", False)

    Call afx.ComboBox1.ClickItem("1360 x 768")

    Call aqObject.CheckProperty(Aliases.MassEffect2Config.
wndAfx.AfxMDIFrame80su.page32770.Afx.page32770.Afx.Afx.
ComboBox1, "wText", cmpEqual, "1360 x 768", False)

    Call afx.ComboBox1.ClickItem("1600 x 900")

    Call aqObject.CheckProperty(Aliases.MassEffect2Config.
wndAfx.AfxMDIFrame80su.page32770.Afx.page32770.Afx.Afx.
ComboBox1, "wText", cmpEqual, "1600 x 900", False)

End Sub
```

As shown in Figure 15.13, running the new "supertest" passes all of the checkpoints for the four Widescreen resolution settings. Note that not all of the steps have pictures. That's because we took a smaller "captured" test and added our own additional code to check for other values. Adding code to a previously captured test does not add screen captures. That's acceptable in this case because the focus of the test was to check the values within the Resolution pulldown box instead of doing a pixel-by-pixel comparison of what's on the screen.

Type	Message	Time	Priority	Has Picture	Link
ⓘ	The application "C:\Program Files\Mass Effect 2\MassEffect2Launch...	11:34:17	Normal		
✓	The window was clicked with the left mouse button.	11:34:18	Normal	▣	
✓	The window was clicked with the left mouse button.	11:34:19	Normal	▣	
✓	The combo box item 'Widescreen (16:9)' was selected.	11:34:20	Normal	▣	
✓	The property checkpoint passed (ComboBox1.wText equals "1088 x...	11:34:20	Normal		
✓	The combo box item '1280 x 720' was selected.	11:34:21	Normal	▣	
✓	The property checkpoint passed (ComboBox1.wText equals "1280 x...	11:34:21	Normal		
✓	The combo box item '1360 x 768' was selected.	11:34:22	Normal		
✓	The property checkpoint passed (ComboBox1.wText equals "1360 x...	11:34:22	Normal		
✓	The combo box item '1600 x 900' was selected.	11:34:23	Normal		
✓	The property checkpoint passed (ComboBox1.wText equals "1600 x...	11:34:23	Normal		

FIGURE 15.13 Happy result of the Resolution setting test.

Data-Driven Testing

Another strategy for efficiently developing and maintaining your automated tests is Data-Driven Testing. The values (data) for each test parameter are provided separately from the test instructions. Special test steps indicate where the data values from the table get used. The results are verified in the same way as when they are individually specified.

To do this in TestComplete, you create a table of values you want to cycle through in your test, and define a Table Checkpoint to indicate where the table data gets used by the tests. For example, to test each of the video resolutions for *ME2*, you need to provide the kind of data that's in Table 15.1, which contains an entry for each Resolution and Aspect Ratio combination that is available for the video settings.

TABLE 15.1 Table of *Mass Effect 2* Screen Resolution Test Inputs

Aspect Ratio	Resolution
Normal (4:3)	800 x 600
Normal (4:3)	1024 x 768
Normal (4:3)	1152 x 864
Normal (4:3)	1280 x 960
Normal (4:3)	1280 x 1024
Widescreen (16:9)	1088 x 612
Widescreen (16:9)	1280 x 720
Widescreen (16:9)	1360 x 768
Widescreen (16:9)	1600 x 900
Widescreen (16:10)	900 x 600
Widescreen (16:10)	1280 x 768
Widescreen (16:10)	1280 x 800
Widescreen (16:10)	1600 x 1024
Widescreen (16:10)	1680 x 1050

To incorporate the data table into a test, you can create a new test from scratch or start with one that already checks for a pair of Aspect Ratio and Resolution values. To update an existing test, hold down the shift key to select the test operations that will be affected by the data in the table. To incorporate the data from Table 15.1, begin by selecting the "Widescreen (16:9)" and "1280 × 720" steps as shown in Figure 15.14.

Next, right-click on the selected items and select Make Data Loop, which will bring up the Data-Driven Loop Wizard. Provide a useful data name, such as VideoSettings, and click Next. Select Excel Worksheet as the data source type and click Next again. Provide the test data filename and browse to the worksheet within the file that contains your test data. Specify which records (rows) in the spreadsheet contain the data you want to feed to the test. To test all of the values in the data table, specify the first row in your data table as the starting row and select To The End for the End

	Item	Operation	Value	Description	▲
	Run Teste...	MassEffect2L...	...	Runs the "MassEffect2Launcher" teste...	
	⊟ ☐ MassEffect2Config				
	⊟ ☐ wndAfx				
▭	Afx	Click	81, 78	Clicks at point (81, 78) of the 'Afx' object.	
▭	C...	ClickItem	"Widescreen (16:9)"	Selects the 'Widescreen (16:9)' item of ...	
▭	C...	ClickItem	"1280 x 720"	Selects the '1280 x 720' item of the 'Co...	
	⊟ ☐ wndAfx2				
▭	C...	ClickItem	"On"	Selects the 'On' item of the 'ComboBox' ...	
▭	Afx	Click	23, 8	Clicks at point (23, 8) of the 'Afx' object.	
▭	wndA	Click	52, 16	Clicks at point (52, 16) of the 'wndAfx1'...	
▭	dlgSa	SaveFile	"C:\Documents and ...	Saves the 'C:\Documents and Settings\...	▼

FIGURE 15.14 Data driven test step selection.

Record value. If you want to execute only a portion of the entire table, such as the four Widescreen (16:9) resolutions, specify the starting and ending rows for those values in the spreadsheet. Lastly, you need to indicate which columns in your table correspond to which test parameters. Figure 15.15 shows the last screen in the process of setting up the table for automation.

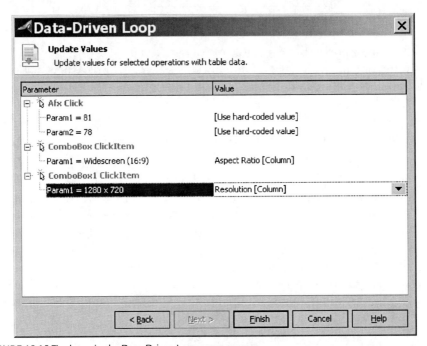

FIGURE 15.15 Final step in the Data-Driven Loop setup process.

The data-driven approach is especially easy to modify or extend for new Aspect Ratios and Resolutions that can be added over time, without impacting any of the test logic or code. All you have to do is change or add rows in the spreadsheet and re-run the test.

Figure 15.16 shows how the data driven elements were incorporated into the original test. The data-driven loop is inserted and within the loop the variables from the table are used instead of a single set of hardcoded values for the Aspect Ratio and Resolution. Now it only takes one playback to check the results for all 14 combinations. As new screen types are supported or old ones are removed, all you need to do is update the spreadsheet and rerun the exact same test code. Likewise, if your team is doing Agile game development, you can continue to update the test parameter table with whatever new values or changes are introduced in each sprint. If you happen to be in a situation where your team is involved in developing its own test automation solution for a proprietary game console or device, consider including this convenient feature.

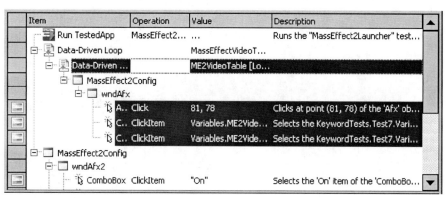

FIGURE 15.16 Data-Driven test items.

Summary

Automated testing is not free—it's profitable! Capture/playback testing is a good way to start. It produces reusable recordings of the tests you are already performing manually. Apply the right test development strategies to provide the most economic and reliable way to test your game. Be creative about using capture/playback to automate controller, keypad, or network inputs and check screen, audio, and network responses. Automating only a small portion of your testing will provide noticeable benefits in the long run. Once you invest some time to learn, practice, and develop basic capture/playback skills, they will become matter of habit in a short period of time.

Exercises

1. Provide examples of how your capture/playback tests could account for each of the following player types described in Chapter 10: Button Masher, Achiever, Customizer.

2. Describe how you could use combinatorial tables as inputs to a data-driven test.

3. Describe how you would incorporate Cleanroom testing principles into your test automation strategy.

4. Are you happy or sad that you reached the end of this book? Elaborate.

A

ODD-NUMBERED ANSWERS TO EXERCISES

CHAPTER 1 – TWO RULES OF GAME TESTING

1. Don't panic.

3. Trust no one.

5. d.

CHAPTER 2 – BEING A GAME TESTER

1. Trust no one.

3. c.

5. Check if the megazooka ammo is still in your inventory and if anything else you were carrying is gone. Check if this problem occurs on other levels, with other character types, and while wearing other armor. Check if this occurs when you are not carrying a weapon other than the knife, and with no weapon at all—just the megazooka ammo. Check if this bug occurs when the ammo is in different inventory slots. Drop the megazooka and pick it up again while you still have the ammo to see if it still reads "0 ammo." Try manually reloading the megazooka. Try picking up more megazooka ammo while you are using the empty megazooka. Get two megazooka ammo packs and then pick up the empty megazooka.

7. Outline text:

> Enter Town
>
> Edit Trooper
>
> Select next character by swiping
>
> Select next character by scrolling
>
> Select previous character by swiping
>
> Select previous character by scrolling
>
> Swipe to end of trooper list
>
> Scroll to beginning of trooper list
>
> Scroll to end of trooper list
>
> Swipe to beginning of trooper list

Advantages: shorter, fewer chances of making an error in writing or executing the test, easier to reuse across versions and platforms, different testers may find different defects by running the test differently.

Disadvantages: does not specify all the details that should be checked after each step, developers may not be able to reproduce problems without more details about each step, may not get repeated exactly the same way each time or when run by a different tester.

Note that both the last advantage and the last disadvantage result from running the test differently from one time to another.

CHAPTER 3 – WHY TESTING IS IMPORTANT

1. Yes.

3. Correct answers to this question should be along the lines of: when you are placed in a particular location in the game world, when you type in a name for something in the game (a player, town, pet, etc.), when you change a game option (language, difficulty, etc.), when you gain a new ability (skill, level, job, unlocked item, etc.), when you set the selling price of an item.

5. RespawnItem defect type opportunities:

Function—1 through 19 (random selection), 20-24 (setup and use flags), 25-26 (play respawn sound)

Assignment—9, 10 (2 instances), 12 (2 instances), 15 (2 instances), 17 (2 instances), 20, 27

Checking—2, 6, 11, 16

Timing—26

Build/Package/Merge—21

Algorithm—14, 22, 23

Documentation—7 (a literal string is used to report an error)

Interface—0, 7, 24, 26

CHAPTER 4 – SOFTWARE QUALITY

1. Your total released defects are 35 + 17 = 52. The table in Figure 4.1 has a column for 100,000 but not for 200,000, so double the defect count values in the 100,000 column. A defect count of 66 indicates a 4.9 sigma level and 48 is 5 sigma. Your 52 defects don't reach the 5 sigma level, so your game code is at 4.9 sigma.

3. The new PCE for the requirements phase is 0.69. The new PCE for design is 0.73. The new code PCE is 0.66.

CHAPTER 5 – TEST PHASES

1. The main responsibilities of a Lead Tester are: managing the test team, designing and implementing the overall project test plan, and "owning" the bug database.

3. False.

5. False.

7. False.

9. Put briefly, a test plan defines the overall structure of the testing cycle. A test case is one specific question or condition the code is operated and evaluated against.

CHAPTER 6 – THE GAME TESTING PROCESS

1. The Expected Result is the way the game should work according to its design specification. The Actual Result is anomalous behavior observed when you played the game, caused by a software defect.

3. Remove the old build and all related save data. Verify and amend your hardware setup to meet the spec of the new build. Install the new build.

5. False

7. False.

9. True.

11. Your answer should look something like the following sequence. Check for any steps or details you missed in your answer.

a. Look on the table next to the bed. You will see an odd plastic box with a coiled cord looped on one side. This is a "telephone."

b. The looped cord is connected to a bracket-shaped piece on the top of the telephone. The brackets end in two round cups. This is the "receiver."

c. Pick up the receiver and notice that one cup has many more holes than the other. Put the cup with the fewest holes to your ear. You should hear a loud, steady hum.

d. Push the numbered buttons in the following order: 5-5-5-1-2-3-4. When you hear a voice answer, begin talking.

CHAPTER 7 – TESTING BY THE NUMBERS

1. The original two testers, B and Z, were progressing at a steady rate which was not quite enough to keep up with the goal. Tester D was added in January, but the team's total output was not improved. This could be due to effort diverted from testing to provide support to D or to verify his tests were done properly. On January 8, C and K were thrown into the mix while B took a day off. We can presume C and K knew what they were doing as the group output went up and they almost caught up with the goal line. K and Z did not participate after that and the output went back down even as B returned. Ultimately only D was left on the project as presumably the others were reassigned to more vital testing. D completed 7 tests on the 12th, but it remains to be seen if he can sustain this output and hold the fort until this project can get its testing staff back up to where it should be. The two important observations here are that you can't treat every tester as an identical plug-in replacement for any other tester—they each have their own strengths and skill sets—and adding more testers does not guarantee a proportional increase in team output, especially during the first few days.

3. Tester C made the best use of her test opportunity to find the most defects per test. However, other testers such as B and Z were able to perform many more tests and find a few more defects. Since "Best Tester" is based on the combined overall contribution to tests completed and defects found, C is not in the running. It's still important to identify C's achievements and recognize them. If B and Z could have been as "effective" as C, they could have found about 6 more defects each; a very significant amount.

5. Some positive aspects of measuring participation and effectiveness: some people will do better if they know they are being "watched," some people will use their own data as motivation to improve on their numbers during the course of the project, provides a measurable basis for selecting "elite" testers for promotion or special projects (as opposed to favoritism for example), testers seeking better numbers may interact more with developers to find out where to look for defects.

Some negative aspects: effort is required to collect and report this tester data, it can be used as a "stick" against certain testers, may unjustly lower the perceived "value" of testers who make important contributions in other ways such as mentoring, could lead to jealousy if one person constantly wins, testers may argue over who gets credit for certain defects (hinders collaboration and cooperation), some testers will figure out a way to exceed at their individual numbers without really improving the overall test capabilities of the team (such as choosing easy tests to run).

CHAPTER 8 – COMBINATORIAL TESTING

1. Full combinatorial tables provide all possible combinations of a set of values with each other. The size of such a table is calculated by multiplying the number of choices being considered (tested) for each parameter. A pairwise combinatorial table does not have to incorporate all combinations of every value with all other values. It is "complete" in the sense that somewhere in the table there will be at least one instance of any value being paired up in the same row with any other value. Pairwise tables are typically much smaller than full combinatorial tables; sometimes hundreds or thousands of times smaller.

3. Use the template for three parameters with three values and four parameters with two values in Appendix C to arrive at Table A.1. The cells with "°" can have either a "Yes" or "No" value and your table will still be a correct pairwise combinatorial table.

TABLE A.1 *FIFA 11* Match Settings Test Table with Seven Parameters

Row	Half Length	Referee	Weather	Difficulty	Pitch Wear	Game Speed	Offsides
1	4 min	Lenient	Dry	Amateur	None	Slow	**On**
2	10 min	Average	Rainy	Legendary	High	Slow	**On**
3	20 min	Strict	Snowy	Amateur	High	Fast	**On**
4	4 min	Average	Snowy	Legendary	None	Fast	**Off**
5	10 min	Strict	Dry	Legendary	None	Fast	*
6	20 min	Lenient	Rainy	Legendary	None	Fast	*
7	4 min	Strict	Rainy	Amateur	High	Slow	**Off**
8	10 min	Lenient	Snowy	Amateur	High	Slow	**Off**
9	20 min	Average	Dry	Amateur	High	Slow	**Off**

5. If you provided the right parameters and values to *Allpairs*, you should get the tests shown in Table A.2 (the "pairings" column has been left out). If your input table had the parameters in a different order that was used for this solution, verify that you have the same number of test cases as Table A.2. Five hundred forty full combinations have been

reduced to 23 pairwise tests. If your result doesn't seem right, redo the input table following the same ordering of the parameters that appears in Exercise 3 and try again.

TABLE A.2 *HALO Reach* Shields and Health Custom Game Settings

Case	Damage Resistance	Shield Multiplier	Shield Recharge Rate	Immune to Headshots	Immune to Assassination
1	Unchanged	Unchanged	0%	Unchanged	Unchanged
2	10%	Unchanged	10%	Disabled	Disabled
3	2000%	Unchanged	200%	Enabled	Enabled
4	Unchanged	NoShields	10%	Enabled	Unchanged
5	10%	NoShields	0%	Unchanged	Enabled
6	2000%	NoShields	0%	Disabled	Disabled
7	Unchanged	Normal	200%	Disabled	Enabled
8	10%	Normal	10%	Unchanged	Unchanged
9	2000%	Normal	0%	Enabled	Disabled
10	2000%	1.5×	10%	Unchanged	Enabled
11	Invulnerable	1.5×	200%	Unchanged	Disabled
12	10%	1.5×	200%	Disabled	Unchanged
13	Invulnerable	4×	0%	Disabled	Unchanged
14	Invulnerable	4×	10%	Enabled	Enabled
15	Unchanged	4×	200%	Unchanged	Disabled
16	Unchanged	1.5×	0%	Enabled	~Disabled
17	10%	NoShields	200%	Enabled	~Unchanged
18	2000%	Unchanged	~10%	~Disabled	Unchanged
19	Invulnerable	Unchanged	~0%	~Unchanged	~Enabled
20	Invulnerable	NoShields	~10%	~Disabled	~Disabled
21	Invulnerable	Normal	~200%	~Disabled	~Enabled
22	10%	4×	~0%	~Enabled	~Enabled
23	2000%	4×	~200%	~Unchanged	~Unchanged

CHAPTER 9 – TEST FLOW DIAGRAMS

1. Your answer should at least describe the following kinds of changes:

a. Change "Ammo" to "Arrows" and "Gun" to "Bow"

b. "DropSound" would be different for the arrows (rattling wood sound) than for the bow (light "thud" on grass, "clank" on cobblestone), so you need two distinct events for "DropArrowsSound" and "DropBowSound."

c. If you have both the bow and some arrows, dropping the bow will not cause you to lose your arrows, so flow 8 should connect to the "HaveAmmo" state.

d. It's not really possible to pick up a loaded bow, so eliminate the "GetLoadedGun" flow (9).

e. "ShootGun" (now "ShootBow") may make more of a "twang" or "whoosh" sound if there is no arrow, so change "ClickSound" to "NoArrowSound" or something similarly descriptive.

f. Firing a bow requires more steps than shooting a gun. You could add some or all of the states and flows for the steps of taking an arrow from the quiver, loading the arrow onto the bowstring, pulling the string, aiming, and releasing the arrow. Your reason for doing this should remain consistent with the purpose of the TFD. For example, with a bow and arrows, you could load the arrow to go to an "ArrowLoaded" state, but then unload the arrow to go back to "HaveBowHaveArrows" to make sure the arrow you didn't fire was not deducted from your arrow count.

3. From Exercise 2, your updated TFD should at least have a "GetWrong-Ammo" flow going from "HaveGun" to a new "HaveGunWrongAmmo" state. From that state you would have a "DropWrongAmmo" flow going back to "HaveGun" and a "ShootGun" flow with a "ClickSound" action looping back to "HaveGunWrongAmmo" the same way flow 3 does with the "HaveGun" state. Your Minimum path must include all of the new flows, passing through the "HaveGunWrongAmmo" state. For Baseline path generation, you may choose the same baseline that applies to Figure 9.10 or define a different one. At some point, you need to have a derived path that gets to the "HaveGunWrongAmmo" state and passes through the "ShootGun" loop. Swap your test case with a friend and check each other's results step by step. It may help to read out loud as you go along and trace the flows that are covered with a highlighter.

CHAPTER 10 – CLEANROOM TESTING

1. The answer is specific to the reader.

3. It is possible to have the same exact test case appear more than once in a Cleanroom test set. This would typically involve values that have high usage frequencies but, like the lottery, it's also possible that infrequent value combinations will be repeated in your Cleanroom table.

5. From Exercise 4 you should have produced inverted usage values for the Casual user profile as follows

Look Sensitivity: 1 – 32%, 3 – 4%, 10 – 64%

Look Inversion: Inverted – 90%, Not Inverted – 10%

Autolook Centering: Enabled – 70%, Disabled – 30%

Crouch Behavior: Hold – 20%, Toggle – 80%

Clench Protection: Enabled – 75%, Disabled – 25%

The random number set that was used to produce the table in Figure 10.12 generates the following inverted usage test data:

1. Look Sensitivity = 1, Look Inversion = Inverted, Autolook Centering = Enabled, Crouch Behavior = Toggle, Clench Protection = Enabled

2. Look Sensitivity = 10, Look Inversion = Inverted, Autolook Centering = Enabled, Crouch Behavior = Toggle, Clench Protection = Enabled

3. Look Sensitivity = 1, Look Inversion = Inverted, Autolook Centering = Enabled, Crouch Behavior = Toggle, Clench Protection = Enabled

4. Look Sensitivity = 10, Look Inversion = Inverted, Autolook Centering = Enabled, Crouch Behavior = Toggle, Clench Protection = Enabled

5. Look Sensitivity = 3, Look Inversion = Inverted, Autolook Centering = Disabled, Crouch Behavior = Toggle, Clench Protection = Disabled

6. Look Sensitivity = 10, Look Inversion = Inverted, Autolook Centering = Enabled, Crouch Behavior = Toggle, Clench Protection = Enabled

7. The path produced from the inverted usage values will depend on the random numbers that you generate. Ask a friend or classmate to check your path and offer to check theirs in return.

CHAPTER 11 – TEST TREES

1. The bug fix affects "sound," "Orks," and "weapon," so you should run the collection of tests associated with the following nodes on the tree:

Options – Sound

Game Modes – Skirmish – Races (Orks)

Races – Orks

3. The keys here are to indicate on your diagram how many spells are required to enable each new lesson and to notice where the same spell unlocks different lessons. A correct tree is drawn with a vertical orientation in Figure A.1.

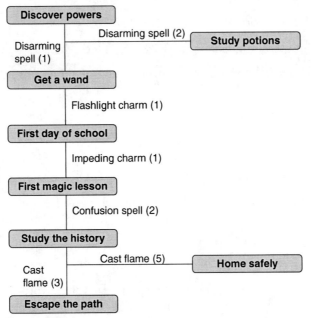

FIGURE A.1 *School of Wizardy* test tree solution.

CHAPTER 12 – AD HOC TESTING AND GAMEPLAY TESTING

1. False.

3. Free testing is an unstructured search for software defects. It results in additional bugs being discovered. Play testing is a structured attempt to judge the quality, balance, and fun of a game. It results in suggestions and feedback that the designers can use to tweak and polish the game.

5. This is gameplay testing. The testers are playing the game, not testing the game.

CHAPTER 13 – DEFECT TRIGGERS

1. The answer is specific to the reader.

3. Representing the "snap back" behavior on the TFD requires a state to represent your avatar at the starting location and another state to represent you standing at a gun or ammo location. A "MoveToGun" flow would take you from the "PreMatch" location to the "standing" location. A flow with a "PrematchTimerExpires" event would take you from your standing location to the "NoGunNoAmmo" state, accompanied by an action describing the "snap back" to the starting position. For the case where you don't move from the initial spawning location, add a "PrematchTimerExpires" flow from the "PreMatch" location to "NoGunNoAmmo" but without the snap back action.

5. Besides the Normal trigger testing, which you are accustomed to, here are some ways to utilize other defect triggers for this hypothetical poker game:

Startup: Do stuff during the intro and splash screens, try to bet all of your chips on the very first hand, try to play without going through the in-game tutorial.

Configuration: Set the number of players at the table to the minimum or maximum, set the betting limits to the minimum or maximum, play at each of the difficulty settings available, play under different tournament configurations.

Restart: Quit the game in the middle of a hand and see if you have your original chip total when you re-enter the game, create a split pot situation where one player has wagered all of his chips but other players continue to raise their bets, save your game, and then reload it after losing all of your money.

Stress: Play a hand where all players bet all of their money, play for long periods of time to win ridiculous amounts of cash, take a really long time to place your bet or place it as quickly as possible, enter a long player name or an empty one (0 characters).

Exception: Try to bet more money than you have, try to raise a bet by more than the house limit, try using non-alphanumeric characters in your screen name.

CHAPTER 14 – REGRESSION TESTING AND TEST REUSE

1. The first stage of your defect model should have states for an undamaged meatshield, damaged meatshield, and a destroyed (by the chainsaw) meatshield, as shown in Figure A.2.

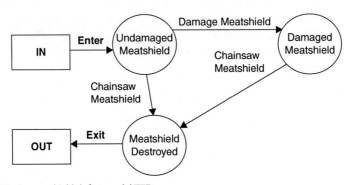

FIGURE A.2 Basic meatshield defect model TFD.

Additionally, you should tack on a few more states and flows to make sure you check what happens if the meatshield is dropped and picked up and to verifiy that the meatshield can actually be destroyed. Figure A.3 shows a TFD that incorporates these added elements. For the final touch, put actions where they're appropriate.

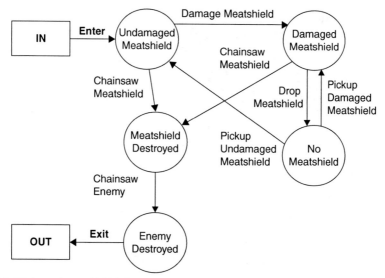

FIGURE A.3 Enhanced meatshield defect model TFD.

3. The following events or situations are missing the player's name. Either blank information is shown or only the player's jersey number (8) is shown.

   a. At 0:59 after the captains meet the referee at midfield, the Bohemians FC lineup is shown. Player 8's number is shown without a name.

   b. At 1:03, a graphic shows the Bohemians FC formation, but there is no name below the number 8 jersey.

   c. At 1:32, scrolling through the team roster shows the #8 player is wearing the captain's armband, but his name does not appear.

   d. As the game begins, each player's name appear above them when the have possession of the ball. From 1:50 to 1:55, player 8 dribbles the ball towards the goal his name does not appear. Likewise when he attempts a shot from 1:58 to 2:00.

   e. At 2:35, player 8 gets the ball again and is subsequently fouled. A free kick is awarded and when scrolling through players to change the kicker, player 8's name is blank.

   f. When player 8 takes the kick from 2:55 to 3:00, his name never appears.

g. At 3:20, player 8 receives the ball at midfield and heads towards the goal, scoring at 3:28. A popup badge appears on the screen to indicate the goal scorer but only the number 8 is shown.

h. Once play resumes at 3:42, the goal notification pops up above the scoreboard. The time of the goal is properly shown, but the name of the goal scorer is not. You can compare that to what's displayed at 4:30 when the opposing team scores.

i. The video skips ahead to the end of the match and again, player 8's name is missing from his goal.

j. After the match, at 5:28, the Player Ratings screen shows the players' names below their image, except for player 8 (above and to the right of the goalkeeper).

CHAPTER 15 – CAPTURE/PLAYBACK TESTING

1. Some appropriate examples for the target player types are:

Button Masher—Perform repeated presses, clicks, or selection of the same item. Check that the proper selection or result occurs each time. Minimize the wait time between presses so things happen as quickly as possible to determine if the game code can or cannot process them.

Achiever—Achievers may do many intermediate saves during their attempts to complete a quest or mission, or to earn an achievement. Put a bit of effort into tests that save and retrieve saved files, verifying the file name, contents, and timestamp. Also, create or keep some saved files on hand that are just below the threshold for earning an achievement so you can verify that achievements are properly award once the criteria are met.

Customizer—Focus testing on game settings preferences screens, especially values that automatically change based on a related value, and those that expand or reduce the choices for other options. Also be sure to test that preferences and customizations such as avatar clothing can be properly saved and retrieved.

3. Table-Driven testing is the most convenient way to incorporate usage percentages. You could have a tool generate sets of input data according to your percentages and store the data in a file you use to drive the tests. Another perspective to consider is that you could use the automation tool to record how different people use the game and derive usage percentages from that data to define your usage-based test profiles that would feed into TFD flow percentages or combinatorial test generation.

BASIC TEST PLAN TEMPLATE

Game Name

    1. Copyright Information

Table of Contents

SECTION 1: QA TEAM (and areas of responsibility)

    1. QA Lead

        a. Office phone

        b. Home phone

        c. Mobile phone

        d. Email/IM/VOIP addresses

    2. Internal Testers

    3. External Test Resources

SECTION II: TESTING PROCEDURES

    1. General Approach

        a. Basic Responsibilities of Test Team

            i. Bugs

        1. Detect them as soon as possible after they enter the build

        2. Research them

        3. Communicate them to the dev team

        4. Help get them resolved

        5. Track them

     ii. Maintain the daily build.

     iii. Levels of Communication. There's no point in testing unless the results of the tests are communicated in some fashion. There are a range of possible outputs from QA. In increasing levels of formality, they are:

        1. Conversation

        2. ICQ/IM/Chat

        3. Email to individual

        4. Email to group

        5. Daily Top Bugs list

        6. Stats/Info Dump area on DevSite

        7. Formal Entry into Bug Tracking System

  2. Daily Activities

   a. The Build

     i. Generate a daily build.

     ii. Run the daily regression tests, as described in "Daily Tests" which follows.

     iii. If everything is okay, post the build so everyone can get it.

     iv. If there's a problem, send an email message to the entire dev team that the new build cannot be copied, and contact whichever developers can fix the problem.

     v. Decide whether a new build needs to be run that day.

b. Daily Tests

    i. Run though a predetermined set of single-player levels, performing a specified set of activities.

        1. Level #1

            a. Activity #1

            b. Activity #2

            c. Etc.

            d. The final activity is usually to run an automated script that reports the results of the various tests and posts them in the QA portion of the internal Web site.

        2. Level #2

        3. Etc.

    ii. Run though a predetermined set of multiplayer levels, performing a specified set of activities.

        1. Level #1

            a. Activity #1

            b. Activity #2

            c. Etc.

            d. The final activity is usually for each tester involved in the multiplayer game to run an automated script that reports the results of the various tests and posts them in the QA portion of the internal Web site.

        2. Level #2

        3. Etc.

    iii. Email showstopper crashes or critical errors to the entire team.

    iv. Post showstopper crashes or critical errors to the daily top bugs list (if one is being maintained).

3. Daily Reports

    a. Automated reports from the preceding daily tests are posted in the QA portion of the internal Web site.

4. Weekly Activities

    a. Weekly Tests

        i. Run though every level in the game (not just the preset ones used in the daily test), performing a specified set of activities and generating a predetermined set of tracking statistics. The same machine should be used each week.

            1. Level #1

                a. Activity #1

                b. Activity #2

                c. Etc.

            2. Level #2

            3. Etc.

        ii. Weekly review of bugs in the Bug Tracking System.

            1. Verify that bugs marked "fixed" by the development team really are fixed.

            2. Check the appropriateness of bug rankings relative to where the project is in the development.

            3. Acquire a "feel" for the current state of the game, which can be communicated in discussions to the producer and department heads.

            4. Generate a weekly report of closed-out bugs.

    b. Weekly Reports

        i. Tracking statistics, as generated in the weekly tests.

5. Ad Hoc Testing

    a. Perform specialized tests as requested by the producer, tech lead, or other development team members.

    b. Determine the appropriate level of communication to report the results of those tests.

6. Integration of Reports from External Test Groups

    a. If at all possible, ensure that all test groups are using the same bug tracking system.

    b. Determine which group is responsible for maintaining the master list.

    c. Determine how frequently to reconcile bug lists against each other.

    d. Ensure that only one consolidated set of bugs is reported to the development team.

7. Focus Testing (if applicable)

    a. Recruitment methods

    b. Testing location

    c. Who observes them?

    d. Who communicates with them?

    e. How is their feedback recorded?

8. Compatibility Testing

    a. Selection of external vendor

    b. Evaluation of results

    c. Method of integrating filtered results into bug tracking system

SECTION III: HOW TESTING REQUIREMENTS ARE GENERATED

1. Some requirements are generated by this plan.

2. Requirements can also be generated during project meetings, or other formal meetings held to review current priorities (such as the set of predetermined levels used in the daily tests).

3. Requirements can also result from changes in a bug's status within the bug tracking system. For example, when a bug is marked "fixed" by a developer, a requirement is generated for someone to verify that it has been truly killed and can be closed out. Other status changes include "Need More Info" and "Can't Duplicate," each of which creates a requirement for QA to investigate the bug further.

    a. Some requirements are generated when a developer wants QA to check a certain portion of the game (see "Ad Hoc Testing").

SECTION IV: BUG TRACKING SOFTWARE

1. Package name

2. How many seats will be needed for the project?

3. Access instructions (Everyone on the team should have access to the bug list)

4. "How to report a bug" instructions for using the system

SECTION V: BUG CLASSIFICATIONS

1. "A" bugs and their definition

2. "B" bugs and their definition

3. "C" bugs and their definition

SECTION VI: BUG TRACKING

1. Who classifies the bug?

2. Who assigns the bug?

3. What happens when the bug is fixed?

4. What happens when the fix is verified?

SECTION VII: SCHEDULING AND LOADING

1. Rotation Plan. How testers will be brought on and off the project, so that some testers stay on it throughout its life cycle while "fresh eyes" are periodically brought in.

2. Loading Plan. Resource plan that shows how many testers will be needed at various points in the life of the project.

SECTION VIII: EQUIPMENT BUDGET AND COSTS

1. QA Team Personnel with Hardware and Software Toolset

    a. Team Member #1

        i. Hardware

            1. Testing PC

                a. Specs

    2. Console Debug Kit

        a. Add-ons (TV, controllers, memory cards, hubs, etc.)

   ii. Software Tools Needed

      1. Bug tracking software

      2. Other

  b. Team Member #2

  c. Etc.

2. Equipment Acquisition Schedule and Costs (summary of who needs what, when they will need it, and how much it will cost)

COMBINATORIAL TEST TEMPLATES

TABLES OF PARAMETERS WITH TWO TEST VALUES

TABLE C.1 Three Parameters, Two Values Each

Test	ParamA	ParamB	ParamC
1	A1	B1	C1
2	A2	B1	C2
3	A1	B2	C2
4	A2	B2	C1

TABLE C.2 Four Parameters, Two Values Each

Test	ParamA	ParamB	ParamC	ParamD
1	A1	B1	C1	D1
2	A2	B1	C2	D1
3	A1	B2	C2	D2
4	A2	B2	C1	D1
5	A2	B1	C1	D2

TABLE C.3 Five Parameters, Two Values Each

Test	ParamA	ParamB	ParamC	ParamD	ParamE
1	A1	B1	C1	D1	E1
2	A2	B1	C2	D1	E1
3	A1	B2	C2	D2	E2
4	A2	B2	C1	D1	E2
5	A2	B1	C1	D2	E2
6	A*	B2	C*	D2	E1

TABLE C.4 Six Parameters, Two Values Each

Test	ParamA	ParamB	ParamC	ParamD	ParamE	ParamF
1	A1	B1	C1	D1	E1	F1
2	A2	B1	C2	D1	E1	F1
3	A1	B2	C2	D2	E2	F1
4	A2	B2	C1	D1	E2	F2
5	A2	B1	C1	D2	E2	F2
6	A1	B2	C2	D2	E1	F2

TABLE C.5 Seven Parameters, Two Values Each

Test	ParamA	ParamB	ParamC	ParamD	ParamE	ParamF	ParamG
1	A1	B1	C1	D1	E1	F1	G1
2	A2	B1	C2	D1	E1	F1	G2
3	A1	B2	C2	D2	E2	F1	G2
4	A2	B2	C1	D1	E2	F2	G2
5	A2	B1	C1	D2	E2	F2	G1
6	A1	B2	C2	D2	E1	F2	G1

TABLE C.6 Eight Parameters, Two Values Each

Test	ParamA	ParamB	ParamC	ParamD	ParamE	ParamF	ParamG	ParamH
1	A1	B1	C1	D1	E1	F1	G1	H1
2	A2	B1	C2	D1	E1	F1	G2	H2
3	A1	B2	C2	D2	E2	F1	G2	H1
4	A2	B2	C1	D1	E2	F2	G2	H2
5	A2	B1	C1	D2	E2	F2	G1	H1
6	A1	B2	C2	D2	E1	F2	G1	H2

TABLE C.7 Nine Parameters, Two Values Each

Test	ParamA	ParamB	ParamC	ParamD	ParamE	ParamF	ParamG	ParamH	ParamJ
1	A1	B1	C1	D1	E1	F1	G1	H1	J1
2	A2	B1	C2	D1	E1	F1	G2	H2	J2
3	A1	B2	C2	D2	E2	F1	G2	H1	J2
4	A2	B2	C1	D1	E2	F2	G2	H2	J1
5	A2	B1	C1	D2	E2	F2	G1	H1	J2
6	A1	B2	C2	D2	E1	F2	G1	H2	J1

TABLE C.8 Ten Parameters, Two Values Each

Test	Param A	Param B	Param C	Param D	Param E	Param F	Param G	Param H	Param J	Param K
1	A1	B1	C1	D1	E1	F1	G1	H1	J1	K1
2	A2	B1	C2	D1	E1	F1	G2	H2	J2	K2
3	A1	B2	C2	D2	E2	F1	G2	H1	J2	K1
4	A2	B2	C1	D1	E2	F2	G2	H2	J1	K1
5	A2	B1	C1	D2	E2	F2	G1	H1	J2	K2
6	A1	B2	C2	D2	E1	F2	G1	H2	J1	K2

TABLES OF PARAMETERS WITH THREE TEST VALUES

TABLE C.9 Three Parameters, Three Values Each

Test	ParamA	ParamB	ParamC
1	A1	B1	C1
2	A2	B2	C2
3	A3	B3	C3
4	A1	B2	C3
5	A2	B3	C1
6	A3	B1	C2
7	A1	B3	C2
8	A2	B1	C3
9	A3	B2	C1

TABLE C.10 Two Parameters with Three Values, One Parameter with Two Values

Test	ParamA	ParamB	ParamC
1	A1	B1	C1
2	A2	B2	C1
3	A3	B3	C1
4	A1	B2	C2
5	A2	B3	C2
6	A3	B1	C2
7	A1	B3	C*
8	A2	B1	C*
9	A3	B2	C*

TABLE C.11 One Parameter with Three
Values, Two Parameters with Two Values

Test	ParamA	ParamB	ParamC
1	A1	B1	C1
2	A2	B2	C1
3	A3	B1	C1
4	A1	B2	C2
5	A2	B1	C2
6	A3	B2	C2

TABLE C.12 Four Parameters, Three Values Each

Test	ParamA	ParamB	ParamC	ParamD
1	A1	B1	C1	D1
2	A2	B2	C2	D1
3	A3	B3	C3	D1
4	A1	B2	C3	D2
5	A2	B3	C1	D2
6	A3	B1	C2	D2
7	A1	B3	C2	D3
8	A2	B1	C3	D3
9	A3	B2	C1	D3

TABLE C.13 Three Parameters with Three Values,
One Parameter with Two Values

Test	ParamA	ParamB	ParamC	ParamD
1	A1	B1	C1	D1
2	A2	B2	C2	D1
3	A3	B3	C3	D1
4	A1	B2	C3	D2
5	A2	B3	C1	D2
6	A3	B1	C2	D2
7	A1	B3	C2	D*
8	A2	B1	C3	D*
9	A3	B2	C1	D*

TABLE C.14 Two Parameters with Three Values, Two Parameters with Two Values

Test	ParamA	ParamB	ParamC	ParamD
1	A1	B1	C1	D1
2	A2	B2	C2	D1
3	A3	B3	C1	D1
4	A1	B2	C1	D2
5	A2	B3	C2	D2
6	A3	B1	C2	D2
7	A1	B3	C2	D*
8	A2	B1	C1	D*
9	A3	B2	C*	D*

TABLE C.15 One Parameter with Three Values, Three Parameters with Two Values

Test	ParamA	ParamB	ParamC	ParamD
1	A1	B1	C1	D1
2	A2	B2	C2	D1
3	A3	B1	C2	D2
4	A1	B2	C2	D2
5	A2	B1	C1	D2
6	A3	B2	C1	D1

TABLE C.16 Three Parameters with Three Values, Two Parameters with Two Values

Test	ParamA	ParamB	ParamC	ParamD	ParamE
1	A1	B1	C1	D1	E1
2	A2	B2	C2	D2	E2
3	A3	B3	C3	D1	E2
4	A1	B2	C3	D2	E1
5	A2	B3	C1	D2	E1
6	A3	B1	C2	D2	E1
7	A1	B3	C2	D1	E2
8	A2	B1	C3	D1	E2
9	A3	B2	C1	D1	E2

TABLE C.17 Two Parameters with Three Values, Three Parameters with Two Values

Test	ParamA	ParamB	ParamC	ParamD	ParamE
1	A1	B1	C1	D1	E1
2	A2	B2	C2	D2	E1
3	A3	B3	C1	D2	E2
4	A1	B2	C2	D1	E2
5	A2	B3	C2	D1	E2
6	A3	B1	C2	D1	E2
7	A1	B3	C1	D2	E1
8	A2	B1	C1	D2	E1
9	A3	B2	C1	D2	E1

TABLE C.18 One Parameter with Three Values, Four Parameters with Two Values

Test	ParamA	ParamB	ParamC	ParamD	ParamE
1	A1	B1	C1	D1	E1
2	A2	B2	C2	D1	E1
3	A3	B1	C2	D2	E1
4	A1	B2	C2	D2	E2
5	A2	B1	C1	D2	E2
6	A3	B2	C1	D1	E2

TABLE C.19 Three Parameters with Three Values, Three Parameters with Two Values

Test	ParamA	ParamB	ParamC	ParamD	ParamE	ParamF
1	A1	B1	C1	D1	E1	F1
2	A2	B2	C2	D2	E2	F1
3	A3	B3	C3	D1	E2	F2
4	A1	B2	C3	D2	E1	F2
5	A2	B3	C1	D2	E1	F2
6	A3	B1	C2	D2	E1	F2
7	A1	B3	C2	D1	E2	F1
8	A2	B1	C3	D1	E2	F1
9	A3	B2	C1	D1	E2	F1

TABLE C.20 Three Parameters with Three Values, Four Parameters with Two Values

Test	ParamA	ParamB	ParamC	ParamD	ParamE	ParamF	ParamG
1	A1	B1	C1	D1	E1	F1	G1
2	A2	B2	C2	D2	E2	F1	G1
3	A3	B3	C3	D1	E2	F2	G1
4	A1	B2	C3	D2	E1	F2	G2
5	A2	B3	C1	D2	E1	F2	G*
6	A3	B1	C2	D2	E1	F2	G*
7	A1	B3	C2	D1	E2	F1	G2
8	A2	B1	C3	D1	E2	F1	G2
9	A3	B2	C1	D1	E2	F1	G2

TEST FLOW DIAGRAM (TFD) TEMPLATES

POWER-UPS

Power-ups are items that give your character some kind of temporary bonus. You might need to drive over them, run over them, trigger a special item in a puzzle, or hit a special sequence on your game controller or keypad. The TFD template in Figure D.1 covers acquiring the power-up, using its abilities, canceling the power-up, checking for power-up expiration, and stacking power-ups. This same template could also be used for RPG and adventure games where a player can trigger temporary effects from a weapon, get a temporary boost from an item, or receive temporary "buff" spells from other characters.

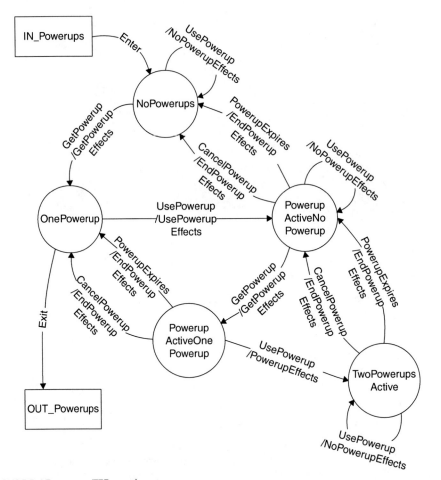

FIGURE D.1 Power-ups TFD template.

CRAFT ITEM

Crafting an item in a game world requires the player to have the ingredients and the skill to craft that particular type of item. Besides being trained in the right skill, the character must also have raised his skill to a sufficient level to make a crafting attempt of the target item. Some or all of the ingredients are normally consumed, whether or not the crafting attempt was successful. These factors are incorporated into the TFD template in Figure D.2.

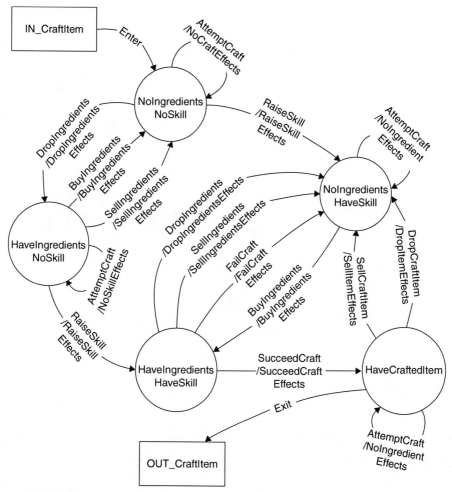

FIGURE D.2 Craft item TFD template.

HEAL CHARACTER

Whether it's medics, magic, or a well-deserved nap, nothing beats a timely heal to get you through a tough mission, level, or battle. Get a friend to resurrect you or respawn to start over. You can also change "Heal" to "Repair" and use the TFD template in Figure D.3 when it's your car or robot that's taking a beating.

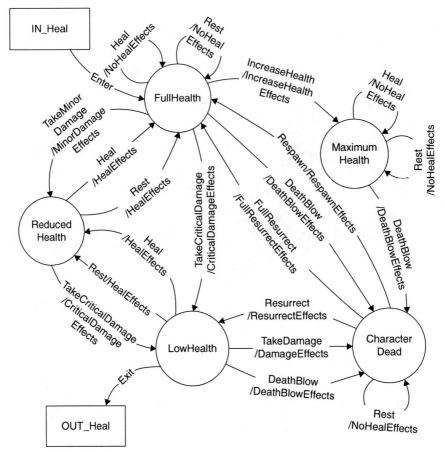

FIGURE D.3 Heal character TFD template.

CREATE/SAVE

Games are full of custom elements. You can create characters, teams, playbooks, song lists, and skateboards. You also need to save them if you want to see them the next time you fire up the game. The TFD template in Figure D.4 handles creating, deleting, filling up your save slots, and restarting the game without saving your changes. If you're using this for something besides character creation, replace "Character" with the name of the type of element you are testing.

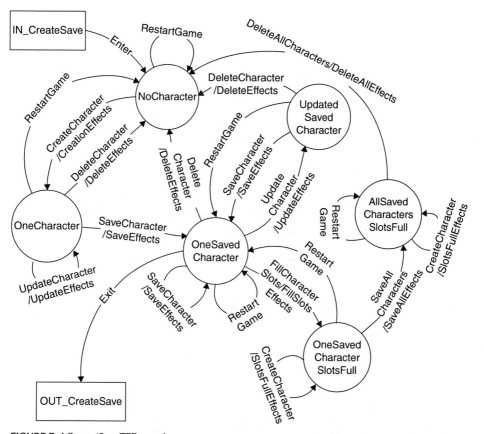

FIGURE D.4 Create/Save TFD template.

UNLOCK AND BUY ITEM

Simulation, RPG, adventure, and even sports games tend to have featured items that you can purchase once you have unlocked the ability to purchase the item and have enough points to actually buy it. The "items" could be weapons, spells, clothing, furniture, mini-games, new vehicles, or new levels. To unlock them, you might have to complete a specific task or mission, defeat a particular opponent, raise your character's level, or achieve a result under special circumstances. Test your purchasing power using the TFD template in Figure D.5. Some of these criteria are documented in the game and some are hidden. Shhhh…

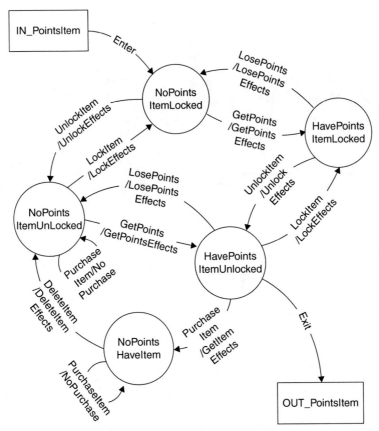

FIGURE D.5 Unlock and buy item TFD template.

UPDATE SONG LIST

It's very effective when games incorporate popular music. You might find today's hits blasting from a car radio or a street basketball court. Music can also be a more integral part of gameplay, such as in a dancing, musical instrument, or karaoke game. The TFD template in Figure D.6 reflects the player's ability to add and delete songs, order them, map them to game events, and trigger them from within the game. Depending on the game, triggering could be user controlled—such as tuning to a particular in-game radio station—or event-driven, such as the music played when the home team scores a touchdown. Just remember that "New Order" on the TFD refers to the order of songs in the list, not the electronica supergroup.

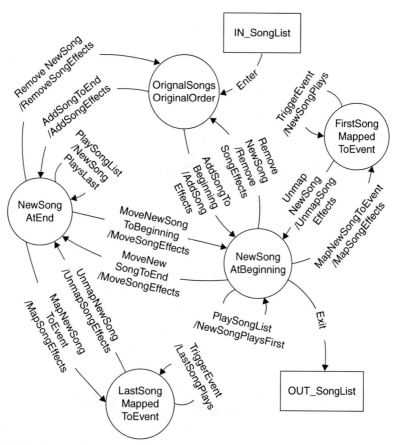

FIGURE D.6 Update song list TFD template.

COMPLETE A MISSION OR QUEST

Many games will reward points, money, items, or access to new parts of the game if you can complete a particular mission, quest, or other designated goal. It's common for these missions to be broken into multiple objectives that must be completed individually in order to achieve success and earn the reward. These objectives could be things such as capturing a set of territories or villains, winning a series of competitions, or completing a set of bonus words. The TFD template in Figure D.7 is constructed for

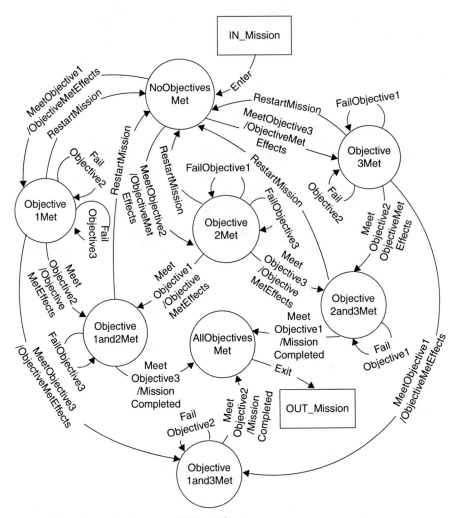

FIGURE D.7 Complete a mission or quest TFD template.

goals with three objectives, but you can also use it for two objectives by knocking out the states and flows that deal with Objective3.

GET WEAPON AND AMMO

The TFD template in Figure D.8 is an enhancement of the diagram from the walkthrough in Chapter 9. A state and flows have been added for handling the case where the weapon has maximum ammo. You can also apply this TFD structure to game elements which have a similar relationship, such as cars and fuel or spells and mana. Just replace "Gun" and "Ammo" with the corresponding elements.

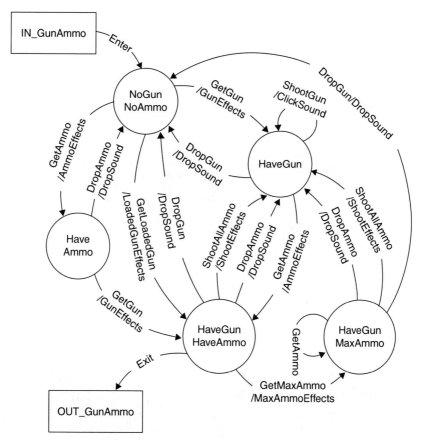

FIGURE D.8 Get Weapon and Ammo TFD template.

REFERENCES

CHAPTER 1

[SCUBADOC 11] Scubadoc's Diving Medicine Online. Panic attacks and the blue orb syndrome. Available online at *http://www.scuba-doc.com/bluorb. htm*, accessed June 2011.

CHAPTER 2

[2DMOVESET 10] 2Dmoveset.com. Indomitable Detective Chun-Li. Available online at *http://ssf4.2dmoveset.com/?cid=1&t=0*, accessed December 2010.

[APTEST 10] ApTest. Bug and defect tracking tools. Available online at *http://www.aptest.com/bugtrack.html*, accessed December 2010.

[ASHERON 01] 2001. A note on the hotfix. No longer available online at *http://classic.zone.msn.com/asheronscall/news/ASHEletterJan2.asp*.

[BIOSHOCK 10] FilePlanet. BioShock2 – Patch v1.03. Available online at *http://www.fileplanet.com/209922/200000/fileinfo/BioShock-2---Patch-v1.03*, accessed December 2010.

[NEUMANN 94] Neumann, P. G. 1994. *Computer Related Risks.* Addison-Wesley Professional.

[PERSON 10] Personality Test Center. Discover your personality type. Available online at *http://www.personalitytest.net/cgi-bin/q.pl*, accessed December 2010.

[PETERSON 96] Peterson, I. 1996. *Fatal Defect: Chasing Killer Computer Bugs.* Vintage.

[SUITE101 10] suite101.com. Judgers and perceivers at work. Available online at *http://trainingpd.suite101.com/article.cfm/judgers_and_perceivers_at_work*, accessed December 2010.

[TECHEXCEL 10] TechExcel. Try DevSuite Live. Available online at *http://www.techexcel.com/try_devsuite_live.html*, accessed December 2010.

[UFC 10] PlayStation.Blog. UFC Undisputed 2010 – PlayStation 3 Exclusive Content. Available online at *http://blog.eu.playstation.com/2010/04/30/ufc-undisputed-2010-playstation-3-exclusive-content/*, accessed December 2010.

CHAPTER 3

[FIFAULTIMATE 09] YouTube.com. 2009. FIFA 09 Ultimate Team. Available online at *http://www.youtube.com/watch?v=irPtocBaLyU*, accessed June 2011.

[GAMEDEV 04] GameDev.net. 2004. A Quick Guide to FMOD. Available online at *http://www.gamedev.net/reference/articles/article2098.asp*, accessed December 2010.

[JEUX 04] JeuxOnLine. 2004. Version 1.70i Release Notes. Available online at *http://forums.jeuxonline.info/showthread.php?t=351712*, accessed June 2011.

[WOLFENSTEIN 04] Return to Castle Wolfenstein. Wolfenstein: Enemy Territory source code download. Available online at *http://returntocastlewolfenstein.filefront.com/file/Wolfenstein_Enemy_Territory_Source_Code;23091*, accessed June 2011.

[ZAM 11] ZAM Dark Age of Camelot. Vanish. Available online at *http://camelot.allakhazam.com/ability.html?cabil=73*, accessed June 2011.

CHAPTER 4

[CAMINOS 04] Caminos, R. 2004. Cross-platform user interface development. Gamasutra.com. Available online at *http://www.gamasutra.com/gdc2004/features/20040326/caminos_01.shtml*, accessed June 2011.

[CROSBY 80] Crosby, P. 1980. *Quality is Free*, Signet.

[FAGAN 11] Michael Fagan Associates. Improved Fagan inspections and continuous process improvement. Information about course available online at *http://www.mfagan.com*, accessed June 2011.

[SPC 11] BPI Consulting, LLC. SPC for Excel: Statistical Analysis Software. Software purchase download available online at *http://www.spcforexcel.com/ spc-for-excel-software*, accessed June 2011.

[SQAP 03] IEEE. Software quality assurance plan (SQAP) template. sqap.pdf. Available online at *http://wilma.vub.ac.be/~se3/dox/IEEEstandards/sqap.pdf*, accessed June 2011.

CHAPTER 10

[BARTLE 96] Bartle, R. A. 1996. Hearts, clubs, diamonds, spades: Players who suit MUDs. Available online at *http://www.mud.co.uk/richard/hcds.htm*, accessed March 2011.

[CUMMINGS 10] Cummings, I. Game flow and the strategy pad. Available online at *http://maddennfl.easports.com/blog.action?blogId=GameFlowandStrategy Pad*, accessed March 2011.

CHAPTER 11

[HOWDOYOU 09] How do you select lands? Available online at *http://www. gamefaqs.com/boards/956484-magic-the-gathering-duels-of-the-planeswalk- ers/50038227*, accessed March 2011.

[ISTHERE 10] Is there any option to choose the mana you tap? Available online at *http://www.gamespot.com/ps3/puzzle/magicthegatheringduelsof theplaneswalkers/show_msgs.php?topic_id=m-1-57617593&pid=614187*, accessed March 2011.

[NOWAY 10] No way to choose which mana to tap? Available online at *http://www.gamefaqs.com/boards/978319-magic-the-gathering-duels-of-the- planeswalkers/55260446*, accessed March 2011.

[WIKIA 11] List of Final Fantasy Tactics A2: Grimoire of the Rift Jobs. Available online at *http://finalfantasy.wikia.com/wiki/List_of_Final_Fantasy_Tactics_ A2:_Grimoire_of_the_Rift_Jobs*, accessed March 2011.

CHAPTER 12

[EDWARDS 89] Edwards, B. 1989. *Drawing On the Right Side of the Brain*. Tarcher/Perigee.

[JANIS 82] Janis, I. 1982. *Groupthink: Psychological Studies of Policy Decisions and Fiascoes, 2ⁿᵈEdition.* Cengage Learning.

[SUDMAN 02] Sudman, S. and B. Wansink. 2002. *Consumer Panels.* South-Western.

CHAPTER 13

[ELDER 11] The Elder Scrolls IV: Oblivion. Downloads available online at *http://www.strategyinformer.com/pc/theelderscrollsivoblivion/patch/12732.html?details=1*, accessed April 2011.

[UNREAL 11] Unreal Wiki. What happens at map startup. Available online at *http://wiki.beyondunreal.com/What_happens_at_map_startup*, accessed April 2011.

[IEEE 06] XBOX 360 System Architecture. 2006. Available online at *http://ieeexplore.ieee.org/xpls/abs_all.jsp?arnumber=1624324*, accessed April 2011.

CHAPTER 14

[NAVARRO 05] Navarro, A. 2005. Does code decay? Assessing the evidence from change management data. Available online at *http://gsyc.escet.urjc.es/~anavarro/talks/seminario_2005_11_02.pdf*, accessed on May 2011.

[SOFTWAREROT 11] Wikipedia. com. Software rot. Available online at *http://en.wikipedia.org/wiki/Software_rot*, accessed on May 2011.

[UPDATE 2 11] Epic Games Forums. Official—Title update #2 has landed. Available online at *http://gearsforums.epicgames.com/showthread.php?t=653638*, accessed on May 2011.

CHAPTER 15

[DEVGURU 05] A beginners guide to creating and displaying your first XML document. Available online at *http://www.devguru.com/features/tutorials/xml/beginning_xml.html*, accessed April 2011.

[SMARTBEAR 11] Automated test performance tips. Available online at *http://www.automatedqa.com/techpapers/testcomplete/test-playback-performance-tips/#tip_6,* accessed April 2011.

INDEX